JOURNEYS from
CHILDHOOD to MIDLIFE

Journeys from Childhood to Midlife

Risk, Resilience, and Recovery

Emmy E. Werner and Ruth S. Smith

CORNELL UNIVERSITY PRESS

ITHACA AND LONDON

First published 2001 by Cornell University Press
First printing, Cornell Paperbacks, 2001

Library of Congress Cataloging-in-Publication Data
Werner, Emmy E.
Journeys from childhood to midlife : risk, resilience, and recovery
/ Emmy E. Werner and Ruth S. Smith.
p. cm.
Includes bibliographical references and index.
ISBN-13: 978-0-8014-8738-5 (pbk. : alk. paper)
ISBN-10: 0-8014-8738-2 (pbk. : alk. paper)
1. Developmental psychology—Hawaii—Longitudinal studies.
I. Smith, Ruth S., 1923– . II. Title.
BF713.W47 2001
305.2'09969'41—dc21   2001001415

Cornell University Press strives to use environmentally responsible suppliers
and materials to the fullest extent possible in the publishing of its books.
Such materials include vegetable-based, low-VOC inks and acid-free papers
that are recycled, totally chlorine-free, or partly composed of nonwood fibers. For
further information, visit our website at www.cornellpress.cornell.edu.

5   7   9   Paperback printing   10   8   6   4

❏

To our husbands and the children of Kauai

❏

CONTENTS

□

TABLES

❏

FIGURES

ACKNOWLEDGMENTS

Many thanks to the Sidney Stern Memorial Trust, Los Angeles, and the Experiment Station of the College of Agriculture and Environmental Sciences at the University of California, Davis, for financial assistance in the midlife follow-up of the children of Kauai.

Laura Jelliffe and Christine Lee provided invaluable help in coding questionnaires and abstracting relevant information from the records made available to us by the circuit courts of Hawaii, the state's Department of Health, and the Department of Social Services, Division of Vocational Rehabilitation. Leanne Friedman, our computer programmer, provided the technical skills for the data analyses. Kathleen Tebb and Stanley Jacobsen each typed parts of this manuscript with precision, patience, and good humor.

We thank Nancy Henderson and Mervlyn Kitashima for permission to reprint excerpts from "Lessons from My Life," published in *Mentoring for Resiliency* (copyright 2000) and HarperCollins Publishers for permission to quote from Barbara Kingsolver's *High Tide in Tucson* (copyright 1995).

Frances Benson, Ange Romeo-Hall, Susan Tarcov, Bob Tombs, and Heidi Young at Cornell University Press transformed our manuscript into this book. We thank them all.

Most of all, our thanks go to the men and women from the 1955 birth cohort on Kauai who taught us that ordinary people have an enormous capacity to overcome the odds—despite hard times and hurricanes. Our *aloha* and *mahalo* go to them, their parents, and their sons and daughters—the *keiki-o-ka-aina*—the children of the land.

EMMY E. WERNER

University of California, Davis

RUTH S. SMITH

Koloa, Kauai

❏

JOURNEYS from
CHILDHOOD to MIDLIFE

❑

CHAPTER ONE

Introduction

Life is not a matter
of holding good cards,
but of playing
a poor hand well.
Robert Louis Stevenson (1850–1894)

This book is about ordinary people who have lived in extraordinary times. Their journey from birth to midlife has spanned two centuries and two millennia—from the middle of the twentieth century to the beginning of the twenty-first. They are Americans, born and raised in the western-most county of the United States, on the island of Kauai, descendants of immigrants from Europe and Asia, and of the local Hawaiians.

Born in 1955, at the midpoint of the post–World War II baby boom, they belong to a generation of some 76 million people nationwide. Because of the rapid development of communication technology and the widespread presence of television in their lives, more members of this cohort were exposed to important social events as they unfolded in the United States than had been possible in previous generations. Among these were the civil rights and women's movements; the assassination of President John F. Kennedy; the war in Vietnam and the War on Poverty; the drug scene of the "counterculture"; and, closer to home, recurrent cycles of economic downturns and natural disasters.

The members of this cohort grew up in a period of rapid growth in educational and employment opportunities for women and minorities. They married later than their parents, had fewer children, and divorced more frequently than previous generations. On their journey to midlife they have been confronted with persistent dilemmas that center on balancing their commitment to work, family life, and personal growth in an economic and social climate that has changed dramatically from that of their parents' generation.

Our study takes a look at the problems they encountered, and the resilience they displayed when faced with adversity along the way. It has monitored, with relatively little attrition, the impact of a variety of biological and psychosocial risk factors, stressful life events, and protective factors on the development of some five hundred men and women at six stages of their lives: infancy, early and middle childhood, late adolescence, young adulthood, and the threshold of midlife.

The principal goals of our investigation were to document, in natural history fashion, the course of all pregnancies and their outcomes in the entire island community from birth to age forty, and to assess the long-term consequences of perinatal trauma, poverty, parental psychopathology, and adverse rearing conditions on the individuals' adaptation to life (Werner, Bierman, and French, 1971; Werner and Smith, 1977, 1982, 1992; Werner, 1999, 2000a).

Our study began at a time when the systematic examination of the development of children and youths exposed to potent biological and psychosocial risk factors was a rarity. In the mid-1950s, when the men and women in this cohort were born, behavioral scientists tended to reconstruct the events that led to school failure, delinquency and crime, and serious mental health problems by studying the history of individuals in whom such problems had surfaced. This *retrospective* approach can create the impression that a poor developmental outcome is *inevitable* if an individual is exposed to perinatal trauma, poverty, parental psychopathology, or chronic family discord, since it examines only the lives of the "casualties," not the lives of the "survivors."

Today, our perspective has changed. A handful of *prospective* longitudinal studies in the United States and Europe have now followed individuals from birth to adulthood and have demonstrated that there are large individual differences among men and women in response to adversity in their lives. Our study, complemented by their findings, provides us with a rare opportunity to examine the interplay between protective factors in the individual, the family, and the community that contribute to resilience in the formative years and to recovery in adulthood.

DEFINITION OF CONCEPTS

For nearly half a century, since the late 1950s, behavioral scientists have been interested in the *negative* impact of a wide range of biological and psychosocial risk factors on the development of children. But in contrast to *retrospective* studies, *prospective* longitudinal studies have fairly consistently shown that even among individuals exposed to multiple stressors, it is unusual for more than half to develop serious disabilities or persistent problems (Robins, 1978).

During the last two decades of the twentieth century, behavioral scientists interested in developmental psychopathology began to shift their focus from negative developmental outcomes to individuals who had made a successful adaptation to life despite great odds (Anthony and Cohler, 1987; Masten and Garmezy, 1985; Rutter, 2000; Werner and Smith, 1982, 1992). A rapidly growing body of literature has now accumulated that deals with the phenomenon of *resilience*—the dynamic process that leads to positive adaptation within the context of significant adversity (Luthar, Cicchetti, and Becker, 2000).

Investigators who are interested in this phenomenon have studied high-risk individuals with good developmental outcomes: persons who sustained high competence under considerable stress and individuals who successfully recovered from serious trauma (Werner, 1995). Under each of these conditions, behavioral scientists have focused their attention on *protective factors and mechanisms* that buffered or ameliorated a person's reaction to a stressful situation or chronic adversity so that his or her adaptation was more successful than would be the case if the protective factors were not present (Masten, 1994). Resilience is thus conceived as an end product of buffering processes that do not eliminate risks and adverse conditions in life but allow the individual to deal with them effectively (Rutter, 1987).

So far, the study of resilience has been primarily the domain of developmental researchers who deal with children and adolescents who successfully coped with adversity. They usually define the positive developmental outcomes in their study populations in terms of multiple criteria. These include absence of significant developmental delays or serious learning and behavior problems, and the mastery of developmental tasks (Havighurst, 1972) or stages of psychosocial development (Erikson, 1959).

Only recently, with the aging of the baby boomers, has the focus of research on resilience and protective factors shifted to early and middle adulthood. The study of resilience in later life is still an uncharted territory. Among researchers who explicitly address the life course significance of resilience, Staudinger, Marsiske, and Baltes (1993) have proposed connections between the developmental psychopathological approach to "resilience," which has its roots in studies of "high-risk" children, and the concept of "reserve capacity," a construct from life-span developmental theory, referring to an individual's potential for change and continued personal growth, even as she or he ages. There is then great value in research on resilience at different points in the human life cycle.

Related Research

Our current understanding of the roots of resilience and of factors or mechanisms that protect individuals against the psychosocial risks associated with adversity comes from a small body of literature generated by pediatricians, psychologists, psychiatrists, and sociologists. Relatively few investigators have followed populations of children and youths into adulthood to monitor the long-terms effects of risk and protective factors that operated during the individuals' formative years. Studies with such a life-span perspective are quite heterogenous. They vary in their selection of subjects (clinic populations vs. community cohorts), definition and measures of quality of adaptation, and the timing and frequency of their assessment in the individuals' lives. Most of these studies have focused on the lives of Caucasians who were born *before* World War II.

Studies Conducted in the United States

Among prospective studies with a life-span perspective are several investigations that trace the long-term effects of poverty and economic misfortune on the individuals' life course. Especially relevant are publications from the Berkeley Guidance Study and the Oakland Adolescent Growth Study, originating from the Institute of Human Development at the University of California at Berkeley (Clausen, 1993; Elder, 1999). Data on the development of 136 members of the Berkeley cohort, born in 1928–29 (who experienced the Great Depression as preschoolers), are available from birth to 21 months, 11/12, 17/18, 30, and 41/42 years (with a subsample followed to ages 53–54 and 61–62). Data on 99 members of the Oakland cohort, born in 1920–21 (who experienced the Great Depression as adolescents), are available from age 10, 17/18, 37/38, and 48/50 years (with a subsample followed to ages 61–62 and 68–70).

In *Adult Lives: Looking Back at the Children of the Great Depression*, John A. Clausen (1993) used the concept of "planful competence," comprising self-confidence, intellectual investment, and dependability, as an organizing principle for the life course of these individuals. For both men and women, planful competence in adolescence predicted greater educational attainment and fewer life crises in every decade up to their fifties. For the men it predicted greater occupational attainment and for the women happier and more enduring marriages.

In *Children of the Great Depression*, G. H. Elder Jr. (1999) examined the impact of sudden financial misfortune on the life course of the Berkeley and Oakland cohorts. For members of the Berkeley cohort, who experienced economic upheavals in their families as young children, an easy temperament (for both males and females), physical attractiveness (for females), and positive mother-child relationships buffered the impact of father's (negative) behavior during hard times. For members of the Oakland cohort, who experienced the Great Depression as adolescents, personal assets, such as intelligence (for the males) and physical attractiveness (for the females) were protective buffers against the trauma of financial hardships, as was a high degree of achievement motivation. Sons and daughters from economically deprived homes sought more advice and companionship among trusted persons outside the immediate family circle, for example, teachers and friends, than did children unaffected by economic misfortune.

In some circumstances, military service served as a positive turning point in the lives of the economically disadvantaged men. Low-achieving youths who had experienced economic hardships tended to join the armed forces at the earliest possible moment. Service in the military enabled these youths to acquire additional education and occupational skills they would not have had otherwise. They married later in life (when they were more self-sufficient) and had generally more stable unions than did nonveterans. Follow-up studies into midlife showed that their occupational achievements were significantly better than could have been expected on the basis of their economically deprived background and functioning in their youth. They had gained significantly more psychological strength from adolescence to midlife than had nonveterans. They also reported more frequently that their lives had become more satisfying and abundant than did the nondeprived (Elder, 1986).

Another cohort that grew up in the shadows of the Great Depression has been followed by Vaillant and his associates in Boston. He has traced the life course of some 456 men, born between 1926 and 1931, who spent their childhood years in the high-crime neighborhoods of that city. These men had originally served as the nondelinquent control group for the studies on crime and delinquency conducted by Glueck and Glueck (1968). They were followed from their mid-teens (age 14) to their mid-forties (age 47), with major assessments at ages 25 and 31. Even though a generation separates the men from the children of Kauai, Vaillant's reports of their resilience and upward social mobility are of considerable importance for our own investigation.

Vaillant and Milofsky (1980) applied Erikson's model (1959) of psychosocial development to the life course of these underprivileged males and contrasted their findings with longitudinal data collected on ninety-four Harvard men, born in the early 1920s (Vaillant, 1977, 1993). They noted that the stages the men had attained in midlife (career consolidation, intimacy, and generativity) appeared quite independent of childhood social class (whether poor or affluent) or education (whether high school graduate or graduate from an elite college). Instead, psychological maturity in adulthood, in *both* the inner-city and the Harvard men, correlated strongly with childhood experiences that were conducive to the development of trust, autonomy, and initiative.

Vaillant and Vaillant (1981) also assessed the relationship between the mental health status and career accomplishments of the inner-city men and their previous success at tasks assessing Erikson's fourth stage of psychosocial development, industry. Capacity to work in childhood (judged by working regular part-time jobs, household chores, school achievement, and participation in extracurricular activities) was significantly correlated with the career success of these underprivileged men in adulthood. The same variable—childhood industry—was also a stronger predictor of the men's capacity for satisfying interpersonal relationships and good mental health in adulthood than was poverty or being a member of a multiproblem family.

By midlife, males who had grown up in multiproblem families as children were, on the whole, indistinguishable from the offspring of more stable working-class families in terms of mean income, years of steady employment, criminality, and mental illness (Long and Vaillant, 1984). For these underprivileged men, childhood IQ showed a stronger relationship to upward social mobility than it did for men who had grown up in more affluent and stable homes. Many of the upwardly mobile men from the multiproblem homes in inner-city Boston had joined the armed forces and had utilized the G.I. Bill of Rights to obtain additional education and vocational training—like the Berkeley men in Elder's studies who were children of the Great Depression.

Snarey and Vaillant (1985) extended their study of social mobility among the men in Boston's inner city to three generations, including both their parents and their children. Two-thirds of the men and 60 percent of their offspring had moved from lower- and working-class status into the middle class. Among the variables that captured most of the variance in social mobility in these cohorts were maternal education, maternal occupation, childhood IQ, and measures of ego strength and intellectualization, that is, the capacity to isolate ideation from affect.

Another large-scale investigation that has explored both criminogenic and protective factors in childhood that have long-term effects on adult development in midlife is the Cambridge-Somerville Project. McCord (1983) reported findings from a thirty-year follow-up of 506 males who were first identified between the ages of 8 and 15 years as "predisposed to delinquency." Several childhood variables maximally distinguished between men who had become criminals and the majority who had not. Maternal self-confidence and education and maternal affection, coupled with consistent discipline, seemed to overcome the negative effects of father's absence, lack of affection, or permissiveness.

How diverse events across multiple life domains shape life histories and how such histories are linked with psychological resilience are questions that have also been explored by Carol Ryff and her associates in the Wisconsin Longitudinal Study (WLS)—a long-term study of a random sample of over nine thousand Wisconsin high school graduates who have been followed into midlife (in 1964, 1975, and 1992/93). The WLS cohort, mainly born in 1939, precedes by about a decade the bulk of the baby boom generation. It provides early indications of trends and problems that will become important as the baby boomers pass through midlife.

The data available from this study provide a record of social background, youthful aspirations, schooling, military service, family formation, labor market experience, and social participation as the original respondents passed through their twenties, thirties, and forties into their fifties. Ryff and her associates have constructed life histories of some 168 women in this sample and found four primary pathways to resilience among these midlife women (Ryff, Singer, Love, and Essex, 1998).

The first pathway comprised women with generally positive beginnings (high abilities, no alcoholism in childhood homes) who subsequently experienced upward job mobility and perceived their achievements in life favorably, despite two or more adversities encountered in midlife, such as the death of a parent or being involved in the care of a seriously ill person.

The second subgroup comprised women who grew up with alcohol problems in childhood and had, in addition, experienced three or more acutely stressful events, such as the death of a parent, child, or spouse; divorce; job loss. However, these women could rely on strong social support and employment that was stable or led to upward occupational status. They reported high psychological well-being in midlife despite their early and later-life adversities.

The third group of women showed primarily advantages in early life. All had parents who were both high school graduates, no alcohol problems existed in the childhood homes, and the women had high starting abilities (grades, IQ). Later, however, they were confronted with various forms of adversity (poor social relationships; downward occupational mobility; job loss; divorce; single parenting; caregiving demands from ill parents). Thus, their lives were characterized by stressful events occurring largely in adulthood, but they began their journeys with important early strengths that facilitated their recovery from adverse experiences in midlife.

A fourth group of women came from intact families with no alcoholism, but with one parent who had not graduated from high school. As life unfolded, these women confronted an array of adversities (job loss, downward mobility; living with alcohol problems in their marriage; divorce or single parenthood), yet they managed to express a high sense of psychological well-being and satisfaction with themselves in midlife.

Ryff and her associates conclude from their preliminary findings that there are diverse pathways through adversity to resilience for these middle-aged women, but that the protective roles of good early starting resources, of high-quality social relationships, of advancement on the job, and of a favorable self-evaluation seem central to their resilience in adulthood.

Among contemporaries of the children of Kauai is a cohort of 229 black teenage mothers, born in the mid-fifties, who have been followed by Furstenberg and his associates, from their first prenatal visit to a Baltimore hospital until thirty years later, when they had entered midlife. In *Adolescent Mothers in Later Life*, Furstenberg, Brooks-Gunn, and Morgan (1987) explored the processes that led to the recovery of the majority of the teenage mothers in their twenties and thirties, and examined what part of their improvement was explained by their own competence and determination, by the support of their kith and kin, and by educational and social services.

In general, the situation of the young mothers improved significantly over time. Using path analyses, Furstenberg and his associates focused on two key indicators of well-being in adulthood: economic independence and low fertility. Both indicators were strongly related to expressions of well-being voiced by the women. Among variables that were positively related to the teenage mothers' later success were parental education (ten grades or more), small family size (fewer than four children in family of origin), and not having been on welfare as a child. Parental education was positively linked to the educational achievement and vocational aspirations of the daughter. The keys to economic independence for these teenage mothers in later life were graduation from high school, restriction of further childbearing, and/or a stable marriage.

The analyses of the latest follow-up phase of this study is still in progress (Furstenberg, 1999), but preliminary results seem to indicate that the mental health of the former teenage mothers is actually improving in midlife, and that they generally feel better about their current economic and social circumstances than they did in earlier years. These women had made substantial gains in occupational success in midlife—as we discovered in our own longitudinal study as well.

Studies Conducted in Europe

The Lundby study is a prospective longitudinal study of the mental health of some 2,550 persons, including 590 children, living in two adjoining parishes in southern Sweden that began in 1947. The mean age of the children was 8 years when the original data were obtained. Marianne Cederblad and her associates interviewed a subsample of 148 individuals when they were between 42 and 56 years old. All had been exposed to three or more psychiatric risk factors (such as parental mental illness, alcoholism, family discord, or abuse) in childhood, but three out of four were functioning well in midlife (Cederblad, 1996; Cederblad, Dahlin, Hagnell, and Hansson, 1994, 1995).

Among the protective factors Cederblad found to be associated with positive mental health in adulthood in this "high-risk" group were intellectual capacity and self-esteem in childhood; an internal locus of control and a desire to improve one's lot in adolescence; a trusting relationship and shared sense of value with one of the parents; and growing up in a small family (four or fewer children). Cederblad interpreted these findings within the framework of Antonovsky's salutogenic model (1987) of mental health that focuses on an individual's capacity for comprehensibility, manageability, and meaningfulness.

Another Swedish study by Per-Anders Rydelius (1981) followed a group of 4–12-year-old children of alcoholic fathers over a twenty-year period and found that the daughters of alcoholic fathers had fewer social adjustment problems in adulthood than the sons. The men had been more often involved in aggressive acting-out behavior as boys and were more prone to criminal behavior, alcohol abuse, and/or drug addiction in adulthood than the women.

A few prospective studies have also examined the adult adaptation of children who were exposed to schizophrenia or affective disorders (Anthony, 1987). Among the first to keep an eye on the long-term development of such high-risk children was the Swiss psychiatrist Manfred Bleuler (1984), who followed 184 offspring of schizophrenic patients from childhood to adulthood. In his clinic sample, only 9 percent of the sons and daughters of schizophrenics developed schizophrenia themselves. Nearly three out of four in his sample were healthy in adulthood—proportions similar to those reported by Cederblad in her Swedish sample. Eighty-four percent of the married offspring of schizophrenics had successful marriages, and the majority were successful in their work life, achieving a higher social status than had their parents.

Among potent protective factors found in the lives of the healthy offspring of schizophrenics were early childhood opportunities to receive some good parenting from the afflicted mother or father, to attach to the well parent or to a warm-hearted parent substitute, such as a grandmother, and to engage in responsible chores that offered the youngster a sense of purpose, such as caring for a younger sibling or for the sick parent.

The Copenhagen High-Risk Study has traced 207 children of schizophrenic mothers and 104 matched controls from age 15 to ages 25 and 42. At the time of the most recent follow-up of this group, at a mean age of 42 years, the sons and daughters of schizophrenic mothers had lived through most of the risk period of developing schizophrenia. By then, a significantly larger aggregation of schizophrenia (16.2%), other nonaffective, nonorganic psychoses (4.6%), and Cluster A (schizoid, paranoid) personality disorders (21.3%) had occurred among these high-risk men and women than among the controls (1.9%, 0.9%, and 5.0%, respectively).

Taken together, nearly 43 percent of the offspring of schizophrenic mothers received a lifetime diagnosis within the schizophrenia spectrum. There was also a significantly higher rate of substance abuse (23.9%) among them, about double the rate of the controls (Parnas, Cannon, Jacobsen, H. Schulsinger, F. Schulsinger, and Mednick, 1993). Still, more than half of these "high-risk" individuals had exhibited no psychopathology from mid-adolescence through midlife.

As in the Swiss study, Mednick and his colleagues found in Denmark that being reared by a caregiver less pathological than the schizophrenic mother (father, grandmother, other relatives) was associated with significantly better outcomes for the high-risk males in adulthood—unless the father was absent as well. For the high-risk females, the absence of the father in childhood appeared less damaging in adulthood than for the high-risk males, but maternal absence was related to daughters' antisocial tendencies in adulthood. Generally, the daughters of schizophrenic mothers appeared more resistant to both biological stressors and breakdown of parenting than the sons (Mednick, Cudeck, Griffith, Talovic, and F. Schulsinger, 1984).

Two other investigations of children who successfully recovered from serious trauma deserve special note. One is a follow-up study into midlife of twenty-four child survivors of the Holocaust who were sent from concentration camps and orphanages to a therapeutic nursery school in England at the close of World War II. Excerpts from follow-up interviews after 30–40 years, conducted by Sarah Moskovitz (1983) and published in her book *Love despite Hate: Child Survivors of the Holocaust and Their Adult Lives*, reveal an extraordinary affirmation of life among these individuals. *All* of these resilient survivors considered *one* woman to be among the most potent influences in their lives—the nursery school teacher who provided warmth and caring and taught them "to behave compassionately."

The other study focused on the adult lives of children of guerrilla fighters who spent their earliest years with their mothers in a maximum security prison during the Greek Civil War. Mando K. Dalianis (1994), a pediatrician and child psychiatrist, took care of their medical needs while she was a fellow prisoner and followed them in midlife when they had grown into competent and caring adults. The most striking qualities shared by these child survivors in adulthood was their compassion for others in need. The common thread that ran through their eyewitness accounts was the impact of a few caring persons on their lives—the Greek "godmothers," women prisoners who had shared food and clothing with the imprisoned children, played with them, sung with them, and taught them how to read.

In both the American and European studies that have followed individuals from their formative years into midlife, we can discern a common core of individual dispositions and sources of support that ameliorate or buffer a person's response to constitutional risk factors (such as parental mental illness or alcoholism) or stressful life events (such as economic hardships or serious caregiving deficits). These findings have been replicated in two or more longitudinal studies, in different historical eras, across different generations, and in different geographical contexts.

An "easy," engaging temperament, intellectual competence, an internal locus of control, a positive self-concept, and the ability to plan ahead are among the protective factors that make it possible for many individuals to successfully overcome adversity in their lives. So is the role model of a competent, educated mother who values her child, and affectionate bonds with alternate caregivers, including grandparents, and with supportive teachers. Growing up in a smaller family (with four or fewer children) is an advantage as well.

Just as a person's vulnerability is relative, depending, at each stage of life, on complex interactions between constitutional risk factors and stressful life events, resilience is governed by similar dynamic interactions among the protective factors within the individual, the family environment, and the larger social context (Cohler, 1987). Gender makes a difference as well.

Males tend to be more vulnerable than females to the effects of biological insults, serious caregiving deficits, and economic hardships in childhood. Females tend to become more vulnerable than males in adolescence, especially with the early onset of childbearing. In the third and fourth decades of life, the balance tends to shift back again in favor of the women (Werner and Smith, 1992).

ISSUES ADDRESSED IN THIS BOOK

What have we learned from previous research that gave direction to our present undertaking?

1. Prospective studies that focus on psychological, social, and biological processes that lead to varied pathways in resilience and diverse outcomes among "high-risk" men and women are rare. Ours is the only one so far that has followed members of the baby boom generation from

birth to age forty, and focuses not only on the stability of resilience from childhood to adulthood, but also on the ability of high-risk individuals to "bounce back" in later life after a difficult youth.

2. We know much less about the lives of adult women who overcame a traumatic childhood and youth than we do about the adult lives of men who overcame early adversity. Our study allowed us to fill some of the gaps in our present knowledge about the different ways men and women deal with adversities in adult life and how their resilience (or vulnerability) shapes their expectations for the second half of life.

3. The protective factors that have been replicated in previous studies focus mainly on individual dispositions, the immediate family, and the school environment. Our data allowed us to take a look at other sources of support in the adult lives of "high-risk" individuals, at work, among their spouses and friends, and in the community at large, that foster the process of resilience.

4. We had some tentative clues about turning points between adolescence and young adulthood that lead to positive changes in life trajectories—such as the positive impact of military service and continued education on the work lives of disadvantaged men. We expected to find additional turning points in the lives of our cohort members in their thirties and forties. We also expected to find significant differences in the individual dispositions and *early* life experiences of the men and women who took advantage of such "second" or "third" chances and those who did not, since we had a database that extended downward to infancy and preschool age.

5. We wanted to identify the protective factors within the individuals and the external sources of support that enabled *most* men and women to achieve a positive midlife adaptation by the time they reached age forty. These included *biological* variables, such as perinatal risk factors and the individual's health status from early childhood to adulthood; *psychological* dispositions, such as temperament, cognitive skills, and planfulness; and the *sources of social support* that were available in infancy, early and middle childhood, adolescence, and adulthood. We also wanted to identify the risk factors and stressful life events that continued to exert a negative impact on a *minority* of individuals who had reached age forty *without* the sense of generativity that permeated the lives of most men and women in our study.

Whenever possible, we compared our results with census data from Hawaii and the U.S. mainland and with preliminary findings made available by the MacArthur Foundation Research Network on Successful Midlife Development (MIDMAC), an interdisciplinary research project begun in 1989 whose goal is to identify the major biomedical, psychological, and social factors that permit some people to become fit, psychologically healthy, and socially responsible adults. At the core of MIDMAC is MIDUS (Midlife in the United States), a cross-sectional survey of a nationally representative random sample of 7,240 men and women, ages 25 to 74 (who speak English and are accessible by telephone). Among them are some 1,000 men and women in the age range 35–44. They are, like the children of Kauai, members of the "baby boom generation"—albeit a bit more affluent than our study cohort.

The Plan of This Book

In Chapter 2, we describe the historical context of the study and the social and economic changes that have affected the men and women in this birth cohort on their journey to midlife. In Chapter 3, we give an overview of the methods we used to assess their development from the pre/perinatal period to ages 1, 2, 10, 18, 32, and 40 and the criteria we used to judge their adaptation to life in adulthood.

In Chapter 4, we give an overview of how the "ordinary" men and women in our study are faring at age forty. We look at their educational and occupational accomplishments and their relationships with their marital partners, children, parents, siblings, and friends. We note their contributions to their community and how they have coped with stressful events in their adult lives. We examine the sources of emotional support they draw on and the transforming experiences that have made them the kind of persons they are at forty. We also take a look at their expectations for the next decade of their lives.

In Chapter 5, we turn to the life histories of the men and women who have managed to grow into competent, confident and caring adults, despite perinatal stress, poverty, parental psychopathology, and family discord in their lives. We examine the protective factors and processes that have enabled them to overcome the odds—and the paths they have taken to achieve a high degree of psychological well-being at midlife.

We subsequently take a look at what has happened in adulthood to their peers who had developed serious coping problems in childhood and adolescence. We examine the progress of the teenage mothers (in Chapter 6), illustrate the recovery of most youngsters who had struggled with serious mental health problems in their teens (in Chapter 7), and trace the life trajectories of the delinquent youths, most of whom have turned out to be responsible citizens at age forty (in Chapter 8). In Chapter 9, we document how the majority of individuals with learning disabilities have coped successfully in adulthood.

In Chapter 10 and 11, we examine the long-term effects of risk and protective factors, and the links between individual dispositions, sources of support and stress in the formative years, and quality of adaptation in adulthood. In the last chapter we summarize the major lessons we have learned from our journey across four decades of the life span and discuss the implications of our findings for developmental research and social policy.

To make our findings more accessible, we have placed all tables in an appendix. Here the interested reader can find a detailed account of the results of the statistical analyses that support the discussion in the text. Appendix I also contains the path diagrams that trace the links between protective factors in childhood, adolescence, and adulthood and quality of adaptation at age forty for the men and women in this cohort. Throughout this book, we present vignettes drawn from our extensive files and interviews to illustrate the process of resilience and recovery that has characterized the lives of most individuals in our study. For the tale is best told by men and women who have struggled and succeeded against the odds.

❑

CHAPTER TWO

The Context of the Study

The men and women whose lives we followed from birth to age forty were born in 1955 on the island of Kauai, in the youngest state of the union. The "Garden Island" lies at the northwest end of the Hawaiian chain, some hundred miles from Honolulu. Roughly circular in shape and about thirty miles in diameter, the island was created millions of years ago by molten lava bubbling out of a rift in the floor of the Pacific Ocean.

The island has great natural beauty: spectacular mountains and valleys, cliffs and canyons, lush rain forests and swamps, and miles of magnificent beaches. The ancient Hawaiians named it Kauai-a mano-ka-lani-po, "the fountainhead of many waters from on high and bubbling up from below." As the oldest of the Hawaiian Islands and the last of the independent Hawaiian kingdoms, its history and legends reflect a certain maverick quality and independence of spirit that have come to characterize its people.

THE PEOPLE OF KAUAI: ORIGINS

The island was first settled around 500 A.D. by canoe voyagers from the Marquesas and Society Islands, and populated around 1000 A.D. by migrations from Tahiti. The Polynesian voyagers who came to Kauai developed an elaborate hierarchy of royalty *(ali'i)*, priests *(kahunas)*, and warriors and commoners *(kanaka maoli)* that would see little change for nearly a millennium.

The landing of Captain James Cook, England's great seagoing explorer, near Waimea, Kauai, in 1778 was a major turning point in the island's history. Kauai became an important source for the sandalwood trade and a strategic location for whalers to replenish their supplies.

The first Christian mission was established by New Englanders on Kauai in 1820. They promptly set about teaching the children of the Hawaiian royalty, and, later, the common people to read and write their native tongue and English. The newcomers and their descendants intermarried with the local Hawaiians, acquired land rights, and began diverse agricultural projects—growing coffee, rice, mulberries, pineapples, and sugar.

In 1835, a twenty-year-old American by the name of William Hooper founded the first sugar plantation on the island, on land leased to him by the king of Kauai. The plantation and the adjacent town were named Koloa, meaning "long sugar," after the thirty-foot-tall plant that had originally come from New Guinea. Sugar soon became the king of the island's economy, and its growth led to the introduction of the many ethnic groups that today, in various mixtures, constitute Kauai's polyglot population.

The native Hawaiian population, in the meantime, was diminishing rapidly because of diseases introduced by foreigners, and had been reduced by approximately 75 percent by the time an official census was taken in 1853. Imported sources of labor had to be sought by the plantation owners. A few Chinese had already settled on Kauai by the 1850s, some engaged in trade and some in growing rice. Portuguese laborers—recruited largely from Madeira and the Azores—began to arrive in large numbers between 1878 and 1887. At the same time, Germans and Scots brought their technical skills to the growing sugar industry.

Far cheaper, however, was the importation of Japanese to work on the plantations. They arrived in large numbers in the 1890s, and by the turn of the century some 40 percent of the population of the island was Japanese. Several thousand Puerto Ricans and Koreans were brought to Kauai in the early 1900s. Beginning in 1907 and continuing until 1931, large numbers of Filipino men were imported, the majority without wives or families. They provided an additional source of cheap labor and served as a buffer against the impact of strikes, which had harassed the plantations for some time. Filipino men were also brought to the island in the 1940s to ease the wartime labor shortage.

The parents of the 1955 birth cohort had been a part of these immigrant families, some as first generation, others as second or third genera-

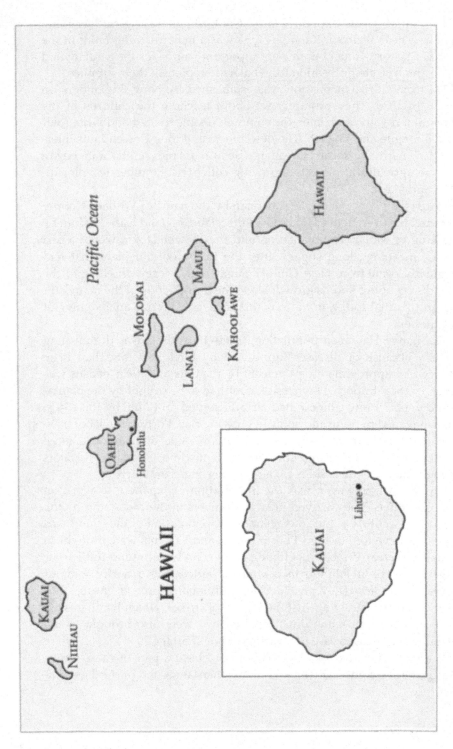

Figure 1. The Hawaiian Islands

tion. They brought to Kauai a mixture of tongues (Cantonese and Hakka, Japanese and Korean, Spanish and Portuguese, Ilocano and Tagalog). They belonged to a variety of religions, including Buddhism, Shintoism, Catholicism, and mainstream and fundamentalist Protestant faiths. Their lives would be shaped by a great sense of family and work ethic but also by a certain plantation mentality, a paternalistic dependence on the supervisors, engineers, and bosses who were Caucasian *haoles* (Hawaiian for "strangers").

Of all the births occurring on Kauai during our study, 33.7 percent were of Japanese ancestry, 22.9 percent Hawaiian and part Hawaiian, 17.9 percent Filipino, 6.5 percent Portuguese, and 2.5 percent Anglo-Saxon Caucasians. The remaining 17 percent were principally mixtures of ethnic groups other than Hawaiian, mostly children of Japanese-Filipino parentage, and a few children of Chinese, Korean, and Puerto Rican descent (see Table 1 in Appendix I).

SOCIAL AND ECONOMIC CHANGES

While their parents had experienced the hardships of the great Depression and of several wars (World War II, the Korean War), the children in the 1955 cohort were born into a period of relative peace and prosperity. They were four years old when, in August 1959, the territory of Hawaii became the fiftieth state of the union and they became full-fledged citizens of the United States.

During their childhood and adolescence, the Hawaiian Islands were experiencing social and economic changes of a magnitude that had not been seen since the early days of European and American contact. Military spending (especially during the Vietnam War era) poured millions of dollars into the islands' economy, making the military the number one business in the new state. By the 1960s, tourism had become the number two industry—soon surpassing the sugar and pineapple industries.

The population expanded rapidly. It rose from 28,000 residents on Kauai in 1955 to nearly double, some 55,000, in 1995. Real estate values rose dramatically as well, and land issues and environmental concerns became inseparable from politics. Clashes between untrammeled entrepreneurial activities and the protests of environmentalists often polarized the island community. The shift from an agricultural to a tourist-oriented economy brought with it an influx of mainlanders to Kauai—mostly from California and other western states. The "hippies" of the 1960s were followed by the surfers, hotel workers, and entrepreneurs of the visitor industry in the 1970s. The drug scene and waves of religious seekers and fringe cults invaded the hospitable island as well and changed forever what was once a conservative rural setting.

The young people in our cohort were learning about new life styles. A number of individuals in our cohort began to experiment with hard drugs in their teens and young adulthood and now have criminal records for narcotic offenses that make it difficult for them to find and keep a job. Others resented the haoles "who stole the waves." Later, in the 1990s, some would become political activists on behalf of the cause of Hawaiian sovereignty, proclaiming that—a century earlier—their land had been stolen in the "illegal overthrow of the Hawaiian monarchy."

Most men and women in our cohort went on with the ordinary business of living: they graduated from high school, found a job, married, and had children. Few were concerned with controversial social issues. But, as they came of age, social laws were changing and educational opportunities expanded.

In 1970, the repeal of Hawaii's law against abortion marked a major turning point in the state's legal history, at a time when the young women in our cohort were reaching childbearing age. Before that time, Hawaii had a century-old criminal abortion statute. Public attitudes about abortion had begun to change in the late 1960s. Hawaii became the *first* state in the union where a fundamental change in the law, rather than a simple modification of the conditions under which abortions were permissible, occurred. That this happened three years before the U.S. Supreme Court decision of 1973 (in Roe v. Wade) declared restrictive abortion laws unconstitutional speaks to the capacity for social change that had come about in the islands during their short history as the youngest state of the union.

The state of Hawaii also has a liberal no-fault divorce law, which was last amended in 1973 when the men and women of the 1955 birth cohort came of age. After the affirmation (by both parties) that a marriage is irretrievably broken (MIB), a divorce becomes final in Hawaii no later than one month from the date of the decree. To protect the children in a divorce, the courts in Hawaii can automatically order an assignment of future earnings of a parent who is delinquent in child support and of income in the amount adequate to ensure that past-due payments and payments due in the future will be paid. As our study proceeded, the wages of a number of delinquent fathers were garnished to protect the court-ordered payments for their children. Thus the members of this birth cohort have had both options and obligations as marriage partners and parents that were quite different from those of earlier generations on Kauai.

By the time the members of the 1955 birth cohort graduated from high school and were ready to enter the workforce, the energy crisis had brought the first of a series of economic recessions to Hawaii. In 1982, when our cohort had reached their late twenties, Hurricane IWA hit Kauai and wrought much destruction. Ten years later, in 1992, Hurricane INIKI caused even more devastation. Both of these natural disasters halted economic progress on the island.

INIKI, in particular, left Kauai devastated, emotionally and economically. The island's major industry, tourism, was especially hard hit. Only about 15 percent of the hotel rooms and condominium units on the island (some 1,200 out of 7,600 rooms) were still usable after the hurricane cut its destructive path across Kauai. Many homes were totally destroyed; others partially so. It took between two and six months to restore electricity in different parts of the island.

In the aftermath of the hurricane, there were many stories of heroism, rallying to the support of friends and neighbors, and a camaraderie that had not existed prior to this natural disaster. The construction industry flourished, with workers arriving from other islands and the U.S. mainland to take advantage of the new building boom, but their influx also put additional stress on available living resources.

Of the seven sugar plantations that had provided the primary economic support for the parents of the men and women in our cohort, only three remained in business in the nineties (with two of them combined in one operation to cut production costs). The oldest plantation, founded in Koloa in 1835, closed in 1996. But the tourist business, which had come to a near halt after INIKI hit, began to recover in the mid-nineties.

EXPANSION OF SERVICES FOR CHILDREN AND YOUTH

In spite of the natural disasters and economic slowdown, the expansion of health, educational, and social services continued on the island throughout the nineties. When our study began, the people of Kauai already had easy access to health facilities provided by the plantations and the territorial government, but private services were very limited. In 1955, only thirteen physicians were practicing on the island. Forty years later, more than eighty medical doctors resided on Kauai. The three hospitals that served the islanders when the study began still exist; a new walk-in clinic has been added to one of them.

The Department of Health, the Department of Social Services and Housing, the Department of Education, Division of Vocational Rehabilitation, and the Family Court, all of which played an important role in the lives of high-risk members of our cohort when they were children and teenagers, continue to provide services and have expanded and adapted their programs to meet the changing needs of their offspring. Newly added programs include the Children's Advocacy Center (CAC), the Friends of CAC, and the Boy's and Girl's Clubs. Some private organizations, such as Rehabilitation Unlimited Kauai and the Serenity House, that provided services when the men and women in our cohort were in their teens, have closed.

Mental Health services have proliferated. The number of therapists in private practice has significantly increased, with a greater emphasis on public-private partnerships in the provision of social and mental health services. The passage of state licensing laws for social workers and marriage and family therapists has contributed to an increase in the quality of training of these practitioners.

Educational opportunities in both the public and private sector have continued to expand on Kauai. Preschools, both Head Start and small private schools, including a Hawaiian language immersion school, are being utilized by two-thirds of the parents in our cohort who have young children. Three public high schools, which served the members of the birth cohort when they were adolescents, now enroll their teenaged offspring. Two new middle schools have opened, and two new elementary schools have been added to the fifteen that were in place at the time of our ten-year follow-up. Several private high schools with small student populations have opened as well.

Kauai Community College (KCC), a part of the statewide system of the University of Hawaii, opened its doors in 1968. Nearly every other member of our cohort took some courses at KCC. Now a substantial number of their college-age offspring are enrolled, including sons and daughters of women from the 1955 birth cohort who were teenage mothers. KCC also offers continuing education courses as well as distance learning courses and courses for the Elder-Hostel Program.

In 1994, a class action suit was filed in the Federal District Court on behalf of individuals, from birth to age twenty, who lived in Hawaii, were eligible for educational and mental health services for developmental disabilities, but were not receiving these services at that time. The court ruled that the state had failed to provide adequate services and approved a consent degree requiring such services, in a statewide system of care, to be fully implemented by June 30, 2000. The implementation plan is being closely monitored by the federal government, and many new programs have been instituted statewide in an attempt at compliance. On Kauai a gamut of services—remedial education, therapy, family counseling, respite help, and home-based services—are being directed to this "special needs" population. Although the numbers served by this special program are small, they demonstrate a commitment on the part of Kauai and the rest of the state to a comprehensive system of care for *every* youngster with developmental disabilities.

Kauai at a Crossroads

At the beginning of the new millennium, Kauai stands at a crossroads. Following the prosperity of the poststatehood decades, the devastation caused by Hurricane INIKI, and a nine-year economic slump, there are many reasons to feel ambivalent about the future. A pessimist might point to the apparent lack of promising job opportunities, to the slow recovery of existing businesses, the closing of the plantations, the critical conditions in the educational system, the dissatisfaction with the players in the political system, and the erosion of the state's famed "aloha" spirit. An optimist could see new opportunities—significant improvements in the state of the tourist industry, successful attempts at diversifying agriculture, greater emphasis on and investments in high-tech industries and health care, the introduction of small innovative businesses—all resulting in expanding horizons and a reduction of insularity.

A new spirit of compromise is alive in the community that came with the growing awareness of its residents that in any future planning process, *both* economic *and* environmental factors must be considered, and that an informed citizenry must be an important part of any decision-making process. That spirit provides hope. The challenge for the *keiki o ka aina*, the children of the land, is now one of balancing their role as members of a world community with the spirit of independence that has characterized the island since its earliest days as an ancient kingdom. As onlookers who have been privileged to document their lives and witness their vulnerabilities and their resilience, we wish them well.

Age of Participants in the Kauai Longitudinal Study by Historical Events

Date	Events	Age
1955	Birth of cohort members	
1956–57	Two-year follow-up	2
1959	Statehood for Hawaii	4
1964	Beginning of War on Poverty and major U.S. involvement in Vietnam	9
1965	Ten-year follow-up	10
1970	Liberalized abortion law approved	15
1973	Eighteen-year follow-up	18
1974	End of War in Vietnam; energy crisis; birth cohort enters workforce	19
1975–80	Serious economic recession in U.S.	20–25
1982	Hurricane IWA hits Kauai	27
1985–87	Thirty-year follow-up	30–32
1991	Serious economic recession in U.S.	36
1992	Hurricane INIKI hits Kauai	37
1995–96	Forty-year follow-up; closing of oldest sugar plantation on island	40
1997	Continued recession on Kauai	42
1999	Tourist industry begins to recover	44

❏

CHAPTER THREE

Studying Lives over Time

The spirit of *kokua*—Hawaiian for "cooperation"—has remained steadfast among the people of Kauai, despite the many social and economic changes that altered the context of their lives during the second half of the twentieth century. Our study has been the beneficiary of that kokua for four decades now. Thanks to this spirit which becomes contagious if you are exposed to it—we were able to carry out a unique longitudinal study that drew on the professional skills and commitment of individuals from several disciplines (pediatrics, psychology, psychiatry, public health, sociology, and social work) and from several institutions (the University of California at Berkeley and Davis, the University of Hawaii, and the Departments of Education, Health, Mental Health, and Social Services of the state of Hawaii and the county of Kauai).

The Kauai Longitudinal Study has monitored the impact of biological and psychosocial risk factors, stressful life events, and protective factors on the development of the men and women who were born on the island in 1955, at ages 1, 2, 10, 17/18, 31/32, and 40. As our study progressed, we began to take a special interest in those high-risk children who, in spite of exposure to birth complications, discordant and impoverished home lives, and uneducated, alcoholic, or mentally disturbed parents, went on to develop healthy personalities, stable careers, and strong interpersonal relationships—children who grew into competent, confident, and caring adults. Along the way, we tried to identify the protective factors and processes that contributed to the resilience of these children and to the recovery in adulthood of most troubled teenagers.

Finding a community that was willing and able to cooperate in such an effort was not an easy task. We chose Kauai for a number of reasons, not the least of which was the receptivity of its people to our endeavors. Coverage by medical, public health, educational, and social services on the island was comparable to what one would find in communities of similar size on the U.S. mainland in the mid-1950s. We also thought the population's relatively low mobility would make it easier to keep track of the study's participants and their families over time. We give here a brief account of how we assessed the individual members of the 1955 birth cohort and the family context in which they lived at each stage of our longitudinal study.

The Prenatal and Perinatal Periods

Early on in the study, public health nurses and social workers who were local residents, knew the community well, and had the trust and co-operation of the women who were to give birth in 1955 recorded their reproductive histories and interviewed them in each trimester of pregnancy. They paid special attention to any physical or psychological trauma that had occurred during the period of gestation. The local physicians submitted monthly a list of pregnant women who had come to them for prenatal care and monitored any complications that occurred during the prenatal, labor, delivery, or perinatal period.

A clinical rating, based on the presence of conditions thought to have a possibly deleterious effect on the fetus or newborn, was made for each child. After reviewing the extensive records, two pediatricians on the research staff scored the severity of some sixty selected complications or events that could occur during the prenatal, labor, delivery, and neonatal periods as follows: 0-not present; 1-mild; 2-moderate, and 3-severe. After all conditions were scored, they assigned to each baby an overall "pre/perinatal stress score," ranging from 0 to 3. This was based on clinical judgment, taking into account the number, type, and severity of unfavorable conditions present. In general, the numerical value of the overall score was the same as the value assigned to the most severe condition present. (See Summary of Scoring System for Prenatal/Perinatal Complications in Appendix II.)

About 10 percent of the cohort (N: 69) were exposed to moderate pre- or perinatal stress. About 3 percent (N: 23) suffered severe pre- or perinatal complications. One out of every six children (N: 116) had physical or intellectual handicaps of perinatal or neonatal origin that required long-term medical, educational, or custodial care.

Year 1

In the postpartum period and when the infants were one year old, public health and social workers interviewed the mothers at home. The mothers rated their babies on a number of temperamental characteristics, such as activity level, ease of handling, and social responsiveness. They also reported if the infants had any distressing habits, such as temper tantrums or irregular feeding or sleeping habits. The interviewers checked a series of adjectives that characterized the mother's interactions with her baby at an age crucial for the development of a secure attachment. They also recorded any stressful life events that had occurred between birth and the baby's first birthday that might have had a deleterious effect on the development of his/her sense of *trust*, such as the prolonged absence of the primary caregiver or an incapacitating illness that prevented her from giving adequate attention to the infant.

Year 2

Two board-certified pediatricians conducted a medical examination when the children were approximately two years old. After a systematic appraisal of all organ systems, they rated each child's overall physical status as either superior, normal, below normal, or retarded. Independently, two psychologists assessed the children's cognitive development with the Cattell Infant Intelligence Scale (Cattell, 1940) and their self-help skills with the Vineland Social Maturity Scale (Doll, 1953). They also completed an adjective checklist describing the behavior of the toddler, focusing especially on the degree to which the child had developed a sense of *autonomy* and was able to perceive himself as an agent capable of controlling his own body and making things happen. They also asked the mother about any stressful life events that had occurred between the infant's first and second birthday, including the birth of a younger sibling.

We rated the quality of the early family environment along three dimensions that reflected the material opportunities, intellectual stimulation, and emotional support available to the young child: (1) *socioeconomic status* (SES), based on the father's occupation, standard of living, condition of housing, and crowding; (2) *mother's educational level*, based on number of years of completed schooling; and (3) *family stability*, based on information gained from home visits and interviews (postpartum and at ages 1 and 2) on presence or absence of the father, marital discord, alcoholism, parental mental health problems, and long-term separations of the young child from the mother without an adequate substitute caregiver. The ratings were made by two psychologists on a five-point scale, ranging from 1-very favorable to 5-very unfavorable.

Year 10

The predominant developmental task in this period is the development of a sense of *competence or industry*. We used several perspectives to judge the progress the children in our study had made toward the acquisition of basic social and intellectual skills. One perspective was gained from referrals that had been made to the Crippled Children's Branch of the Department of Health, the Division of Special Services of the Department of Education, and the Division of Mental Health Services for children who had developed major physical, intellectual, or emotional problems that were interfering with their school achievement.

Another perspective was gained from parental interviews in which we asked the primary caregiver about any behavior problems the child had displayed at home and any stressful life events to which he or she had been exposed between the ages of two and ten, such as serious or repeated illnesses of the child, parents, or siblings; chronic family discord; divorce and/or remarriage of the parents; and loss of job or sporadic unemployment of the major breadwinner.

A third perspective came from a questionnaire filled out by the child's current teacher, including grades obtained in reading, writing, and arithmetic, and a checklist of behavior problems observed in the classroom. Last, a clinical psychologist administered two group tests to the children—the Bender-Gestalt Test (Koppitz, 1964) and the Primary Mental Abilities Test (PMA) sampling reasoning, verbal, numerical, spatial, and perceptual-motor skills (Thurstone and Thurstone, 1954). Some 30 percent of the youngsters who had learning and/or behavior problems received additional diagnostic examinations from specialists, such as audiologists, neurologists, ophthalmologists, pediatricians, and psychiatrists.

The combined screening and diagnostic information was reviewed by a panel consisting of a pediatrician, a psychologist, and a public health nurse, who prepared an assessment for each child, that determined the effect of any existing handicap on school progress and the need for future care (medical, remedial education, or mental health services). About one out of every five children in this cohort (142 in all) developed serious learning or behavior problems in the first decade of life that required more than six months of remedial work (all the children with serious behavior problems had learning problems as well). By the time the children were ten years old, twice as many children needed some form of mental health service or remedial education (usually associated with reading problems) as were in need of medical care.

Public health nurses and social workers also made home visits when the child was ten years old and assessed the quality of the caregiving environment via standardized interviews with the primary caregiver, usually the mother, but sometimes a mother substitute, such as a grandparent. Based on this information, three ratings of the home environment were made: (1) a rating of the family's current *socioeconomic status*; (2) a rating of *educational stimulation*, and (3) a rating of *emotional support* provided for the child in the home.

The rating of the family's socioeconomic status combined information on father's occupation, income, steadiness of employment, and conditions of housing. It was based primarily on father's occupation, categorized into one of five levels: (1) professional; (2) semiprofessional, proprietorial, or managerial; (3) skilled trade and technical; (4) semiskilled; (5) day laborer or unskilled work.

The rating of educational stimulation took into account the intellectual interests and activities of the family; the value the family placed on education; and opportunities provided to enlarge the child's vocabulary and to explore the community at large, such as the library and recreational facilities.

The rating of emotional support was based on the information given in the interview on the quality of the relationship between parents and child; the availability (or lack) of positive role models; methods of discipline and ways of expressing parental approval; as well as stressful life events encountered by the child between ages two and ten.

These ratings were made by a clinical psychologist (independent of any knowledge of the children's earlier scores on quality of family environment) on a five-point scale: 1-very high, 2-high, 3-adequate, 4-low, 5-very low.

Some 55 percent of the children in this cohort were rated as living in families of "low" socioeconomic status by age ten. The rating of educational stimulation showed that the families were about evenly divided between those with "adequate" to "high" ratings and those with "low" to "very low" ratings. But regardless of the relatively low educational level of the parents, who worked mostly in semi- and unskilled jobs on the plantations, the majority of their children (two out of three) were rated as getting at least "adequate" emotional support.

Years 17/18

When the youngsters were in their senior year in high school, we obtained permission to search the records of the Office of Guidance and Special Services of the Department of Education, the Department of Health, the Department of Social Services, the Family Court, the Kauai Police Department, and the local hospitals for referrals that had been made for members of this cohort. This screening process helped us locate youths who had become delinquent during their teens (15%), youths who had developed serious mental health problems requiring either in- or outpatient care (10%), and girls who had become pregnant during their teens (8%).

The district superintendent of the Department of Education on Kauai gave us permission to access the verbal, quantitative, and total scores from the School and College Ability Test (SCAT, 1966), and the scores on the reading, writing, and mathematics scales of the Sequential Test of Educational Progress (STEP, 1966). Both the SCAT and STEP were routinely administered to the students in grades 8, 10, and 12 in the local high schools. In addition, a brief biographical questionnaire asking about the youths' educational and vocational plans, marital and health status, and stressful life events experienced in adolescence was mailed to each member of the 1955 cohort.

Two psychologists from the study team conducted an in-depth study via clinical interviews and personality tests of high-risk youths with serious coping problems (mental health problems, learning disabilities, serious or repeated delinquencies, teenage pregnancies) and of control groups without problems, matched by age, gender, ethnicity, and socioeconomic status. We assessed the youths' self-assurance and interpersonal adequacy, their sense of responsibility, intellectual efficiency, and achievement with the California Psychological Inventory (CPI) (Gough, 1969). We used the Novicki Locus of Control Scale (Novicki, 1971) to ascertain their faith in the effectiveness of their own actions.

The semistructured interview explored the youths' attitudes toward school, their current interests and activities, their occupational plans, and their participation in and satisfaction with work and social life. The youths were asked about their preference in friends, the quality of their relationship with their parents, their feelings of security or conflict with their family, and how much they identified with their mother and father. Last but not least, we tried to get their perspectives on their own strengths and weaknesses, and matters about which they worried at this stage of life—questions that permitted us to make a judgment on whether or not they were comfortable with their *identity* and had achieved a secure sense of self.

The interview yielded a number of ratings on a five-point scale from 1-very high to 5-very low. Among the dimensions rated were the youths' overall attitude toward school, their achievement motivation, the realism of their educational and vocational plans, the quality of their relationship with their peers and parents, and their self-esteem.

We also asked about stressful life events they had encountered in their teens and the help they had received from informal and formal sources of support, such as siblings, friends, teachers, ministers, mental health professionals, or community agencies. Contacts with professionals and local social service agencies were independently verified by record search.

Years 31/32

Our principal concern in our follow-up at age 31/32 was to trace the different paths that led most men and women in our cohort from a high-risk childhood or youth to a successful adaptation in adulthood. We wanted to examine the long-term consequences of stressful life events in their earlier lives as well as the protective factors and processes that contributed to their well-being and success in the "age thirty transition period" (Levinson, 1978, 1996). We wanted to assess how well they had accomplished the transition into the world of work, marriage, and parenthood, whether they had developed a capacity for *intimacy*, for closeness and commitment to another, and what sources of support and inner strength they could draw on to deal with stressful events in their adult lives.

We used two perspectives to assess the quality of the adult adaptation of the men and women in our study. One was the perspective gained from a semistructured interview that focused on the developmental tasks of early adulthood. We explored the ways in which each individual had dealt with getting started in an occupation, with choosing a spouse or friend for a long-term commitment, with managing a home and rearing children, with the search for a congenial social group, and the satisfaction gained from present accomplishments in life.

We asked each participant to fill out a Life Events Checklist that included a list of events commonly perceived as stressful in adult life, such as loss of a job, breakup of a long-term relationship, divorce, and illnesses or accidents suffered by the individual, his children, spouse, or parents, as well as deaths of family members or close friends. We also asked each participant to check a list of formal and informal sources of support that had helped him or her cope with these adversities.

We expected that some troubled adolescents, after leaving an adverse home situation, might find opportunities or supportive persons that would bolster their faith in the efficacy of their own actions and lead them on the road to recovery. We therefore asked each participant in the 31/32 year follow-up to complete Rotter's Locus of Control Scale (1966), which assesses the degree to which a person believes that he or she is in control of his life (internal), and the degree to which events are perceived to be a result of fate, luck, or other forces beyond the person's control (external).

We also expected that these "turnarounds" (for better or worse) in adult lives of high-risk individuals might be dependent on temperamental characteristics that make it easier or harder for a person to seek or elicit new opportunities. Hence we asked each of the participants to complete the EAS Temperament Survey for Adults (Buss and Plomin, 1984). It assesses dimensions of temperament, such as excitability, activity level, and sociability, which have a fair degree of stability at different stages of the life cycle.

A second complementary perspective on the quality of adult adaptation of the members of our study group was gleaned from their public records in the community. From the district and circuit courts in Honolulu, Kauai, and the other islands (Maui and Hawaii), we obtained information on every member of the 1955 birth cohort residing in the state of Hawaii who had been convicted of a crime, was a defendant in a civil suit, or whose marriage had ended in a divorce. The files of the criminal, civil, and family courts also contained information on domestic problems, such as delinquent child support payments, child and spouse abuse, and restraining orders issued against the offending spouse or parent.

From the state Department of Health we obtained records of the date and cause of death for members of the 1955 birth cohort who were deceased. The Department of Social Services informed us about special services rendered to cohort members who had physical or mental disabilities. Using code numbers to safeguard confidentiality, we obtained information from the statewide mental health registry of the Department of Mental Health on members of the 1955 birth cohort who had received in- or outpatient treatment, or whose parents had such treatment. Last but not least, the U.S. Veterans Administration provided us with information on cohort members who had served in the armed forces and who had received disability payments or educational benefits.

At the time of the 31/32-year follow-up, the majority of the surviving members of the 1955 birth cohort still lived on Kauai. Some 10 percent had moved to other Hawaiian islands (Hawaii, Maui, Oahu)—most to Honolulu. Another 10 percent had settled on the U.S. mainland, and 2 percent lived abroad. We noticed some selective migration: by age 31/32 many of the resilient individuals who had coped well during childhood and adolescence, in spite of a combination of biological and psychosocial risk factors, had moved to Honolulu, or the U.S. mainland, and some lived abroad (in Europe and Asia). In contrast, most of the individuals who had been troubled teenagers, with learning or behavior problems, records of delinquencies, or teenage pregnancies, still lived on Kauai— many still as dependents of parents or in-laws. The most elusive, however, were individuals who had developed serious mental health problems by age eighteen. Nearly a third in this group could not be traced by mail or telephone, nor were their whereabouts known by their family or former friends. Some were found with the help of the statewide mental health registry, others with the assistance of the Veterans Administration (if they received disability payments after military service).

Year 40

Our forty-year follow-up revealed a pattern of increased mobility, especially for the women. The majority of the surviving members of the cohort (some 66 percent) still lived on Kauai, but one out of four had moved to other islands—most to metropolitan Honolulu. Some 10 percent lived on the U.S. mainland—most on the West Coast. Nearly twice as many women as men had moved from their birthplace to other islands, other states in the union, or abroad. In turn, some of the men who had spent some time in Europe and Asia during their early thirties—most in military service in the US. Army, Navy, or Air Force—had returned to Kauai and civilian life.

Our main focus at this stage were the issues of midlife transition that confronted the men and women in our study group, for this was the time when many were reexamining the life structure they had established previously and reevaluating its meaning and direction. As in the previous stages of the life cycle, we used two perspectives to assess the quality of adaptation of the individuals in our study: one was their own account of their success and satisfaction with work, family, and social life and of their psychological well-being. The other was based on their records in the community.

We used several questionnaires to assess the status of the men and women at age forty. The first one, which also served as a way to reintroduce our study, focused on demographic information, including their current marital and employment status, the number of children in their household, any serious health problems in the family, and any hardships they had encountered when Hurricane INIKI struck the island, including property damage, financial problems, injuries, and posttraumatic stress disorder associated with this major natural disaster that had occurred midway between the thirty-year and the forty-year follow-up.

The second questionnaire focused on the way the individuals were coping with major midlife issues in their work and with the quality of their relationships with their spouses or partners, their children, their (aging) parents, their siblings, and their friends. We explored issues of *generativity* by asking them what contributions, if any, they made to their community through volunteer work, and how satisfied they were with their allotment of time between their own needs, the needs of others who were dependent on them, and their obligations to their church, school, and community at large. We also asked them about their satisfaction with their present lifestyle and accomplishments, their goals for the next decade in their lives, the sources of support they could rely on when the going got tough, and how they felt about their effectiveness in dealing with both opportunities and crises in their lives.

As in the previous follow-up, the respondents also filled out a Life Events Checklist and the EAS Temperament Survey. In addition, they completed an eighteen-item questionnaire that tapped six dimensions of psychological well-being: self-acceptance, positive relations with others, autonomy, environmental mastery, purpose in life, and personal growth. (For a description of the six Scales of Psychological Well-Being, see Appendix II.) These scales, derived from theories of adult development by Ryff and Singer (1996), had proved to be useful indices of successful adaptation in the Wisconsin Longitudinal Study and in the National Survey of Midlife in the United States (MacArthur Foundation Research Network on Successful Midlife Development, 1998).

A second perspective on the quality of the midlife adaptation of the men and women in our study was gleaned from their public records in the community. We examined the files of the criminal and civil courts on Kauai and the other islands (Oahu, Hawaii, Maui) for any violations of the law committed by study members since the last follow-up, and for any relevant information on divorces, as well as domestic and child abuse. The Department of Social Services, Division of Vocational Rehabilitation, provided us with a list of services rendered to men and women in the cohort who had serious mental, physical, and psychological disabilities. The state Department of Health in Honolulu informed us about the dates and causes of death for thirty-three individuals in the birth cohort who were deceased. More males than females had died at each of the previous phases of the life cycle, in early and middle childhood, adolescence, and early adulthood. Most of them had been born and reared in poverty.

The Participants in the Midlife Follow-Up

We have follow-up data at age forty on 489 individuals. They represent 70 percent of the 698 subjects in the 1955 birth cohort on whom we have pre/perinatal stress scores. Among them are 80 percent of the individuals who had successfully overcome multiple adversities in their early childhood (chronic poverty, perinatal stress, parental psychopathology, and a dysfunctional family life) without developing any serious coping problems at years ten and eighteen. We also have forty-year follow-up data on 85 percent of the troubled youths who had delinquency records, learning disabilities, mental health problems, and/or teenage pregnancies. Since we were able to reach a very high proportion of the "high-risk" individuals in our study—including both those *with* and those *without* coping problems—sample attrition did *not* appear to introduce any selective bias in our midlife follow-up.

Our attrition rates with this Pacific-Asian population compare favorably with those of two major longitudinal studies on the U.S. mainland that extended into midlife—one with an Afro-American sample who were members of the "baby boom" generation, the other with a

Caucasian sample who were "children of the Great Depression." On the East Coast, Furstenberg and his associates (1999) managed to reach 229 (57%) out of their original target group of 403 black teenage mothers from Baltimore when the women were in their mid-forties. On the West Coast, researchers from the Institute of Human Development at the University of California were able to follow 136 out of 252 individuals (54%) from the Berkeley Guidance Study from birth to their early forties (Clausen 1993).

The low attrition rates of the Kauai Longitudinal Study are a tribute to the cooperation of an immensely helpful island community, to the education, health, and social agencies of the county of Kauai and the state of Hawaii, to the diligence of our research staff, and foremost to the men and women who were willing to share the stories of their lives with us.

RATINGS OF THE QUALITY OF ADULT ADAPTATION

At both ages 31/32 and age 40, ratings of the quality of adult adaptation were made independently by a developmental psychologist and a Ph.D. in human development on the basis of the individuals' self-evaluation (in the clinical interviews and questionnaires) and their records in the community. The ratings were made independently of any information that had been obtained at previous follow-up stages (see scoring system for the ratings of the quality of adult adaptation in Appendix II).

The following criteria were used to define "successful coping" in adulthood:

Work: The individual is employed and/or is enrolled in school; is (very) satisfied with work and/or school achievement.

Relationship with spouse/mate: The individual is married or in a long-term committed relationship; is (very) satisfied with partner and reports little or no conflict; no record of desertion, divorce, or spouse abuse in court files.

Relationship with children: The individual evaluates children (very) positively; is (very) satisfied with parental role; no record of child abuse or delinquent child support payments in court files.

Relationship with parents and siblings: The individual evaluates father, mother, and siblings positively; reports little or no conflict with them.

Relationship with peers: The individual has several close friends who provide emotional support when needed; is (very) satisfied with the relationship; no record of assault, battery, rape, or other criminal offenses in court files.

Self-assessment: The individual is (very) happy or mostly satisfied with present state of life; reports no dependency on alcohol or drugs; no psychosomatic illnesses; no record of psychiatric disorders in Mental Health Registry.

Some 50 percent of the men and women in this birth cohort on whom we have follow-up data at age 31/32 satisfied our criteria for "successful" adult adaptation. One out of three had developed minor problems in the transition to age thirty, but were functioning adequately. Approximately one out of six had developed serious coping problems that included at least two of the following conditions: a criminal record, a record of mental health problems, evidence of spouse or child abuse, and a poor self-evaluation—a finding similar to that reported by Magnusson (1988) in his follow-up study of young adults in an urban Swedish cohort who are the same age as our study cohort. Men and women were nearly equally represented among the adults with serious coping problems in their early thirties; among individuals with minor coping problems, there were more men than women. Among those without coping problems, there were more women than men.

By age forty, nearly half of the men and women (47.2%) were rated as having made a "good" adaptation in their transition to midlife, about a third (36.7%) were functioning "adequately," and one out of six (16%) were doing poorly, struggling with chronic financial problems, domestic conflict, violence, substance abuse, serious mental health problems, and/or low self-esteem. At age forty, a significantly higher proportion of men than women were in the "troubled" group (M: 23%; F: 8.7%). A higher proportion of women than men (M: 40%; F: 54%) showed positive changes in their life trajectories in the transition from early adulthood to midlife and were rated as having made a "good" adaptation at age forty.

❑

CHAPTER FOUR

Forty Something

"I really never expected things to be a certain way at a predetermined time of my life. I guess I just deal with life's offerings when they arrive—whether they are victories or problems." "I have realized how important every day is and I have learned to appreciate my accomplishments." Two voices—one male, the other female—reflect on being forty and on what they have learned on the journey to the midpoint of their lives.

Like most of the men and women in our study, these two individuals have led "ordinary" lives: getting a decent education; holding down a steady job; living in a committed relationship with a spouse or friend; meeting—as best they could—the needs of growing children and aging parents; and caring for their neighbors and their community. Their accomplishments in the face of repeated cycles of economic uncertainty and natural disasters are a tribute to their competence and determination, to the faith that sustained them, and to the hopes and dreams of their immigrant parents and grandparents who came to Hawaii to find a better life for their sons and daughters.

"Being forty" turned out to be a milestone that brought satisfaction to many of the men and women in this cohort. To our surprise, they rated it as a more satisfying period in their lives than their teens, their twenties, and their thirties. Even childhood, in retrospect, did not seem to hold as many promises as entering midlife for one out of every three women and one out of every four men in our study. Their responses are similar to those reported from participants in the MacArthur Survey of Midlife Development on the U.S. mainland (MIDUS).

In this, the largest and most comprehensive survey of middle age ever attempted, a nationally representative sample of some one thousand men and women from Atlanta, Boston, Chicago, Phoenix, and San Francisco, in the age range 35–44 years, rated the quality of their lives in several domains. They reported significant improvements in their work, their relationship with their spouses and children, their contributions to their community, and in their overall life satisfaction in comparison with previous decades. So did the men and women on Kauai (see Table 2 in Appendix I).

EDUCATIONAL ACCOMPLISHMENTS

Few members of their parents' generation, with the exception of the Japanese immigrants, had been high school graduates. The median years of schooling for their mother's generation was eight grades, and the median years of schooling for their father's generation was six grades. In contrast, some 97 percent of the 1955 cohort had graduated from high school.

By age forty, 88 percent of the men and 80 percent of the women had obtained some additional schooling beyond high school. More than half had attended college—either the local community college, the University of Hawaii, or a college in the western part of the U.S. mainland. Thirteen percent of the men and 15 percent of the women went on to graduate or professional schools, becoming architects, designers, doctors, engineers, lawyers, ministers, pharmacists, public health nurses, social workers, or teachers. The percentage of those who graduated from high school and of those who attended graduate or professional schools in this cohort was comparable to that of the 35–44 year-old men and women in the MacArthur Survey of Midlife Development on the U.S. mainland.

Individuals heading for college, if they came from poor homes, used a stepwise approach in getting an advanced education: the first two years at the Kauai Community College, the next two years at the University of Hawaii in Manoa or Hilo, and then graduate or professional school in Honolulu or on the U.S. mainland. Some 24 percent of the men and 2.5 percent of the women in this cohort joined the armed forces and used their benefits to further their education. Most pursued training in computer and electronic skills.

Thus the local community college and the armed forces became important gateways for higher education for many men and women on Kauai who are now the first college graduates in their family. Others continued to take adult education classes in the community and education programs provided by their employers to upgrade their technical and business skills—especially the women, once they were free of time-consuming child-rearing responsibilities. "Going to school" had become a lifelong process for the men and women who were motivated to improve their knowledge base and, most important, their financial status.

WORK EXPERIENCE

By age forty, 89 percent of the men and 86 percent of the women were in the labor force. The male unemployment rate of 11.3 percent was more than twice as high as that reported in the National Census of 1996 (5.4%) and significantly higher than for the state of Hawaii (6.9%), reflecting the continuing negative impact on Kauai's economy of the devastation caused by Hurricane INIKI. Among the women, only 5 percent were unemployed and actively looking for a job; 9 percent were full-time homemakers with small children. These figures were comparable to those reported for women on the U.S. mainland in the National Census of 1996.

While 56 percent of their fathers had worked in semiskilled or unskilled jobs on the island's plantations, only 3 percent of the sons were still working in agriculture. The most prevalent employment for the men in this generation was in the skilled and technical trades (29.6%) and in managerial positions in business (24.6%).

The majority of the women worked either in administrative positions (30.6%), as salespersons or secretaries (20%), or as teachers, counselors, social workers, or nurses (17.2%). Both employment rates and levels of employment for the women had significantly increased since our follow-up at age thirty. By age forty, a higher proportion of women worked in professional jobs and in semiprofessional and managerial positions than at age thirty, and the proportion of semiskilled or unemployed women had decreased. In contrast, there was a significant increase in the male unemployment rate and a decrease in the proportion of men who held semiprofessional and managerial positions, owing to the downsizing of many local businesses.

Financial worries were very much on the minds of the men who were affected by the lingering economic impact of Hurricane INIKI on Kauai and the continuing sterile economic conditions in the state of Hawaii. Wrote one unemployed painter, "I am not working; there's no jobs available. I've been hustling, putting applications in, but no one calls." Another male who was in the nursery business told us: "The greatest stress in my life right now is dealing with the loss of a job and seniority due to the devastation of Hurricane INIKI. I have to face a 70% reduction in income, just when my teenage daughter is about to enter the local junior college with a 75% increase in tuition. I struggle with the financial stress as well as having to find a new direction in my life at age 40." A craftsman took it more philosophically. He wrote: "We have occasional money problems. My wife worries about our finances, but I tend to go with the flow."

MARITAL STATUS

By age forty, 81 percent of the men and 91 percent of the women had been married at least once. The rates for "never married" women were comparable to those obtained in the National Census of 1994 (9%); the rates for "never married" men were somewhat higher (19% vs. 13%). One percent of the men and women were widowed. About one out of every three marriages had ended in divorce by age forty, a trend similar to that reported for the nation as a whole for this age group (Besharov, 1999). Only a third of the divorced men and women had remarried by age forty—partly because there was no stigma attached to informal "living together" arrangements, and partly because more women could survive financially on their own.

Among the forty-year-olds who were *currently* married (72% of the women; 50% of the men), most were satisfied with their relationship—as were the majority of middle-aged adults in the MIDUS survey. One out of four reported some marital difficulties. The most common sources of stress were financial worries, followed by concerns about personal differences and communication problems; problems with (step)children, and worries about finding enough "quality time" for the proper balance between work, family, and personal relationships.

The women were generally more articulate in expressing their concerns about personal differences with their spouses. One wrote, "My husband is an energetic and intelligent man, but sometimes lacking in common sense. Dealing with him takes a lot of patience." Another commented: "I live with a spouse who is insecure and jealous. Otherwise he is a wonderful man."

The men were less specific in their complaints than their wives, but several admitted to occasional problems with communication. One husband *was* quite specific. He wrote: "Sex could be better, but otherwise the marriage is great."

One out of five among the married men and women mentioned problems with children that affected the marriage. Most lived in families where there were stepchildren from the first marriage of a husband or wife. One male wrote, "In my second marriage I am having some difficulties with the children of the first marriage of my current spouse. My second marriage produced twins on my 40th birthday, and this is stressful." A woman who was remarried to a divorced man wrote, "Having my stepchildren go back to visit their mom worries me. Her values are different than ours."

A number of women complained about their husbands' lack of involvement with household and parenting duties. Their responses were similar to those of many women in the MacArthur Survey of Midlife Development. "I feel that my husband does *not* always live up to *his* half of the bargain of being a father," wrote one. "He hardly ever gives a bath, or changes diapers." Another, a business manager, complained, "I do not get a lot of help from my spouse in disciplining our children and no support in household chores." A third was not happy about her husband's problem-solving skills. "He makes the problems and I need to solve them. It's burning me out. I am responsible for raising and nurturing our three sons. He is too busy working or being with his associates."

Finding the right balance between work, family, and personal relationships was a recurrent theme among the married couples. Many husbands were keenly aware of that problem, and so were their working wives. A businessman wrote, "The daily routines of life with a wife and young child, and the stresses and frustrations of my business struggling in depressed economic times is sometimes hard on me. Compassion for the family is at times difficult when the job and economic survival demand most of my time and self." A teacher told us, "Our lives are so busy, with both parents working in education and with four children; numerous activities; varieties of issues to deal with, being attentive and available to each child can be exhausting at times." A female administrator tried to find more hours in her busy schedule "to raise our family, and to find time for one's self and for my spouse." *Time* seemed to be the commodity that was scarce for all these busy forty-year-olds, whether they were male or female, married or single, with or without children—regardless of their station in life. A professional woman, married with a child, put it succinctly: "Work schedules are the bane of my life."

Divorce and Remarriage

"Lack of time together" was also a theme struck by some of the men whose marriages had ended in divorce by age forty. Long work hours, stressful jobs, and jobs that required frequent separations from their spouses contributed, in their opinion, to the breakup of their marriages. But the most frequently mentioned grounds for divorce by both men and women were personality differences between themselves and their spouses. One of the men wrote, "We are different types of people. She is very active, likes to go places, thinks about today only. I like to relax on the beach, take my time doing things, and think about tomorrow."

Both men and women who had divorced commented on their immaturity and inability to communicate with each other as major reasons for a dissolution of their marriage. Years of unfaithfulness and disloyalty had also tried the patience of some of the spouses who had sought a divorce. "My husband was not ready for the responsibility of a marriage," wrote one woman. "He wanted to party all the time. He left us for another girl." A divorced male wrote: "My wife was fooling around behind my back."

Alcohol and drug abuse had also taken their toll on some marriages. One divorced woman wrote, "Coor's Lite was more important to my husband than sex." Another wife was physically abused. "I feel stepped on, used, abused. Have suffered mental, emotional, and financial abuse. He spent too much money, I got blamed for not paying the bills. I had no say in anything."

One woman took the initiative to get a divorce after a belated discovery of her sexual orientation. She wrote, "I separated from my husband after twelve years of marriage and am now in a relationship with a woman. It is somewhat stressful as far as coming out to family and friends, but I have to realize and come to terms with my sexual preference."

Four out of ten men and three out of ten women in this cohort had made use of Hawaii's liberal divorce laws, which made the dissolution of their marriages easier than did laws in other states of the union. But they had not taken this step lightly. Their comments suggested that their generation was asking more from matrimony than had their parents and grandparents. They wanted marriage to be a partnership with equality between husband and wife and to be emotionally satisfying for both spouses. On the whole, they thought that a bad marriage was worse than no marriage at all, so they were willing to divorce, even when they had young children. The minority in this group who risked a second marriage generally were satisfied with the choice of their new partners and their commitment to the responsibilities of parenthood.

CHILDREN: HOPES AND EXPECTATIONS

By age forty, two out of three men and four out of five women in this cohort had children. The average number of children who had been born to these forty-year-olds was significantly lower than for their parents' generation (2.5 vs. 4.5), but higher than the national average (1.7). The children ranged in age from their late teens to young infants. Some of the forty-year-old women were pregnant with their first child; others were planning to have a child in the fifth decade of their lives.

An overwhelming proportion of these forty-year-olds (93.4% of the fathers; 87.1% of the mothers) derived great satisfaction from watching their children grow. A male teacher wrote, "Looking at the world through the eyes of a child gives me great pleasure. Helping him see the magic! Teaching him." A woman who was a full-time homemaker told us, "There is pure joy in seeing my child grow and learn things. Seeing things through his eyes makes the most simple things seem so fantastic." A salesperson wrote, "Watching the results of all the years of hard work raising our sons gives me great satisfaction. They are wonderful people. They're not just my sons; they are my friends."

Other parents found pleasure in fostering their children's sense of mastery and responsibility. A male technician wrote, "What has been most satisfying to me as a parent is watching my daughter grow and learn, guiding her along the way, being able to confront challenging situations, and also learning myself, day by day, and trying to be a responsible friend and guardian to her." And a woman teacher stressed the importance of shared affection: "The most satisfying thing about being a parent has probably been experiencing the love my children share with me. I feel this when we help each other during our daily lives, play together, have both serious and humorous discussions, and reconcile after disagreements."

More than half of the women (57%) and a third of the men (36%) told us that they were more communicative and affectionate with their children than their own parents had been. "I am not as strict with my son as my father was with me," wrote a lawyer. "I do not hit him. I have much more interaction with my son—talking and showing affection." A manager said, "I try to get more involved and spend more time in my children's daily lives."

One of the mothers, who was a part-time student, wrote, "We are giving our children verbal and non-verbal messages of our love and affection as well as clear limits of what is (un)acceptable. We make a big deal of rituals—celebrating birthdays and holidays and other special occasions. I volunteer at their schools and we get involved in their sports. We plan our family activities, ranging from casual to cultural activities. Our children have a voice in our family and many choices and opportunities." Another, who worked as a secretary, commented, "I strive to keep communication open between my boys and myself, as a very important key to our being a family. As a youngster I wasn't very expressive with my parents and they with me. It was an Oriental upbringing which didn't express emotions verbally."

One out of four parents reported that they were less strict with their children than their own parents had been when they were growing up. A homemaker wrote, "I am more lax in discipline, but more understanding. Close to my son and more in tune with his needs." A salesman said, "We could not talk back to our parents. I give my children the opportunity to explain *their* side. Spanking is *the last resort*."

One out of five stressed the fact their children had more material things than they did when they were young. A firefighter wrote, "Having a smaller family (2 children) compared to me (6 children), I can provide for my children a few of the better things in life." A produce clerk remembered, "We, as young children, didn't have as much as my own children do now. I come from a big family (11 kids). My dad and mom couldn't give us material things we needed, but they gave us their love which was more important."

A few parents also emphasized different values from those they had grown up with as children. A teacher wrote, "My husband and I place more emphasis on church and God than my parents did. We are more involved in our children's Sunday School activities, and spend more time actually talking with them about what we believe in." And a businessman expressed his hope that "even on Kauai, with shopping malls and cable T.V., I have succeeded in instilling in my kids some of the old fashioned values, such as honesty, integrity and work."

Some parents, especially those with teenagers, expressed concern about the negative influences, such as drug use, violence, and the pressure to have early sex, their children were facing in the outside world. One of the mothers wrote, "There is so much pressure on them to take the *easy* way instead of doing it the *right* way (although that may be painful). I try to teach them that our society is governed by rules that we must live by and that our present way of life seems to be drifting away from that. We have become a nation of 'justifiers' which is bringing our society down." Another mother worried about "raising my children in a society that tempts them with so many evil things, things that we parents have had to educate ourselves about."

Despite these worries, 86 percent of the men and 88 percent of the women who were parents in this cohort were satisfied with their present relationships with their children—proportions that were higher than those reported for the MacArthur Survey of 35–44-year-olds on the U.S. mainland (M: 73%; F: 82%).

They also had high expectations for their children. Most of them centered on achievement (60% of the fathers; 67% of the mothers); getting a good education (34% of the fathers; 35% of the mothers); a happy family life of their own (33% of the fathers; 47% of the mothers), and good values (27% of the fathers; 45% of the mothers). A male teacher wrote, "I expect my son to become a competent problem solver, and effective communicator, both orally and written, and a comprehensive reader who respects himself and other people." A businessman hoped that his children "become self-sufficient, educated and responsible in their community."

A significantly higher proportion of mothers than fathers emphasized happiness and moral values. A saleswoman wrote, "I expect my children to be good, respectful people in all their relationships. To follow through on their commitments and responsibilities. To remember that God is ever present in their lives. Most important to get their priorities straight. To find peace and happiness." An artist expected her son and daughter to be "good, responsible, law-abiding citizens. To be productive and effective in our society and enjoy the existence they create for themselves." A manager hoped that her children "would do or be anything they want to be. To live life to its fullest. To explore the world. To have fun, but be responsible."

SOCIAL RELATIONS

Parents

By age forty, one out of every four individuals in this cohort had lost his or her father and one out of six had lost his or her mother. Among the majority whose parents were still alive, three out of four were satisfied with their current relationship with their fathers, and five out of six with their relationship with their mothers. Twenty-seven percent of the men and 34 percent of the women felt that their aging parents were somewhat emotionally dependent on them. A small minority (18.8% of the males; 13.4% of the females) supported their parents financially, especially when they were seriously or chronically ill.

In turn, a third of these forty-year-olds admitted to being emotionally dependent on their parents. Somewhat to our surprise, a significantly higher proportion of men than women still lived with their parents (M: 17.1%; F: 4.9%). Most of them were either unmarried or recently divorced. Twelve percent of the forty-year-old males and 10 percent of the forty-year-old females needed (and received) some financial help from their parents. Among them were sons who had lost their jobs in the declining economy of Hawaii and daughters who were either divorced or single parents.

Siblings

Some 20 percent of the forty-year-old males and some 12 percent of the forty-year-old females also received financial support from their siblings in hard times. The majority of both men and women valued their brothers and sisters for their emotional support in times of crises (M: 58.5%; F: 77.7%) and for their shared interests and activities (M: 70.3%; F: 66%). For nearly half of the men and women, older siblings had become role models they tried to emulate. For the 20 percent who still had small children, siblings were also valued as reliable providers of child care.

Occasionally, child care issues led to some problems for forty-year-old mothers with young children. One woman wrote, "My husband, being the youngest, is constantly being 'counseled' by his siblings on bringing up our only child. My parents, who live nearby, attempt to provide *their* 'guidance' to me to relay to my husband. Each side uses *one* of us—*never both* of us as a couple."

Friends

Friends were among the most important members of the social network of these forty-year-olds. Three out of four men and nine out of ten women valued their friends for their emotional support in times of crisis—true to the spirit of the Beatles song "I get by with a little help from my friends," a song they first heard in 1967, when they were entering their teens. Nine out of ten men and five out of six women shared their social activities with friends they had known since high school. For more than half, friends had become important role models who shared their most deeply held values. For fathers and mothers of young children, friends, like siblings, were also cherished because they could be relied upon as providers of child care.

Community Service

But the network of social relationships also extended into the neighborhood and community at large. In spite of an acute "time crunch," many of the forty-year-olds were involved with volunteer activities (as were their middle-aged peers in the MIDUS Survey). Thirty percent of the men and 45 percent of the women allotted weekly time for church activities. Forty percent of the men and 25 percent of the women participated in athletic activities, mostly in the schools their children attended. One out of four tutored children in school or worked with local youth choirs or dance groups; others gave their time to community organizations that raised money for worthy causes, ranging from homes for foster care children to the restoration of buildings and the preservation of the island's endangered ecology.

Others were active in support groups for individuals with substance abuse or mental health problems. In spite of having to work a double shift at home and in their place of employment, a significantly higher proportion of women than men tended to be regular volunteers in church groups and in community organizations.

STRESSFUL LIFE EVENTS

The fourth decade of life had brought a number of stressful events for many of the men and women on Kauai that tested their mettle (see Table 3 in Appendix I). Foremost was Hurricane INIKI and its aftermath that affected some 85.5 percent of the men and 90 percent of the women in this cohort. Nearly two-thirds changed residence and almost 60 percent changed employment during that time, and for nearly half of the men and women the natural disaster that had struck their island and the continuing recession in Hawaii brought financial problems—more than double the rate that had been reported by them in the third decade of life.

The proportion of men and women who had suffered a personal illness or injury during the fourth decade of life also increased—up from 16.8% at age 30 to 27.4% at age 40 for the men, and from 19.9% at age 30 to 28.9% at age 40 for the women. Among the most frequently reported health problems for both men and women were high blood pressure, back and joint problems, arthritis, allergies, asthma, and anxiety and depression. These were also the most frequent complaints voiced among the participants in the MacArthur Survey of Midlife Development.

Nearly half of the women in this cohort and a quarter of the men were concerned about weight gain. Problems with substance abuse had also substantially increased from the third to the fourth decade of life—up from 10.9 percent at age 30 to 20.5 percent at age 40 among the men, and from 4.5 percent at age 30 to 12.5 percent at age 40 for the women. The illness and death of aging parents had added considerable stress to the lives of one out of every four women and one out of every five men during their fourth decade of life.

On the positive side, a third of the men and women reported the birth of a child during the period between ages thirty and forty, and nearly 30 percent had taken the "plunge" into a first or second marriage. Despite hard economic times, 50 percent of the men and 45 percent of the women had gained a promotion on their jobs.

Still, finances headed the list of current worries for both men (48%) and women (51%). As they had at age thirty, a significantly higher proportion of women than men worried about their children (F: 46.7%; M: 27.4%) and about social issues that would affect their future (F: 30.3%; M: 17.7%). In turn, a higher proportion of men than women worried about work-related issues (M: 22%; F: 12.5%). And for about one out of four of the forty-year-olds health issues had become a major concern.

SOURCES OF EMOTIONAL SUPPORT

At forty, the overwhelming majority of the men and women in this cohort turned to informal sources of support rather than mental health professionals when they needed counsel in stressful times—as they had done in their teens, twenties, and thirties. Leading the list was the support of close friends (M: 70%; F: 73%) or spouse (M: 64%; F: 70%). Indeed, two-thirds of the married men and women thought of their spouses as their best friend.

More than half of the men and women also received emotional support from their parents (M: 52.5%; F: 61.8%). Half of the women and a third of the men relied on the counsel of siblings, and one out of four sought emotional support from other family members (aunts, uncles, in-laws). A significant proportion of men and women also sought advice from their coworkers (M: 28.8%; F: 33.6%) and from their boss or supervisor (M: 17.8%; F: 13.2%). A third of the women and one out of every five men relied on faith and prayer or the counsel of a minister. Teachers were sought out by some 12 percent of the men and women. Mental health professionals of *any* kind (social workers, psychologists, psychiatrists) ranked *last* in the list of sources of emotional support. Their help had been sought by only 5 percent of the men and 10 percent of the women.

DEFINING EXPERIENCES: A MIDLIFE PERSPECTIVE

When we asked the men and women in this cohort to tell us about the experiences that had been most important in making them the kind of person they were, we noted that a significant proportion mentioned calamities and losses in their lives that had become "learning experiences" for them—especially the women (F: 44.3%; M: 28%). An administrative assistant told us, "Being involved in the recovery after Hurricane INIKI made me aware of how many people are so much less fortunate than I am. This made me appreciate even more my family and friends." A designer wrote, "The most important experience was the passing of my father. It has made me realize that we are not permanent fixtures on this planet. It has made me think about everything I do and what effect it has on everyone." And a widow, with teenage children, told us, "The death of my husband and caring for him before he died has helped me to be kind and loving, especially to friends and relatives who are ill. It has made me appreciate life."

One woman who had struggled with substance abuse problems felt that the critical moments in her life were "two episodes of anxiety attacks, requiring hospitalization. The experience has helped me to take one day at a time, to be patient with me and to help myself." And another, a health worker, told us that "my divorce was my first opportunity to see if I could do it *on my own*. It was very difficult, but somehow we (myself and my children) survived. My mom told me some years ago that she was proud of me for deciding to strike out on my own instead of moving back home."

The loss of a father through death or of a spouse through divorce turned out to be a defining experience for men as well. A technician wrote, "My dad dying and my pending divorce will, I believe, show me what kind of person I really am." And a musician told us that "the loss of my father at an early age and the subsequent events that forced me to be independent put things in perspective for me. Living through hard times made me realize that I am a true survivor, no matter how tough things have gotten."

One out of every four individuals in this cohort pointed to the love and encouragement of family members, friends, and teachers as important influences in their lives. A female teacher wrote, "I have had loving and caring people throughout my life who have been my mentors and supporters." Another teacher told us, "My parents were always there for me. I didn't necessarily confide in them, but I knew that they loved me and would support me in whatever I chose to do. I grew up with the special love of my grandfather. I was *Ochijan*'s girl. He worried about me and talked with me whenever I needed advice."

A male administrator gave special credit to his grandparents as well, "the time spent, the special memories, their patience and words of wisdom which still ring true today." Others praised their teachers and coaches who cared about them. Some chose to get their education on the mainland to test their mettle. A teacher wrote us from the Midwest, "I left home after high school to go 3,000 miles away to another school where I realized I can take care of myself."

Travel, associated with getting an education or a job, was a defining experience for one out of five individuals in this cohort. A woman who teaches English as a Second Language wrote us, "Living overseas has enabled me to get to know different cultures and people and has broadened my horizon." Several men and women felt that military service and living overseas were the crucial experiences in their lives. A male teacher credited his college education and his teaching jobs on the mainland (in Washington and Idaho) with making him an independent person who thinks for himself. And a female paralegal wrote, "I think having gone away to a mainland college has broadened my horizon . . . experiencing a new environment, the pain of prejudices and the joy of traveling."

One out of five among the women felt that their work accomplishments had defined their identity at midlife. A divorced mother of teenagers told us, "By getting an education and by my job experience, I have been able to be a better person. I can communicate with people a lot better and have been able to cope with being a single parent." Another woman, a counselor, felt proud "to be able to make a difference, no matter how small, in the lives of the students I work with." And a female business manager wrote, "My mother's encouragement to obtain a college education and be able to stand on my own two feet has paid off. Today I am not totally reliant on my spouse for support. Three promotions in my 14-year-old career have given me much self-confidence."

The same proportion of women considered motherhood to be their defining experience in life. A clerk wrote, "I have realized how important every day is and I have learned to appreciate the accomplishments that my husband and I have made. I feel that becoming a parent has been the most important experience in my life thus far, because it has made me more aware of setting priorities and the importance of a positive outlook in life."

One out of ten individuals reported that their faith was the most important factor in their lives. "Having a Catholic education helped me in overcoming most (if not all) the problems I encountered," wrote a woman who is a teacher's aide. "My Christian upbringing has given me strength and hope for what I feel is a difficult time in my life," said a clerk. "I came to know Jesus Christ as my Lord and Savior, and it's helped me accept things I cannot control," wrote a service worker. "Accepting the Lord Jesus in my Life" and "Accepting Jesus Christ as my personal savior" were common refrains among the men and woman for whom religion had become the focal point of their lives. Theirs had been a rebirth at midlife, usually under trying circumstances, after they had lost a job or a loved one.

Satisfaction with Life and Expectations for the Future

In spite of persistent economic uncertainties, six out of ten among the 40-year-old men and seven out of ten among the 40-year-old women on Kauai felt satisfied with themselves as they were entering the fifth decade of their lives. These proportions are significantly higher than those reported from the 35–44-year-old participants in the MacArthur Survey on the U.S. mainland (M: 54.4%; F: 49.2%).

More than half (M: 53.3%; F: 56.5%) hoped to continue their education. A female homemaker and part-time student wrote us, "In the next ten years, I expect to continue taking classes which interest me and to return to part-time employment. I would hope that my husband would be able to reduce *his* work-load and resume *his* educational interests, too. College classes are more interesting and relevant now. It is I who changed in attitude, and not the classes. My husband is of the same opinion." A married nurse told us, "I expect to retire from my nursing career with approximately 28 years of service. At that time I will be 50 years old. I may work part-time, hopefully in a different field. I may go back to college for some non-credit courses. I'll expect to travel, garden, read, and pursue more creative projects. I expect to be financially stable, and emotionally mature." And a government worker expected "to be closing the financial security chapter and opening the spiritual chapter of my life—keeping healthy and gaining wisdom."

A significantly higher proportion of women than men were anticipating success in their chosen careers or jobs (F: 69.4%; M: 54.2%). A female businesswoman wrote, "I want my own business to be successful. I want to be financially independent, so my husband can retire and relax, and my children can go on deserved vacations. I feel that I am strong, assertive and confident enough to put all my skills, knowledge and feelings together to create a happy non-worried life for all of us." In contrast, an unemployed male, married with children, just hoped to find "a good, steady job."

A significantly higher proportion of women than men were concerned about the future of their children (F: 52.4%; M: 29%). A female service worker told us, "I have three children—14, 12, and 2. It's very hard knowing that I will be starting all over with my two-year-old baby. Because I am older, I am more tired and less patient. Knowing I am going through pre-school, kindergarten and sports all over again is overwhelming sometimes. My expectations for the next ten years are—to start all over again." Undeterred, a forty-year-old salesperson, recently remarried, was planning "to have a baby, retire from the military as a NCO, and get a degree in accounting"—all in the fifth decade of her life!

She was not alone in her desire for another child at age forty. A full-time homemaker wrote, "I expect to raise my 3 months old son the way my parents raised me—to respect your elders and to know right from wrong. I expect to work on my new computer and to further my knowledge in computer set-ups. And to maybe have another baby." Another woman, a travel agent with a three-year-old son, said, "I would like one more child, own my home, be financially secure, so that I could have a part-time job where I could be home with my children and give them lots of love and attention." And a divorced secretary expected to "get married again and have kids."

Others planned to give something back to the community that had nourished them. A female manager, with high-school-age children, who was taking college courses in preparation for a career as a therapist, told us, "My girls all think it is *cool* that their mom has home-work! I have reached a point in my life that I want to *give back* to society. I'd like to spend the rest of my life helping other people." A teacher planned "to make a stronger impact on the community," and a male physician hoped "to continue on my path, develop new skills and improve the lives of others."

A few had humble expectations for the fifth decade of life. A man with marital and employment problems expected "to try to put the past behind me and get my life back." Another, in the process of divorce from his second wife, planned to "live a quiet, unassuming life." A recovering alcoholic, recently retired from the military, confessed, "I am completely up in the air." A self-employed businesswoman who had recovered from mental health problems and substance abuse problems in her thirties was more upbeat with her expectations. "I want to survive the economic downturn, to be happy, and to make a few people laugh!"

INDIVIDUALS WITH SERIOUS COPING PROBLEMS

Most of the men and women in this cohort had managed the transition to midlife without major problems. But one out of six (16%) were doing poorly, struggling with domestic problems, substance abuse, and serious mental health problems, and living in precarious financial circumstances. Two out of three males and four out of five females in this group had been "troubled" teens, with serious learning and mental health problems and a record of delinquencies.

Such a *retrospective* look at the lives of the "troubled" forty-year-olds may give the impression of a high degree of continuity in maladaptation from childhood through midlife. But a *prospective* view shows a different picture. By age forty, only one out of four of the individuals who had been troubled teens were still doing poorly. Three out of four were coping with the demands of midlife without any major problems.

There were a few individuals (M: 13; F: 3) who had experienced a relatively trouble-free childhood and adolescence but who were having serious coping problems at age forty. They scored significantly lower than their same-sex peers on three scales of Psychological Well-Being: Environmental Mastery, Positive Relations with Others, and Self-Acceptance.

The women also scored significantly lower on the Personal Growth scale, and significantly higher on the Distress, Fear, and Anger scales of the EAS Temperament Survey. At age thirty, both men and women in this group had also scored significantly lower than their same-sex peers on the Sociability scale of the EAS Temperament Survey.

The men had been troubled by financial problems and problems with substance abuse; the women reported the loss of a job, the breakup of a long-term relationship, and serious personal illnesses or injuries in their fourth decade of life. And they could count on fewer sources of emotional support during this period than did women who were coping well at age forty.

They also seemed to be less well equipped intellectually to handle the stressful life events they had encountered in adulthood. Both the men and the women in this group had scored lower than their peers on measures of scholastic competence (PMA IQ) and practical problem-solving skills (PMA reasoning factor score) at age 10. The women had done poorly on the STEP reading test in grades 4/5 and had scored in the "external" direction on the Novicki Locus of Control Scale at ages 17/18, expressing little faith in the effectiveness of their own actions—even *before* they had made the transition into adulthood.

But these individuals were the *exception*. As we shall see in the next five chapters, the journey to midlife for *most* men and women in this cohort was more often shaped by their extraordinary resilience and their capacity to recover from and overcome the problems they had encountered in childhood and adolescence.

◻

CHAPTER FIVE

Pathways of Resilience
From Childhood to Midlife

About 30 percent of the individuals in this cohort encountered a combination of potent biological and psychosocial risk factors when they were young. They experienced perinatal stress, grew up in chronic poverty, were reared by parents who had not graduated from high school, and lived in a family environment troubled by chronic discord, parental alcoholism, or mental illness.

Some two-thirds of the children (129 in all) who had experienced four or more of these risk factors by age two *did* develop serious learning and behavior problems by age ten, and/or had delinquency records, mental health problems, and teenage pregnancies by age eighteen. Yet to our surprise, one out of three of these "high-risk" children—72 individuals (32 males and 40 females)—managed to cope successfully with the adversities in their lives. We called them "vulnerable but invincible" (Werner and Smith, 1982).

None of these individuals developed any learning or behavior problems in childhood or adolescence. As far as we could tell from interviews and from their records in the community, as they grew up they managed to do well in their schoolwork and in their homes and social lives; and they set realistic goals and expectations for themselves when they graduated from high school. At the end of the second decade of life, they had developed into competent, confident, and caring persons who expressed a great desire to make use of whatever opportunities came along to improve themselves.

Looking back over the lives of these seventy-two individuals, we contrasted their behavior characteristics and caregiving environments with those of high-risk youths of the same age and sex who had developed serious coping problems at ages ten or eighteen (learning disabilities, mental health problems, serious delinquencies, and/or teenage pregnancies). We found a number of characteristics within the individuals and their families and also outside the family circle that contributed to their resilience.

Infant

Even as infants, these children had temperamental characteristics that elicited positive attention from family members as well as strangers. By age one, both boys and girls were frequently described by their caregivers as "very active," the girls as "affectionate" and "cuddly," the boys as "good-natured" and "easy to deal with"—more often than the babies who later developed serious learning or behavior problems. They also had fewer eating and sleeping habits that distressed their parents.

toddler

As toddlers, these children already tended to meet the world on their own terms. The pediatricians and psychologists who examined them independently at age two noted their alertness and autonomy, their tendency to seek out novel experiences, and their positive social orientation. They were more advanced in communication, locomotion, and self-help skills than children who later experienced serious learning and behavior problems.

elem. School

In elementary school, teachers reported that the resilient children got along well with their classmates. They had better reasoning and reading skills than the children who developed problems. Although not unusually gifted, they used whatever skills they had effectively. Both parents and teachers noted that they had many interests and engaged in activities and hobbies that were not narrowly sex-typed. Such activities provided them with solace in adversity and a reason to feel proud.

high School

By the time they graduated from high school, the resilient youths had developed a positive self-concept and an internal locus of control. On the California Psychological Inventory (CPI), they displayed a more nurturant, responsible, and achievement-oriented attitude toward life than their high-risk peers who had developed problems. The girls in this group, especially, were more assertive and independent than the other girls in this cohort.

Family

Most resilient boys and girls grew up in families with four or fewer children, with a space of two years or more between themselves and their next sibling. Few had experienced prolonged separations from a primary caretaker during the first year of life. All had the opportunity to establish a close bond with at least one caregiver from whom they received plenty of positive attention when they were infants. Some of this nurturing came from substitute parents, such as grandparents or older siblings, or from the ranks of regular babysitters. Such substitute parents played an important role as positive models of identification. Where mothers were employed, the job of taking care of younger siblings contributed to the pronounced autonomy and sense of responsibility noted among the resilient girls, especially in households where the father was absent. Resilient boys were often firstborn sons who did not have to share their parents' attention with many additional children. There was usually a male in the family who could serve as a role model— if not the father, then a grandfather, older cousin, or uncle. Structure and rules and assigned chores were part of their daily routines in adolescence.

 Friends

The resilient children also found emotional support outside of their own families. They tended to have at least one and usually several close friends, especially the girls. They relied on informal networks of kin and neighbors, peers and elders, for counsel and support in times of crisis. Many had a favorite teacher who became a role model, friend, and confidant for them.

activities

Participation in extracurricular activities played an important part in their lives, especially activities that were cooperative enterprises, such as 4-H and the YMCA and YWCA. For still others, emotional support came from a youth leader or from a minister or church group. With their help, they acquired a faith that their lives had meaning and that they had control over their fate.

temperament

Constitutional factors (health, temperamental characteristics) discriminated most between the resilient children and their high-risk peers in infancy and early childhood. The emotional support of alternate caregivers, such as grandparents or siblings, and the child's verbal and reasoning skills gained in importance in middle childhood. By late adolescence, personality characteristics, such as high self-esteem and an internal locus of control, and the presence of external support systems differentiated most between positive and negative developmental outcomes among the high-risk children. As the number of risk factors or stressful life events increased, more protective factors were needed to counterbalance the negative aspects in the lives of these vulnerable children and to ensure a positive developmental outcome.

We were able to obtain follow-up data at age thirty on 63 of the 72 resilient children—88 percent of the original sample. Among our data are interviews, questionnaires, test scores, and agency records for 27 of the 30 resilient males and for 36 of the 42 resilient females. A third of the men and women in this group were of Japanese descent, a third were Filipino, and the others were part Hawaiian. They represented the three major ethnic groups on Kauai.

The resilient men were about evenly divided between those who had settled on Kauai and those who left the island to serve in the armed forces, to work in Honolulu or on the West Coast of the U.S. mainland, or to venture overseas to Japan and Europe. The resilient women had experienced more changes of residence than the resilient men since we last saw them at age eighteen. We traveled thousands of miles to interview them—in their homes on Kauai, in their offices in Honolulu, and in their new residences in California, Oregon, and Washington. One of the women, a sergeant in the U.S. Air Force, was interviewed at an airfield in Colorado; another, the wife of an enlisted man, at an army base in Maryland. Some of the resilient women, in turn, traveled many miles to meet with us. A head nurse had flown from her home in the Western Caroline Islands to attend a conference at the University of Hawaii and to visit her kinfolk on Kauai.

How well did these resilient children fare in adulthood in comparison with the men and women who had grown up under similar conditions of poverty and family instability but who had developed serious coping problems in their teens?

Educational and Vocational Accomplishments

Both the resilient men and the resilient women were highly achievement oriented. With few exceptions, they had pursued additional education beyond high school. Some 40 percent had attended a four-year college (M: 43.5%; F: 38.2%)—a rate more than twice as high as the national average for individuals their age (M: 17.2%; F: 16.0%) and significantly higher than that for men and women with coping problems by age eighteen (M: 15.2%; F: 10.0%).

Equally impressive were the vocational accomplishments of the resilient men and women who entered the workforce during hard economic times. When we saw them at age 31/32, only one man (a recent graduate of a textile design school in the Netherlands) and three women (all mothers of young children) were not in the labor force. Unemployment rates among the resilient individuals were significantly lower than the national average (of 6.5%) for their age group at that time (U.S. Bureau of Labor, 1986).

While their fathers had been in either unskilled or semiskilled jobs, most of the resilient men and women had moved to skilled trade, technical, and managerial positions. None was in an unskilled job, and only about 10 percent held semiskilled jobs. In comparison with their peers who had developed coping problems by age eighteen, a significantly lower proportion of the resilient males held semi- or unskilled jobs (13.0% versus 35.3%). A significantly higher proportion of the resilient males and females were in professional, managerial, and semiprofessional positions (M: 39.1%; F: 45.5%).

Among the resilient men were a youth minister, an engineer who designed satellites, and a career officer in the U.S. Army. Several men had entered professions related to law enforcement: one served as a deputy prosecutor; another as an adult correctional officer. Some worked in advertising and graphic design in Honolulu; others were self-employed in construction work. Several men worked as personnel managers, foremen, or supervisors on the islands' sugar plantations; others had found employment in the tourist industry. One of the men was a commercial fisherman; another managed a pizza parlor.

The jobs held by the resilient women ranged from the more traditional female occupations (accountant, administrative assistant, beautician, bookkeeper, clerk, insurance agent, nurse, preschool teacher, waitress) to less traditional jobs (poet-in-residence in a school, paralegal, president of a trading company, sergeant in the U.S. Air Force, tour director, and writer of children's books).

A higher proportion of the resilient individuals than of the men and women who had been troubled teens reported work-related stress in their adult lives. Interpersonal difficulties with coworkers and bosses were cited as the most frequently encountered stress at work by both the resilient men and the resilient women (M: 26.3%; F: 39.3%). The overwhelming majority of the resilient men and women relied on their own competence and determination in resolving such work-related difficulties (M: 73.9%; F: 61.8%).

With few exceptions (the construction workers with fluctuating income), the resilient men and women had employment that provided them with income sufficient for their styles of life. The majority relied on the income of two wage earners to meet their financial needs. Career or job success was the primary goal of the resilient individuals at this stage of their lives, especially for the women.

While most of the resilient women stressed the cooperative aspects of work, more resilient men focused on the challenge of competition. A supervisor at the local sugar plantation said, "I am a very aggressive person—I'd rather lead than be led. I thrive on that." The young deputy prosecutor mused, "I am always competitive—there is more in life than what I am doing. I want to run for senator some day."

Marriage and Relationship with a Mate

At age 31/32, a higher proportion of resilient women than women with problems in their teens were married, but the resilient men were as reluctant to marry as were men who had been troubled adolescents. Four out of five among the resilient women were currently married, including 15 percent who were in their second marriage. This rate was higher than the national average (of 68.5%) for women their age. In contrast, less than half of the resilient men were married at that time. This rate was lower than the national average (of 64.7%) for men their age (U.S. Bureau of Labor, 1986). Also, among the singles, a higher proportion of men than women did *not* live in a committed long-term relationship (M: 21.7%; F: 8.8%). Whatever the reasons, fear of failure or fear of intimacy, there was a greater reluctance among the males than among the females to make commitments to a partner of the opposite sex.

Expectations from marriage or long-term relationships differed significantly by gender. The majority of the resilient men and women wanted permanency and security (M: 57.1%; F: 73.1%), but a significantly higher proportion of the resilient females than males expected intimacy and sharing from such a relationship (M: 35.7%; F: 73.1%). These were a nurse's expectations from her marriage: "That we can always be friends first, then lovers, then husband and wife." The recently married poet said, "I make it a point to go wherever he goes. I expect my marriage to be a lifetime partnership."

But once committed, the resilient males worked harder at resolving conflicts in marital relationships than did males with coping problems in their teens. The overwhelming majority of the resilient men (64.7%) and about half of the resilient women (48.3%) resolved conflicts by discussion and a joint resolution. The majority reported that their caring and determination made their marriages work.

Divorce and Remarriage

The divorce rates of the resilient men and women were comparable to the rates reported by their peers with coping problems by age eighteen, but nearly twice as high as nationwide rates for this generation (M: 17.4% versus 8.5%; F: 20.6% versus 11.5%). The resilient women, however, had higher rates of remarriage than did the resilient men (M: 8.7%; F: 14.7%).

A higher proportion of the resilient men than the resilient women referred to the negative effects of the breakup of a long-term relationship (M: 45.5%; F: 29.4%). For the men, divorce usually also involved separation from children or stepchildren. A foreman who was divorced from his wife (who returned to her former husband) wrote, "When I was married I was able to relate to my stepdaughter as a friend and real father. Now [after the divorce] I have come to the realization how harsh life really is—how relationships can leave deep within hurts that don't seem to go away."

Half of the divorced men were estranged from their children; the other half reported ambivalent, off/on relationships with their offspring. In contrast, the majority of the divorced women reported that their divorces had no bearing on their present relationships with their children. They generally praised their second husbands for their caring and understanding, as well as for the acceptance of their offspring. Commented a woman (who had taken an overdose of sleeping pills when her first husband deserted her), "My second husband is quiet, considerate— a good family man. He is always there to back me up. He says he likes me as I am—what's in my heart." A sales clerk, whose first marriage ended in divorce because her husband was a drug addict, told us, "My second husband is very patient, understanding—he doesn't treat my first son any differently than the other children. He is hard working and a good father."

Overall, men in this group were more reluctant than women to make long-term commitments in early adulthood; career consolidation seemed to take precedence over intimacy. Childhood experiences of parental discord and psychopathology (especially in the mother) were reexperienced by some men in the context of the breakup of a long-term relationship, and the hurt of a divorce often stunted a still-fragile feeling of trust.

Among the resilient women, there was a heightened expectation for intimacy and sharing in a long-term relationship, which occasionally led to disappointments in a first marriage, but the resilient women were more willing to risk again and to enter a second and happier marriage than were resilient men. Their risk taking in matters of the heart was also related to their greater need to find a permanent and secure home for their children.

PARENTHOOD: HOPES AND EXPECTATIONS

Three out of four among the resilient women had children by age thirty, in contrast to fewer than half of the resilient men (M: 43.5%; F: 76.5%). Most had two children and did not plan to have any more. Many of their children were of preschool age or in the early elementary grades; however, some of the women who had married right out of high school already worried about their teenagers.

Although they had, on the average, a smaller number of children, the resilient men and women valued the positive aspects of parenthood more than did their peers with coping problems by age eighteen. Two out of three among the resilient men enjoyed the opportunity to care for their children and believed in their futures. Fewer than one out of four among the men with coping problems in adolescence had similar perspectives on parenting. Two out of three among the resilient men saw fatherhood as a sign of self-development, and a high proportion considered their spouses as helpful in their parental role. None of their high-risk peers did.

There were some significant differences between the resilient men and women in their hopes and expectations for their offspring. While the majority of parents wanted their children to be competent (M: 54.5%; F: 57.1%), a significantly higher proportion of the resilient mothers expected them to achieve well in school and to be successful in a career (M: 18.2%; F: 61.9%). A loan and collection officer who was the mother of four children said, "I want them to do better than I did—go to college." Added an accountant, the mother of two preschoolers, "I hope both of them go into some kind of profession."

A significantly higher proportion of the resilient men than women considered parenthood a sign of maturity (M: 66.7%: F: 16%) and welcomed the opportunity to care for their offspring (M: 66.7%; F: 20%); a significantly higher proportion of the resilient women than men commented on the pleasure of seeing their children grow (M: 33.3%; F: 64%).

The majority (67.7%) of the resilient women stressed early independence for their offspring, while most (62.5%) of the resilient men tolerated dependence in their young children. But in spite of the obvious pride that the resilient fathers took in their children, there were still large differences between spouses in their active involvement in child rearing. Most of the resilient women reported that they had the major share of child rearing, while most of the resilient men said that both parents shared child rearing equally.

RELATIONSHIPS WITH FAMILY AND FRIENDS

Parents

Among parental problems that exerted a continuing negative effect on the lives of the resilient men and women in adulthood were alcoholism, chronic family discord, divorce, parental illness, and, for the females, maternal mental illness. The overwhelming majority of the resilient men and women handled the stress of such parental problems by detachment or withdrawal, while their troubled peers continued to get enmeshed in the familial discord and pathology that were the norm for their childhoods. Some three out of four among the resilient men and women (M: 71.4%; F: 75.0%) detached themselves emotionally when difficulties arose with their mothers—in contrast to only 16 percent of the high-risk men and 10 percent of the high-risk women with coping problems by age eighteen. Two-thirds of the resilient men and women detached themselves emotionally when difficulties arose with their fathers—in contrast to only 16 percent of the high-risk men and 25 percent of the high-risk women with coping problems by age eighteen.

Comments among the resilient individuals about parents who had caused them pain in earlier years varied from negative to ambivalent to positive. Perhaps the most critical comments came from the women who perceived themselves as abandoned by their mothers in childhood. A woman who was happily married and expected to "grow old and gray" with her husband reflected on her feelings about her mother after her parents divorced when she was in junior high school. "I don't know where she is—she left us all behind. I was watching her fool around with other men. I used to be her maid—to do everything for her." Another, whose parents separated when she was three years old and who was raised by her father with the help of her paternal grandmother, said, "I don't know my real mother at all. She lives on the mainland now. When she comes for vacation to Kauai, she just goes touring around with my sisters."

Reactions to mothers who were mentally ill and who abused their children either emotionally or physically ranged from distant to forgiving. Said the happily married daughter of an epileptic mother who had behaved erratically toward her, "My mom and I have never been close. I believe my mom is slow mentally—not bright—she can be very hurtful and hateful."

Nevertheless, parental illness and impending death also led to compassion and forgiveness. One of the women, whose mother had been a nervous, abusive woman who had beaten her daughters savagely, said, "My mother left us several times when she had her nervous breakdowns for fear she might hurt her children. Shortly before she died from lung cancer, I was able to tell her that I loved her and she told me that she regretted what she had done to me when I was a child."

Similar reports came from the children of alcoholics. The daughter of an alcoholic father reported, "My father used to be so erratic—he drank a lot. He was the Samurai—everything in the family's life centered around him. If he was not in a good mood, you had to walk on tiptoes. He has mellowed a bit since he got sick with cancer ten years ago." The son of an alcoholic father added, "We went through hell. It was a poor marriage—swearing, bitching all the time—my parents separated once and came back together—I grew up in all of this! My dad used to drink daily and get drunk; but two years ago, after an ulcer operation, the doctor told him that if he drank again he had to have more painful surgery. He quit smoking and drinking. Now I can sit and talk with him, now that he is on the wagon."

Parents-in-Law

In contrast to the majority of their high-risk peers with coping problems, almost all of the resilient men and women who were married had good relationships with their in-laws. The majority of the resilient men and women evaluated their parents-in-law positively, especially the parent-in-law of the opposite sex. A higher proportion of the men than women had good things to say about their mothers-in-law (M: 66.7%; F: 60%), and a lower proportion reported problems in their relationships with them (M: 22.2%; F: 48.1%). Conversely, a higher proportion of the women than men gave positive evaluations of their fathers-in-law (M:

44.4%; F: 78.3%), and a lower proportion reported problems in their relationships with them (M: 54.4%; F: 26.9%).

Nearly half of the married women in this group regarded their parents-in-law as important sources of emotional support. This was especially true for women who were not particularly close to their own parents because of family discord, divorce, parental alcoholism, or mental illness. These women recruited substitute parents among their in-laws, just as they had sought counsel and comfort from the parents of their boyfriends in their youth.

When difficulties with their parents-in-law arose, however, the majority of the resilient men and women employed the same defense mechanism they used with their own parents. They detached themselves emotionally and avoided getting enmeshed in in-law problems.

Siblings

The resilient men and women tended to have more satisfying relationships with their siblings in adulthood than did their peers with coping problems—a trend we had already seen in childhood and adolescence. About a third of the resilient men and nearly half of the resilient women reported continuing close relationships with their siblings in their adult lives. Those who were close to their siblings tended to value their emotional support above everything else (M: 47.6%; F: 69.7%). A much smaller proportion shared common interests and activities with their brothers and sisters (M: 14.3%; F: 30.3%), and fewer still shared common values with their siblings (M: 14.3%; F: 9.1%).

Among the group that maintained the closest sibling relationships across the years were the offspring of alcoholic or mentally ill parents. Often a resilient adult continued to play the role of comforter, counselor, or protector that he or she had assumed in late childhood or adolescence. Said a woman of Hawaiian descent who was married and the mother of two children, "My older brother is still my protector. He is in the army, but he sends his paychecks to my mother for me. He stills treats me as a baby." Added a divorced construction worker, offspring of an alcoholic father, "My older sister has always played a big part in my life. Whenever I get into trouble [he had problems with substance abuse], she helps me out."

The strong ties among siblings who experienced a traumatic childhood together continued, even when the resilient sibling moved away. One of the women whom we interviewed in California said, "I am still in touch with my sister, who lives on Kauai. We hung together through the hard times when my mother beat us both. We consoled each other, and we still do."

The resilient men and women who went to college on the mainland often credited a sibling for counsel and support while away from home. The daughter of an alcoholic father who completed a bachelor of science degree at the University of Hawaii told us: "When I first came up to the university, my oldest brother helped me a lot—he was at the university too. I can call him if I need him—he is my counselor." A graduate in business administration from a university in the Pacific Northwest noted, "My sister always tried to provide a family life for me when I was going to school on the mainland."

Some of the resilient women were so closely identified with the role of sibling caretaker that they had a hard time letting go. A paralegal who worked for the federal government said, "I am closest to the youngest. I took care of him when he was growing up. I guess I feel since I am older, he should listen." Commented another, "I became possessive—it is hard to release them. When I finally let go, I found my relationship became pretty good."

While most of the resilient men and women acknowledged that they now led separate lives from their siblings who had grown up, married, and had children of their own, they still felt that they could count on them in an emergency. The exceptions were those who had left behind brothers or sisters who were mired in multiple problems, similar to those their parents had to contend with: financial problems, marital problems, divorce, alcoholism, and mental illness. Most of the resilient men and women refused to get enmeshed in these problems. They often voiced disapproval: "I talk it over with them, but I can't understand their attitude." They eventually detached themselves and withdrew—just as they did when they encountered such problems with parents and in-laws.

In spite of their withdrawal, they did not lose their sense of compassion. One man whose brother had been in constant trouble since his youth said, "He is so much like me in many ways, but also so different. He was creative, a good artist, but something happened in his life. I thought for a long time that he had mental health problems. But I have tremendous respect for him."

Relationships with Friends

Most resilient men and women had at least one or two close friends. They tended to keep their childhood friends—especially the women.

Even if they moved to the mainland, they sought and found friends from the Hawaiian Islands with whom they could relax, speak their island dialect, and "talk story." The majority shared common interests and activities with their friends—mostly outdoor activities, family get-togethers, and shopping. The resilient individuals, however, relied on their friends less often for financial support than did their peers who had been in trouble in their teens. They also shared less often a common set of values with their friends and less often mentioned their friends as role models for their adult lives.

A fairly high proportion, especially among the resilient men, acknowledged that they were loners. They could take or leave the friends with whom they shared their leisure time, and more often than not they kept their own counsel when it came to major decisions in their lives. In this attitude, they differed significantly from their peers with coping problems in adolescence, who depended more often on friends for emotional support in adulthood.

While most of the resilient women (63.6%) were eager to help their friends who encountered problems, the majority of the resilient men (66.7%) tended to withdraw from others' troubles. Friends acknowledged this fact and yet spoke fondly of them, as did one of the women who had gone to school with a resilient male who went to seek his fortune overseas: "He was a special, multitalented person—creative, intelligent, popular. He was also strong-willed, ambitious, and moody. He had no time for a personal relationship. He was well on his way discovering the U.S.A., Mexico, Europe, and North Africa when we finally lost touch with him. I have only good wishes and thoughts for him."

GOALS AND WORRIES

Nowhere were the differences between the resilient individuals and their peers who had been troubled teenagers more apparent than in the goals they had set themselves for their adult lives. Career or job success was the highest priority on the agenda of the resilient men (39.1%) and women (64.7%), but the lowest priority on the agenda of their peers with problems in adolescence. Also high on the priority list of the resilient individuals were self-development and self-fulfillment (M: 34.8%; F: 38.2%). The more traditional goals of a happy marriage, children, and a home of one's own were mentioned by only about one out of four in this group. The lowest priority among their life goals was close relationships with family and friends (M: 8.7%; F: 2.9%).

At age 31/32, worries about finances were on the top of the list for both the resilient individuals and their high-risk peers with problems in their teens, followed by worries about their work for the men, and by worries about their children for the women. The resilient individuals, however, worried less about their spouses than did peers of the same age and sex who had developed problems in their teens, and they worried more about social issues.

We had not anticipated the high proportion of stress-related health problems that the resilient men and women reported. These rates were more than twice as high as those mentioned by their high risk-peers who had developed coping problems in adolescence. More than half of the resilient men (54.5%) and nearly half of the resilient women (41.2%) reported some health problems at this stage of life. The majority of the men reported symptoms that appeared to be related to stress such as chronic back problems, dizziness, fainting spells, ulcers, and problems with being overweight. Most of the health problems among the women were related to menstruation, pregnancy, or childbirth (premenstrual stress syndromes, migraine headaches, emergency D&Cs, toxemic pregnancies, miscarriages, stillbirths, C-sections).

Sources of Support

In contrast to their peers with coping problems in adolescence (who relied mostly on family members and friends), the overwhelming majority of the resilient individuals considered their personal competence and determination to be their most effective resource in dealing with stressful life events (M: 73.9%; F: 61.8%). One of the resilient women, a daughter of an abusive mother, expressed her conviction succinctly: "I am a fighter—I am determined—I will survive. I give it 100 percent before I give up. I will never lose hope." A bookkeeper in a local construction company observed, "When things have to be done, you just *do* it. I am not the type of person to run away—no matter how difficult the problem." Said the aerospace engineer: "I don't let problems take control of myself. I just pick myself up and start all over—you can always try again."

Half of the resilient women and more than a third of the resilient men considered their spouses or mates to be important sources of support. A supervisor at a local sugar plantation who had lived through a traumatic childhood with a quarrelsome, alcoholic father said: "My wife is always there to listen when I have problems—she cares. That helps me to address the problem—I am not a quitter—I learn." A preschool teacher who grew up with an alcoholic father commented: "I used to talk to my mom—now I talk to my husband—he supports me." Her sister said in a separate interview, "Usually, if I am really down, I talk it over with my husband and my sister. That helps it get off your chest and you feel better afterward."

Nearly half of the resilient women and one out of five among the resilient men relied on faith and prayer as an important source of support in times of difficulties (M: 17.4%; F: 41.2%). Such a faith was not narrowly confined to a particular denomination, for in this cohort there was a wide range of religious persuasions, from Buddhism to Catholicism to various mainstream Protestant denominations. Some were born-again Christians, others were Mormon converts.

A construction worker who was a recovering alcoholic had found renewed purpose in his life in the tenets of a Buddhist world youth movement. So had the daughter of an abusive mother. A nurse who worked overseas summed up her faith, "What has helped me most in difficult times is believing in God—knowing that He'd never do anything deliberately to hurt me, and knowing that something good will come out of it all. I know, after a lot of soul searching, that I, as an individual, am responsible for my own life." The Chinese Irish Hawaiian Hispanic entertainer at a Polynesian culture center expressed her belief in a very private way: "I know I have *mana* (the Hawaiian spirit)—I respect it in myself, and its effects have shown throughout my life."

A Japanese American attorney had *his* philosophy of commitment and caring: "I am not active in the church, but I am a believing person. I believe there is a reason for pain and suffering. In real stressful situations, I look at the Bible. I thank God that He gave me the power and strength to be where I am." That statement was echoed by an Assembly of God minister: "I live each day realizing that I can make anything happen when I put my faith in God."

Overall, the resilient women drew on a significantly larger number of sources of support than did the resilient men that included friends, older relatives, siblings, coworkers, mental health professionals, and self-help groups. In contrast, the resilient men tended to rely much more exclusively on their own resources, seeking only occasional help from spouses or parents, or in some cases, from teachers who became their mentors. The men derived less emotional support from their peers than the women did—whether they were siblings, friends, or coworkers.

SATISFACTION WITH THEIR STATUS IN THEIR EARLY THIRTIES

Despite some continuing financial worries and the stress of multiple transitions into work, marriage, parenthood (and for some into divorce and remarriage), the overwhelming majority of the resilient men (66.6%) and women (79.4%) considered themselves to be happy or satisfied—proportions that were significantly higher than we found among their peers who had grown up in more affluent and stable homes.

But not all resilient children had become happy and contented as adults. Two of the women (one the daughter of a psychotic mother) had sought psychiatric treatment. One had attempted suicide with an overdose of sleeping pills when her first husband left her; the other had a "hysterical" pregnancy around the time her enlisted husband was to be transferred to an army base overseas. Two men and one woman had problems with substance abuse during their twenties, but were rehabilitated and active as youth workers in their respective churches by the time they reached their early thirties.

Looking back at their lives, many of the resilient men and women commented with some surprise on their own inner strengths and accomplishments. One woman said, "I feel good about myself—actually going over a lot of hurdles—and I know now I can make it on my own." Others looked forward to new challenges in their lives. One man said, "I have accomplished a lot—some of my goals I have reached, but I am always setting new goals." Another commented, "I just think I am 30 years young. I have so much more to do in my life."

Mused one man, "Ten years go by in a snap, sitting in my living room on my easy chair—and now I am 30. . . . I am still trying to figure out what I am supposed to accomplish. I haven't done the best I could. I can do more." From one of the brightest in this group of accomplished men came this comment: "I don't yet quite know what I am supposed to do with my life, but I am keeping my mind open. At least I try. Somehow I think it will be interesting to see where I'll be ten years from now. I hope it's better than now—I am optimistic and hopeful."

Ten years later, at age forty, we were able to obtain information on sixty of the seventy-two resilient men and women—80 percent of the original sample (M: 24; F: 36). Two individuals, both men, had died in their thirties—one from a chronic childhood disease, the other from a virus he had contracted in his job as a lab technician in a local hospital.

By age forty, one-third of the resilient individuals had moved to other islands, and one out of six lived on the mainland. But there were also some individuals who had returned to their birthplace—among them a woman who had moved back to Kauai to claim her Hawaiian homestead, and a former army recruiter who had retired from active service. As a group, the resilient men and women had not been negatively affected by the economic downturn that had hit Kauai in the aftermath of Hurricane INIKI. Only 15 percent in this group had experienced any economic hardships as a consequence of the natural disaster that destroyed many homes and hotels on the island (in contrast to 30 percent among the troubled teens). None of the men and women who had been in the workforce at age thirty were unemployed at age forty— though the unemployment rate on Kauai in 1996/97 was 11 percent, more than twice the national average (Hawaii State Department of Labor and Industrial Relations, 1998). No one in this group had received any welfare payments or temporary assistance for emergencies, and no one had been in trouble with the law (see Tables 4 and 5 in Appendix I).

VOCATIONAL ACCOMPLISHMENTS

At forty, most of the resilient men and women worked in jobs that were similar to the ones they had held at age thirty. They were predominantly in managerial and administrative positions or worked as skilled technicians. None worked in semi- or unskilled positions in agriculture. Some 60 percent of the men and 40 percent of the women had received promotions in their line of work since our last follow-up. A few individuals who had held "creative" jobs as artists, writers, or designers at age thirty had ventured into their own independent commercial enterprises by age forty. Others planned to do so in the near future. Three out of four among the resilient individuals were satisfied with their work. Rates of job satisfaction for the resilient women were significantly higher than those for the women who had been troubled teenagers. The resilient men in turn reported significantly more time spent at work than did the men who had been in trouble in adolescence.

Marriage, Divorce, and Remarriage

At age forty, nearly three out of four among the resilient individuals were in stable marriages. These rates were significantly higher than for the high-risk troubled teens (59%) and the low-risk men and women who had grown up in a more affluent and stable family context (60.6%). A third of the resilient men had married relatively late, i.e., in the forth decade of life, after they were financially settled; so had one out of six among the resilient females. One out of six among the resilient individuals had divorced by age forty (in contrast to one out of four among their troubled peers). Major reasons given for the break-up of their first marriage were "differences in personality," "being too young when married," and "having little time together." With few exceptions those who did divorce had remarried by age forty and were in happy second marriages.

Five out of six among the resilient women (85%) and two out of three among the resilient men (64.3%) were satisfied with their current marriage or relationship. Financial worries and their living situation (i.e., long work hours and in some cases the need to maintain two homes) put stress on some marriages. That was especially true for the Hawaiian nurse who had returned to claim her homestead on Kauai but whose husband was still working abroad. Still, for her as well as for most other resilient individuals, "a commitment to the family" was the most important goal at midlife; so was the hope "to improve close relationships." When asked about their expectations for the next ten years of life, both men and women echoed a similar refrain: "to be always there for my family" (M); "to have more time with my family, more shared interests and discussion" (M); "to concentrate on improving my marriage and being more involved in the work of my spouse" (F); and "for my marriage to get even better with age" (F).

Those who were still single at age forty (M: 20%; F: 10%) were hopeful that they might eventually marry. Wrote a forty-year-old legal assistant in an attorney's office in Honolulu, "I hope to get married and have twins!" Commented a graphic artist who worked as a designer for the state of Hawaii, "Hopefully I'll find a girl friend, then get married, and have a son or daughter."

Children: Hopes and Expectations

By age forty, the resilient men and women had on the average more children than was the norm for their cohort (2.6 versus 2.4). They also had a higher percentage of adoptions. Some of their offspring were still infants; others were already seniors in high school. Most of the resilient men and women reported the presence of at least one teenager in their household. Almost all (90%) of the parents were satisfied with their relationship with their children and derived great pleasure from watching them grow up. As they had done in their early thirties, both the resilient men and the resilient women took their roles as parents seriously. Their major worry was to find the right balance between their work responsibilities and commitment to their offspring, especially among the men. The resilient women tended to be more concerned with the discipline of their children than mothers who had been troubled teenagers. More than any other group in this cohort, the resilient men and women expected their children to have a better life than they had themselves and to raise a happy family of their own. But above all, they wanted them to be able to obtain a good education and to be "successful."

Said a female bookkeeper, "I want my children to go to college and see them get happily married." Commented an employee at a local bank, "I hope that in the next ten years, I'll be able to look back and be satisfied with the way my children turned out—their accomplishments. If they are happy, I'll be happy." A nurse expected her children to "successfully complete high school and college." A sales clerk on Kauai hoped that her children would become successful young adults, and a legal secretary in a Honolulu law firm expected her children to be "independent and happy."

The resilient men expressed similar hopes for their offspring. A commercial fisherman (with seven children!) aimed to "raise them in a way that I can feel satisfied and see the positive results of their upbringing," and a loan officer hoped "to raise my young family and to see that each child gets a good education and social training to make them successful individuals." "Being a successful father" was the goal of an art director in an advertising agency in Honolulu. And what mattered most to the deputy prosecutor was not the power and prestige of his job and the lure of a political career that had attracted him in his early thirties, but the opportunity "to keep raising my family."

The resilient men and women managed to allocate significantly more time for joint activities with their children than did parents who had been troubled teenagers or who had grown up in more affluent and stable homes. Many of their volunteer activities in the community centered on their children and their children's friends, from coaching baseball, football, basketball, and track (for the fathers) to work with the PTA and choral, dance, and theater groups (for the mothers). Indeed, the resilient individuals at midlife remained committed to a pattern of "required helpfulness" (Rachman, 1979) that they had already practiced in childhood and adolescence. They volunteered more time to help out in school, in church, and in various youth groups than did other parents in this cohort. Resilient women spent significantly more time in these volunteer activities than any other group and significantly less time on being preoccupied with their own needs.

RELATIONSHIPS WITH PARENTS, SIBLINGS, AND FRIENDS

The majority of the resilient men (63.3%) and women (70.3%) reported they were satisfied with their relationship with their parents. A substantial proportion of their aging fathers and mothers (some 40%) were now emotionally dependent on them. A third reported that chronic or serious illnesses (both physical and mental) among parents and in-laws had put a strain on their own life.

Most were satisfied with their relationships with adult siblings and valued them for their emotional support in times of crisis (77%), their shared interests (67%), their shared values (49%), and, for those with young children, their availability for child care (38.5%). "We grew up in a family where siblings always helped each other" and "as the oldest girl I was expected to watch out for my younger sisters" was a recurrent refrain in the tale of sibling relationships, especially among the women.

Most resilient individuals also maintained close ties with their (childhood) friends who shared their interests and who were reliable sources of emotional support. Three out of four among the resilient men and two out of three among the resilient women considered their spouse to be their best friend—rates that were significantly higher than for the men and women who had been troubled teenagers and for their low-risk peers.

Despite their relative success, the resilient individuals worried about finances (55%), their children (35%), their health (35%), and—significantly more often than their peers—about social issues that might affect their future (35%). But they were essentially hopeful—anticipating the next decade of life as one that would give them the opportunity for continued growth for themselves and the people they cared for. Wrote a certified public accountant: "I want to leave a legacy of love, reach out to help others in need." Said an educational consultant who had moved to the Pacific Northwest: "I'd like to resume my creative writing, produce a children's book. I hope to continue to make a difference in children's lives through my job." Another woman, an accountant who lived in southern California, planned to "change jobs or job location that requires a move and making new friends; learn new things; continue to improve myself." And the former poet-in-residence hoped to "continue poetry writing; open up a pottery studio, and develop a spiritual foundation for my creative activities."

The resilient men, on the whole, were more restrained about their expectations for the next decade of their lives than the women: "Live and learn!" wrote a carpenter; "Become more responsible; achieve or come closer to realizing my personal and professional dreams," commented the art director of an advertising agency in Honolulu. "Start my own business," ventured a supervisor in a sugar company. And the Assembly of God minister hoped to "continue to serve Christ, and be an example to my family, friends, church and community."

SOURCES OF EMOTIONAL SUPPORT AT FORTY

As they had at ages 31/32, the resilient individuals considered their own ability and determination to be their strongest assets in times of crisis. "I am stubborn and independent," wrote the female sergeant who was now an information network manager for the U.S. Air Force. "I am self-reliant," echoed a licensed public nurse who resided on the West Coast. "I am strong in times of crises," wrote another. "I am self-sufficient and independent," commented the legal assistant in an attorney's office in Honolulu. "I can always be counted upon to get things done in an emergency," wrote a bookkeeper in a construction company. These are strong words from strong women with big hearts!

The resilient men used similar expressions to define their ability to master stressful situations—an ability they mentioned significantly more often than did men who had been troubled teenagers. "I am determined; when I make decisions I consider all options," wrote the deputy prosecutor. "I am a good problem-solver; decisive; hardworking," commented a personnel manager for a construction firm on Kauai. "I have the ability to overcome adversity, and I am good at damage control," said the minister.

The resilient individuals also sought help from people they respected and trusted. Fewer than 5 percent had consulted mental health professionals in times of trouble, while some 10 percent of their age group had done so between the ages of thirty and forty. Instead, the majority of the resilient men and women relied on the emotional support of their spouses and close friends when the going got tough. More than any other group in this cohort, they also sought the counsel of teachers, mentors, and coworkers (especially the men) and drew strength from their faith and prayers (especially the women). "God through prayer and Bible reading has taught me to have faith," wrote a certified public accountant at age forty. "Praying has helped me a lot to deal with stress; it has pulled me through a lot of things," wrote a woman who had attempted suicide in her thirties when her husband deserted her. "Going to church with my Hawaiian grandmother who has the gift of *mana* (spiritual power) was the most important experience that helped me make the kind of person I am today," said a nurse. "Having been brought up with a religious background helps—it's good to have it—it doesn't matter which denomination," commented a legal secretary who was raised as a Catholic.

Many of the resilient men also professed a faith that gave their lives a sense of coherence. Wrote the head custodian of a high school, "Knowing that God is always on my side helps me get a great appreciation of just living. I pray to God, even if I don't go to church." Others centered their lives in their faith. Wrote a commercial fisherman, "I am a Jehovah's Witness. Bible-study and House-to-House Ministry is a central part of my life." Added the Assembly of God minister, "At the age of seventeen I accepted Jesus Christ as my Lord and Savior and have tried to follow Him ever since."

SATISFACTION WITH LIFE AT FORTY

Most of the resilient individuals considered "age 40" to be the best period of their lives so far. Seventy percent rated themselves as "happy, delighted," or "mostly satisfied" with their lives—rates of satisfaction that were higher than those reported by their peers who had been troubled teenagers and comparable to those of others in the cohort who had grown up in more affluent and stable homes. The resilient individuals also tended to feel more in control of their lives when unexpected or unpleasant things happened to them. Both the resilient males and the resilient females had significantly lower anger scores on the EAS Temperament Survey at age forty than did their peers with a troubled past. Indeed the resilient individuals recorded a *decrease* in anger scores from the third to fourth decade of their lives.

On the Scales of Psychological Well-Being, there were significant differences at age forty between the resilient females and women who had been troubled teens (and those who had grown up trouble-free in more affluent and stable homes) in Autonomy, Environmental Mastery, Personal Growth, Positive Relationships with Others, and Self-acceptance. The resilient males, in turn, appeared significantly more purposeful in their lives at age forty than did men who had been troubled teenagers (see Table 6 in Appendix I).

When asked about their strong points, both the resilient men and the resilient women focused on similar assets: "compassion and caring," "the ability to get along with others," "optimism and a sense of humor," "good planning and problem solving skills," "hard work," and "creativity" were the shared characteristics they enumerated, regardless of their gender or station in life. Their self-descriptions at midlife mirrored their teachers' ratings at age ten and their self-reports on the California Psychological Inventory at age eighteen. But, as at age thirty, the resilient individuals were continuing to pay a price for their efforts to "beat the odds." At forty, a higher proportion reported some stress-related health problems, such as frequent headaches and occasional bouts with depression, than did their age mates.

Two individuals, a man who was the son of an alcoholic father and a woman who was the daughter of parents who had both struggled with depression, had sought help from mental health professionals during their thirties. The male was trying to overcome his substance abuse problem; the female was diagnosed as suffering from an "agitated" depression due to job-related stress (sexual harassment and racial discrimination). Both were recovered by age forty and reported "feeling much better" after they had undergone therapy. The man now held a steady job and was a devoted husband and father. The woman had returned to college to pursue her creative interests in music and writing.

She was writing poetry and planning to publish a collection of her poems.

In Sum

Compassion and a commitment to their family and community characterized the resilient men and women at age forty. With few exceptions, they had made a successful transition into a stage of generativity in which the needs of others—both the younger and the older generation— were of foremost concern to them. The satisfaction and challenges of midlife seemed to far outweigh their occasional worries about health, finances, and their children's future. For most women, age forty held the promise of new opportunities for personal growth and challenges outside the home; for most men, it was a time for a renewed commitment to their family.

CHAPTER SIX

Teenage Mothers
From High-Risk Pregnancy to Successful Midlife Adaptation

In our book *Kauai's Children Come of Age* (Werner and Smith, 1977), we first introduced the teenage mothers in this cohort after we had interviewed them at age eighteen. The twenty-eight girls who bore live children in their teens represented 8 percent of the women born on the island in 1955. The teenage mothers, as a group, had scored within the normal range of intelligence on developmental tests at ages two and ten. Only a minority (N: 5) had been considered in need of remedial education in the elementary grades. But by the time we saw these young women in late adolescence, nearly half had developed some problems in school. One-third had come to the attention of the police and/or mental health agencies because of repeated truancies, sexual misconduct, or substance abuse in their teens. In contrast to the positive anticipation of the future that characterized most interviews with their peers, the responses of the teenage mothers at age eighteen told a depressing tale of lack of opportunities, lack of faith in the efficacy of their own efforts, and, most of all, lack of self-esteem.

Three out of four among the teenage mothers had grown up in families with four or more children. The majority of their parents had not graduated from high school, and there was little educational stimulation at home when they were children. About a third of the teenage mothers had mothers who had borne their daughters when they were adolescents themselves and had been single parents, rearing their children with the help of grandparents. Girls of Hawaiian descent tended to repeat this pattern. They kept their babies or *hanaied* them to their parents, grandparents, close relatives, or friends, practicing an informal adoption custom that has persisted in the islands across generations.

Although the young women were not altogether lacking in emotional support, the interviews with the teenage mothers at age eighteen had not revealed an encouraging outlook for their future. In contrast to peers of the same age, gender, and social class, the majority of the pregnant teenagers had been content to just get by in school (61% vs. 19%). Few expressed any satisfaction with their educational achievements (30% vs. 73%). The majority did not plan to go beyond high school (52%). Vocational plans were undefined or unrealistic for most (59%). Only about a third (35%) had some specific occupational goals. Most planned to marry and to work to earn money but were not committed to a job or a career. By age eighteen, about half of the teenage mothers were married; the others were still living with their parents.

Married or not, the teenage mothers worried a lot, mostly about money. Very few (less than one out of four) thought highly of themselves at this stage of life or felt that they could control their futures. Although most wanted a better life for themselves and their children, they feared that the door to adult life, which was opening to their peers, had already shut for them.

The Teenage Mothers in Early Adulthood

Our information on the experiences of the teenage mothers in early adulthood is based on two sets of data, collected at age 26 (when their children were in the early elementary grades) and at age 31/32 (when their offspring were teenagers themselves).

By the time they were in their early thirties, we had follow-up data on 90 percent of the teenage mothers (26 out of 29), data that included interview and personality questionnaires as well as agency records from the courts, the Departments of Health and Social Services, and the Mental Health Register of the state of Hawaii. One of the teenage mothers had died at age twenty-eight from respiratory distress after a bout with cancer (carcinoma of the tongue) that had spread to her neck and chest.

Our sample of teenage mothers is small and differs in ethnic makeup from the samples in follow-up studies of adolescent mothers on the U.S. mainland. Half of the women in this group were of Hawaiian descent; the other half was about evenly divided between women of Japanese,

Filipino, and mixed ethnic heritage. All had come of age and made the transition into adulthood on a small island. Yet our findings are strikingly similar to those of the large-scale study of Furstenberg and his associates (1987, 1999) for a predominantly black population of teenage mothers in Baltimore and to findings reported by Osofsky (1990) from both Caucasian and black samples in New Orleans and Topeka, Kansas.

EDUCATION

By the time of the 26-year follow-up, some 90 percent of the teenage mothers in our cohort had graduated from high school. The high school completion rates of the teenage mothers on Kauai were higher than those commonly reported on the mainland at that time (U.S. Bureau of Labor, 1986; Furstenberg et al., 1987), in part because of extensive outreach programs for potential dropouts at the three high schools on the island. These included special night classes and programs for pregnant teenagers, tutors, outreach counselors, and special off-campus classrooms. All of the teenage mothers we interviewed at the 31/32-year follow-up had managed to earn a high school diploma or its equivalent, the General Education Diploma (GED).

As was the case in Furstenberg's study, much educational activity took place in the second follow-up phase of our study, between ages 26 and 32, when the women's children were launched in grade school. By age 31/32, the majority of the adolescent mothers on Kauai had obtained additional schooling beyond their high school diploma. Twenty percent had attended the local community college and had obtained associate degrees (in accounting, the computer sciences, nursing, or tourism/management); another 20 percent had received training through federally sponsored programs such as the Comprehensive Employment and Training Act (CETA). Three of the women had been awarded bachelor degrees from four-year colleges, and one woman had obtained a M.S. degree in social work (gerontology). Others (some 14%) had sought technical training in secretarial work and word processing or attended classes in night school.

EMPLOYMENT

Finances were the issue that had worried the teenage mothers the most—both at age eighteen and at age twenty-six. But by their early thirties, the women who had been mothers in their teens had made considerable strides toward economic self-sufficiency. Again, the picture, though not altogether rosy, was not as bleak as we had anticipated when we saw them in adolescence and had improved for most between their mid-twenties and their early thirties. By age twenty-six, when the women had barely launched their children into grade school, the majority had worked in either unskilled or semiskilled jobs in the local hotels and restaurants (as cashiers, cooks, maids, and waitresses), and some 20 percent were unemployed. Only one out of five (those who had obtained some college education, either at the local junior college or at a four-year college off the island) had worked in technical, semiprofessional, or managerial positions. But even then, only two women obtained some form of public assistance—mostly to tide them over in family emergencies associated with the breakup of an earlier marriage. One woman had to rely on public welfare; the other received unemployment insurance.

By the time the teenage mothers had reached age 31/32, their employment picture was much more positive. Only two of the women, mothers of young preschool children, were still at home, and none received welfare payments. In part because of additional education and training, there had been a significant decrease in the numbers of those in unskilled and semiskilled jobs and a significant increase in those who now worked in technical, semiprofessional, and managerial positions—as accountants, administrative assistants, bookkeepers, insurance saleswomen, licensed practical nurses, medical and dental assistants, retail buyers, social workers, statisticians, and managers of small businesses.

The employment experience of these mothers refuted the popular stereotype of teenage mothers as chronic welfare recipients. As with the cohort of predominantly Afro-American women whom Furstenberg and his associates (1987) followed across a similar time span, we found that the rate of employment of the teenage mothers on Kauai had risen steadily during the course of the study and that their levels of employment had increased with educational opportunities sought out by the mothers once their children were of school age.

An important gateway for better opportunities for them was the day and night classes offered (at little expense) by the local junior colleges; however, it was the drive and determination of the majority of the women "to better themselves for the sake of their children" that made the difference in whether or not they used the educational facilities available in the community. Osofsky (1990) also observed in her samples of teenage mothers in Topeka and New Orleans that the mothers' ability to use available community resources made a difference in their lives as did their motivation and capacity to have goals. A thirty-two-year-old single mother of five children (ranging in age from five to fifteen years) told us, "I set a goal at what I wanted—what I believed in—and I didn't stop or give up until I got what I wanted."

MARITAL RELATIONSHIPS IN EARLY ADULTHOOD

When we first interviewed the teenage mothers at age eighteen, about half were married; the other half were not. The same can be said about the adolescent mothers at age twenty-six and at age thirty-two; a little more than half were married; the others were single mothers who had survived one and sometimes two marital breakups. As in the Baltimore study of black adolescent mothers, about half of the teenage mothers married in their twenties, while some 40 percent had separated or divorced. By age thirty-two, some 55 percent of the Asian and Polynesian females on Kauai had married, in contrast to only 34 percent of the black women studied by Furstenberg and his associates (1987).

In comparison with national trends at that time, the proportion of teenage mothers who were married was lower than the norm for U.S. women in their age groups (54.5% vs. 68.5%); but the proportion who were already divorced by age thirty-two was higher (40.9% vs. 11.5%) (U.S. Bureau of Labor, 1986). In contrast to the women in this birth cohort who had waited to have children at a later stage in life, a significantly higher proportion of teenage mothers were unmarried at age thirty-two (44.5% vs. 30.7%). Of those married, a higher proportion were dissatisfied or felt ambivalent about their marital relationships (55.0% vs. 13.9%). A third of the teenage mothers (33%) had had "messy" divorces, as documented in the files of the family courts. Some had been abused by a spouse or their children had been abused; others' husbands had been delinquent in child support payments.

One woman, in response to the question "What has been the worst period of your life?" wrote, "My marriage. For we got married too young, and it was hard raising the kids and trying to keep the relationship together. Also, his abusing was horrible. So I ended up at the Women's Center and got a divorce." Another woman wrote, in response to the same question, "My marriage was the worst period [age 16–21] of my life so far. I was beaten by my husband repeatedly. Most of the time he was unemployed and we had serious financial difficulties." Added another, "The worst period of my life was between age twenty-four and twenty-six. I was divorced and had a relationship with a paranoid schizophrenic and I didn't know it."

The majority of the teenage mothers whose marriages later ended in divorce had reported in the eighteen-year interviews that they never or only infrequently talked to their fathers (58%), and about half believed that their fathers had little or no influence on them. Nearly half of the teenage mothers had told us that their fathers did not understand them and were unconcerned about them. In contrast, a significantly higher proportion of the teenage mothers with stable relationships or satisfying long-term relationships in early adulthood had had good relationships with their fathers in their teens (80% vs. 40%). Marital stability was also related positively to educational and economic achievements when the women were in their mid-twenties and early thirties.

RELATIONSHIP WITH CHILDREN

As in the Baltimore study of black teenage mothers, almost all of the young mothers on Kauai had grown up in large families. Fifty-five percent of the adolescent mothers had a second child before age nineteen, and 10 percent of the young mothers had a third child before age twenty-one. The second and third follow-up phases of our study, however, found that the vast majority had been able to control their fertility—as had the teenagers in Baltimore (Furstenberg et al., 1987).

In May 1971, when these young women were still in their teens, Hawaii became the first state in the union to allow abortions at the request of the woman. Although the young women of Hawaiian descent were responsible for nearly half (43%) of all the teenage pregnancies, they contributed only 20 percent of the abortions among the women in this cohort, in contrast to members of other subcultures such as the Japanese and the Caucasians, who were more apt to choose to abort. The choice of abortion seemed more strongly related to the instability of the relationship with the putative father of the child than to conflicting educational and career goals (Gonsalves, 1982).

Significant in their attitudes toward their own offspring was the fact that many of the teenage mothers on Kauai came from a subculture that valued a nurturant maternal role and prized children highly—a characteristic that still distinguishes contemporary Hawaiians from other American ethnic groups. This pride in their children was very obvious in the spontaneous comments the young mothers made when we interviewed them at ages 26 and 31/32. Said one woman, "My husband and I are better parents now, with the energy to play and surf with our boys, than if we had waited until we were older to start our family." All the women interviewed at age 26 (when their children were in grade school) agreed that it was hard to start a family as an adolescent mother, but none would trade their children for an easier time then or now.

Similar statements recurred when the women were in their early thirties and their children were teenagers themselves. Wrote a single mother of five who by age thirty-two managed a small computer business of her own, "Growing up with my children, being young and energetic, helped me to become a friend and yet a mother to four sons and one daughter. We enjoy each other's company." A social worker, mother of three, who by then lived and worked in southern California with her husband, added, "The most satisfying thing about being a parent has been receiving unconditional love from my children and seeing the personal growth in each child." Another came right to the point, "What's been most satisfying is when they say 'Love you, Mom' and when their faces show their excitement." A mother of four, who worked as a janitor for the local Head Start program, wrote with great pride, "The best period of my life so far was when my fourteen-year-old daughter (born when she herself was seventeen years old) went to play community basketball and made it. It's a boys' basketball team, and she is on the first string. She made two winning baskets for her team with only five seconds to go and the team won."

Personality Characteristics of Teenage Mothers

A comparison of mean scores on the California Psychological Inventory (CPI) of the adolescent mothers at ages 18 and 26, revealed significant differences on the subscales that had differentiated the teenage mothers from their peers at age 18 (Werner and Smith, 1977). The teenage mothers at age 26 scored significantly higher on the scales measuring Capacity for Status, Social Presence, Responsibility, Socialization, Tolerance, Achievement via Independence, and Intellectual Efficiency than they had at age 18. They appeared to be more poised, self-confident, nonjudgmental, responsible, socially mature, and independent than they had been in late adolescence. Above all, they tended to have a greater faith in the efficacy of their own actions than they had expressed at age

18. On both the Novicki Locus of Control Scale at age 26 and the Rotter's Locus of Control Scale (1966) at age 31/32, the adolescent mothers tended to show significantly higher internal control than they had at age 18. In their early thirties, they were more inner-directed than were women of the same age who had not become mothers at such an early age.

The majority of the teenage mothers felt more in charge of their own lives at age 31/32 than they had at age 18. In response to our question "What do you consider your strong points?" they tended to give answers such as "Aggressiveness. If I want something, I make sure that I do my utmost to achieve what I want and usually nothing stops me" (from a single mother of five who was a technician with a large construction firm); or "I am assertive, innovative, not afraid to go out on a limb for ideas I believe can work" (from a woman who was a vice president of a real estate company that managed small shopping centers); or "I keep on trying even when the going gets rough" (from a licensed practical nurse who was happily married and the mother of four children).

When we asked these young women about the most important thing that had happened to them in their lives so far, a number pointed with pride to their personal achievements. "I went from teenage unwed motherhood to accomplishing my goal of completing a master's degree, which enabled me to support myself and my daughter," wrote the social worker who had specialized in gerontology. "When I first moved here [to California], all I had was my clothes. But now I've got a job, a car, and a place to stay, and lots of friends," wrote a divorced mother of three. "I am trying to learn more things so I can better myself. I am always looking for challenges for my future," said a teenage mother whose marriage had lasted for fourteen-plus years. "A lot has changed since I attended different seminars for self-improvement," wrote a sales representative and operation supervisor of a local credit union. "Most of all, *I* have changed and I see and do things in a positive way."

For some teenage mothers, an internal locus of control was the result of a painful struggle. One woman escaped an abusive husband and struck out on her own with her two sons. "It took me a while to like myself after my marriage," she commented. "But I am really a pleasant person. For a long time I couldn't stand up for myself. . . . I was terrified of my husband, but he taught me a lot. . . . I finally realized what kind of a person I wanted to be; now I have succeeded." In contrast, another woman attributed her confidence and belief in herself to a very supportive husband and success in her career: "I learned I can really do what

I want. . . . I became more ambitious and independent because my husband and my boss kept telling me I can be anything I want to be."

Teenage mothers whose lot had improved by age twenty-six—some 50 percent—had had less anxious, insecure relationships with their caregivers as infants and a stronger feeling of security as part of their families in adolescence than had teenage mothers whose lot had not improved by their mid-twenties. A higher proportion of the more successful teenage mothers had mothers who held a steady job when they were children, and a smaller proportion had problems in their relationship with their father in adolescence.

Sources of child care for teenage mothers whose lot had improved and who were going to school differed from those of the adolescent mothers who had not sought further education and who, at age twenty-six, were found mostly in unskilled or semiskilled positions. A higher proportion of teenage mothers whose lives had improved by their mid-twenties relied on help from siblings, friends, or in-laws, and enrolled their children in Head Start programs. Among those whose lot had not improved, child care was mostly in the hands of the women's parents, possibly increasing their dependency. The more positive outcomes by age twenty-six were related to a balance of high social support and a moderate number of stressful life events reported by the women.

Six years later, by age 31/32, some 60 percent of the teenage mothers reported that they were in stable relationships, had work that satisfied them, had good relationships with their children and other family members, and could rely on several sources of support in times of difficulties. Women in this group rated themselves as happy or satisfied with their present stage of life. In contrast, some 40 percent of those who had borne children in their teens felt ambivalent or dissatisfied with their present status in life.

When we contrasted these two subgroups of teenage mothers, we found significant differences among them, which dovetail with the findings of the Baltimore study (Furstenberg et al., 1987). The parents of the more successful teenage mothers at age 31/32 had achieved higher levels of education—an average of ten grades—than had the parents of the less successful teenage mothers (whose fathers, on the average, completed only seven grades and whose mothers, on the average, had nine grades of schooling). The more successful teenage mothers had significantly higher mean scores on the Reasoning factor of the Primary Mental Abilities (PMA) test when they were age ten (109.4 vs. 97.5), had participated more in school activities during their teens, and had identified more with their fathers than had the less successful teenage mothers. By age twenty-six, a significantly higher proportion in this group had already worked in skilled, semiprofessional, and/or managerial positions (87.8% vs. 14.3%).

The more successful adolescent mothers at age 31/32 also had a higher proportion of stable marriages and/or relationships (75.0% vs. 33.3%) and reported a significantly lower number of stressful life events since age 18 than did the teenage mothers who were still ambivalent or dissatisfied with their status in life.

TEENAGE MOTHERS AT AGE FORTY

At age forty, we were able to reach 85 percent (23/27) of the surviving teenage mothers. Only two women, both of whom had delinquency records in adolescence, were doing poorly at that stage in their life. One had a criminal record and was incarcerated at the time of our follow-up; the other had chronic problems with substance abuse. All the other teenage mothers (92%) had made a satisfactory adaptation to midlife. Some 80 percent were married or remarried (one was recently widowed), 18 percent were divorced, and only one woman was still single. Their marriage and divorce rates were comparable with those of the other women in the cohort who bore children at a later age.

Contrary to the popular stereotype of the "welfare-dependent" teenage mother that has often been depicted in the popular media, none of these women relied on public assistance by age 40. A third of the women were in managerial or administrative jobs; one out of four was a secretary, sales person, or clerical worker; one out of five was either a preschool teacher or parent educator; two out of ten worked as nurses in local hospitals or in service jobs. Two were married, full-time homemakers, who took care of their elementary-age children.

The former teenage mothers had been highly motivated to obtain additional education not just for themselves but also for their children. A third of these women had sons and daughters who were now enrolled in college, either in junior colleges, or in four-year colleges, such as the University of Hawaii at Manoa (in Honolulu) and Hilo (on the island of Hawaii), Brigham Young University in Provo, Utah (for those of Mormon faith), and Gonzaga University, a Jesuit-run institution in Spokane, Washington. Enrollment rates for the offspring of these teenage mothers were only slightly lower than those reported for the cohort as a whole (33.3% vs. 39.2%).

There was only one daughter among the offspring of teenage mothers who had dropped out of the twelfth grade of the local high school because she was pregnant. She planned to obtain her general education diploma (GED) and to enroll her son in an early childhood education program for Hawaiian children, the Queen Lili'uokalani Children's Center, which employs teenage mothers as parent aids.

Pride in the educational accomplishments of their children permeated their responses to our question about what had been most satisfying to them as parents. "I saw to it that both my children graduated from high school and pursue their present interests as full-time students at a community college," wrote one former teenage mother. "I am very satisfied with my daughter, who is now thriving in college—as she did in high school," wrote another. "I am so pleased to grow with my children and to learn from them as well," commented a third. "Young adults have such great potential and talent."

Their expectations for the next decade of life reflected a similar concern for continued personal growth: "I want to continue my nursing, upgrade my skills, and be able to counsel teenagers," wrote a former teenage mother who now provided health care. She and her son had both finished high school with a GED. "I want to get my children into college," commented another woman who managed a business by age forty. "I want to continue to support my children in their efforts to become productive and happy individuals who make a positive contribution to society," wrote a teacher at a local children's center. "I want to give something back to my community—be involved in projects to help children, especially those who have been abused," wrote one teenage mother who had been abused herself when she was an adolescent.

When asked about the most important experiences that had helped make them the kind of person they were at age forty, most teenage mothers gave credit to an adult in their family, or to a teacher or counselor in school, who believed in them and gave them unconditional emotional support after they discovered that they were pregnant. Often it was a grandmother (*ohana*) who helped with the rearing of their young children (and on occasion adopted them). Later it was marriage to a supportive spouse, "with the constant challenge to learn the concept of sharing, to live in harmony, to take responsibility for myself and my husband, to give and seek love," wrote a woman who was a single parent in her teens and still managed to go to college.

"The experience of others who have gone through it" was a valuable lesson for many teenage mothers, as was membership in self-help support groups. "Being able to see the world and all the different kinds of people who all need love, some more than others," was the most important life experience for a woman who had traveled and entertained in Hawaii and Japan while her mother and grandmother took care of her daughter. "Work, work, work," had mattered most to another. A strong belief in God and the teachings of the Bible were important to former teenage mothers who had grown up in fundamentalist Christian churches, like the Latter Day Saints and the Seventh-Day Adventists.

Perhaps because of their prolonged dependence on other members of their household, the teenage mothers were more concerned with securing their independence in midlife than were other women in this cohort who were spared the trials and tribulations of early childbearing and rearing. Obtaining financial independence and a home of one's own were important goals for them in the fifth decade of their lives—as well as the chance "to be my own self and not to worry about what others might think."

For despite their remarkable upward-bound journey that had taken them from a miserable adolescence to a contented midlife, some of the former teenage mothers still had a hard time accepting themselves unconditionally. They still felt somewhat isolated from other people of their age, perhaps because they were psychologically "older" (and also wiser) than others who had just turned forty. We certainly were struck by the maturity of their answers to our questions.

Without doubt they were more satisfied with their economic and social circumstances than in earlier years, and many felt they had accomplished a great deal despite the often desperate circumstances in which they had begun their childbearing and rearing. "If you make a mistake, you learn from it" was the lesson that one of them took from her life. "I created opportunities to better myself, so I can be a good and loving parent," wrote another.

Our findings dovetail with those reported by Furstenberg (1999), who was able to follow, in 1996, two-thirds (N: 229) of his original sample of black teenage mothers in Baltimore. At midlife, these Afro-American women had become strong individuals who were prepared to lend a guiding hand to younger kin. That same sense of generativity was present among the Asian American women who had been teenage mothers on Kauai. With substantial gains in occupational success during their thirties (and the stabilizing effect of marriage for the majority), they had become a rock of strength for their children and were looking forward to becoming indulgent grandmothers.

In Sum

On the whole, the former teenage mothers on Kauai appeared in a much more favorable light when we compared their status in their early thirties and at age 40 with their lives at 18 and 26. In almost all respects, except for some stress-related health problems such as asthma and high blood pressure, they were better off than when we had seen them in their late teens and in their mid-twenties. Six out of ten had obtained additional schooling, nine out of ten were gainfully employed at a time of serious economic recession on the island, and eight out of ten were in skilled, technical, and managerial positions. Both their rates of employment and the levels at which they were employed had steadily improved over time.

Much positive growth and improvement in their mental health had taken place in their thirties, when their children were becoming less dependent on them. By age forty, the marriage and divorce rates of the teenage mothers were similar to those of women in the cohort who had started their childbearing later. On the average, they had the same number of offspring as was typical for their age group. A third of their offspring were enrolled in college by the time the teenage mothers had turned age forty. They looked with considerable pride at their children's accomplishments.

This improvement in the lives of most teenage mothers on Kauai was related to their motivation and competence, to opportunities that opened up for them through additional education and vocational training in local junior colleges and Project Head Start, and to the encouragement of supportive family members, teachers, principals, and counselors. The development of the women's personal resources and the support of kith and kin all acted as protective buffers that contributed to positive changes in their life trajectories from high-risk pregnancy to successful midlife adaptation.

One of the teenage mothers who became the manager of a publishing company in Honolulu and who had a daughter who was enrolled in the

University of Hawaii summed it up succinctly: "Marriage [and preg-nancy] at 15 and a divorce at 28 taught me a lot. So was the support of my family in however I chose to lead my life and any decision that I've ever made! Now [at forty] I'll continue to strive for personal growth. I look forward to spending more quality time with my second husband and to become an overindulgent grandparent. Most of all, I plan to make a difference in my community for the next generation."

Perhaps the story of their remarkable metamorphosis is best told by a happily married mother of seven children (four had attended Head Start, three were college students) who was the district coordinator for the Parent-Community Networking Centers in Hawaii's Department of Education. Merv called it simply "Lessons from My Life." She told her story on July 1, 1997, at the University of Maryland at a conference aptly titled "Building Hope."

WHY DID SOMETHING HAVE TO MAKE A DIFFERENCE FOR ME?

Now, [my] story: When I started to think [about] why did something have to make a difference for me, I came up with a list. The first risk factor on top of the list was for where I was at that time in my life grow-ing up on the island of Kauai, I was culturally wrong. My mother is Hawaiian, born and raised on the island, and my father is from New Jersey. Where I grew up was what we call Hawaiian Home; it's similar to the idea of a Native American reservation. This land is designated for Hawaiians, you must be Hawaiian to live there, and you even have an opportunity to have a home. But I wasn't Hawaiian; half of me was, and the other half was something that was not normal in that time. This was back in [the] early sixties. Though Hawaii is the melting pot of the world today, and there is a mixture of all kinds of cultures and people and ethnicities, they didn't mix back then. The Hawaiians stayed in one place; the Japanese stayed in one place; the Chinese stayed in one place; the Filipinos stayed in one place. So when we came along, people didn't know how to treat us. We were different. We weren't Caucasian, or white, or *haole*, the Hawaiian word for foreigner, and we weren't Hawaiian. We were different, so we were culturally wrong. And we were treated differently.

Number two, we lived in a blended family. My mother had three chil-dren from a first marriage. My father had six children from a first mar-riage. Then they proceeded to have four more. And I was the oldest of the four. It created some difficulties, just the idea of blending families. The six of my father's children were here in the states and in all of my life, I have met only one of those six brothers and sisters. It is a *puka*, a void for me that I have family here that I don't even know. But I understand that it was a very bitter and ugly divorce, so there were no connections. So the blended family created its difficulties.

Number three, we were poor. I'm not sure why because my father was in the military service. That is why he was on Kauai. He was in the military, and he had a paycheck, and he did go to work. But we didn't have anything. There were times when there was no food on the table. We never, ever, ever had new clothes, never. I cannot remember a time going to elementary school with a brand new dress. We never had shoes. It's a good thing in Hawaii you don't need them; it doesn't get cold enough. Bare feet are fine, and that's how we existed. If we were lucky, we had "flip flops." We call them rubber slippers. If we were lucky, we had a new pair of rubber slippers that may have cost twenty cents from the Ben Franklin store. [We] never had the things that we were supposed to have.

In the beginning of the year, they have this long list of supplies that students need to bring to school. If you don't have food on your table, and you don't have clothes to wear, do you think you have money to buy all those supplies? No. So, you walk into the classroom and from day one, not only are you "at risk" because you look different and you sound different, but because you don't have everything you need. Somebody is on your case for what you don't have. And again, it wasn't my fault. I had no clue why. It was just that this is the way it was.

Number four, my father was an alcoholic. When he wasn't working, he was drunk. And when he was drunk, mom was angry. Lucky for us, mom didn't drink. The difficulties that came from an alcoholic father in our home created some stuff that I would hope most young people don't have to experience, but I know they do. My mother would rage when dad was drunk. I remember walking into the kitchen one day where she had grabbed his bottles, and busted [them], and was going after him. There was blood all over the kitchen, and there was blood all over her. As children, you don't stick around to watch your parents hurt each other. You take off. For us, on an island and in the country, we took off in the cane fields. We took off down to the beach. We took off into the mountains—wherever we could go, because you don't stick around. I remember watching my mother chase my father down with the car. He was drunk. She was angry, and she chased him with the car through the pasture fence, knocked him over. I don't know how the man lived to die a natural death, but he did.

I remember a time when I was in the second grade when my mother was institutionalized because she had a nervous breakdown. What was very difficult for me was that the elementary school was on a little one-lane road, and the hospital was right across the street. So I would sit in my classroom and I would look out the window and know that my mother is over there. I didn't understand why she had to be there with all those funny people and why she couldn't go home. What else was very difficult was, as wonderful as children are, they can be cruel in the things they say. Now, not only was I this strange-looking girl with the *haole* father, but now [I'm] the strange-looking girl with the *haole* father bullying whose Hawaiian mother is nuts. That's what I was in elementary school. And it became difficult trying to deal with these problems.

Out of the seven children who grew up in this Kauai home, six of us are really fine. There's only one, a sister two years older than I, who has not been able to change it around. She has a major drug problem, she is homeless somewhere on the island. I have no clue where she is. She's been through one abusive relationship after another. Still, six out of the seven is not bad. We love her with all our heart and continue to hope for her and continue to be there whenever we can help her.

How come the six of us are really basically okay? I can only share my understanding of what made a difference for me. I'm going to share four things. When I was asked, "What made a difference for you?" these were the four things I came up with. What's been very exciting is that it has fit into the research really nicely. I didn't learn about the research until a few years ago, and I hadn't paid attention to it until a few years ago. As I did learn more about it, it was exciting to me that it just fit.

The first thing that I think made a difference for me was that we were ① expected as children to work, and we were expected to work hard. If we didn't, we would get lickings. We would get beat. That was all there was to it. If we didn't do our jobs, when mom and dad came home, we would get the belt or whatever was handy. We had a one-acre piece of land, which is a lot for Hawaii. We had to take care of it. As children, we took care of the yard, the house, the clothes, each other, and the cars. We did everything. My father cooked when there was something to cook, and my mother simply coped. I asked her one day, "Mom, what do you do?" Because we did everything. We did laundry by hand for nine people. If there's no food, there's no washing machine. If there's no food, there's no lawn mower to clean the yard. So we did it with sickles and hoes and what we call cane knives.

I remember once we were late. We had played too long with our friends, and mom and dad were on their way home, and we hadn't done our chores. So we decided to set fire to the yard to burn down the bush we were supposed to take care of. We thought that was the fastest way to do it, and we didn't want to get the belt. So we burnt nearly the whole community down. I mean, the fire took care of what it was supposed to take of and then it went further and further, and all the neighbors came out with their water hoses, and we managed to get it under control. When mom and dad came home, it was already dark, so they couldn't see the burnt backyard, so we didn't get the belt until the next day.

Children do whatever it takes not to get punished. That's what I did. Like I told you, laundry by hand, scrubbing the floor on hands and knees. And if you missed one little spot, you'd get the belt and you did it again. If you missed one piece of food on the dish, you'd get the belt and our father dumped it back in the sink again. You did it over until it was done right. This made a difference for me. It doesn't sound like a wonderful opportunity, but what it did was teach me how to dig in my heels and work. When things got rough, I learned to dig in my heels and say, "How am I going to make this happen?" versus, "This is too hard, I quit." I think we're raising a generation of young people now who say too quickly, "This is too hard, I quit." We need to give them the opportunity to do meaningful work.

I have seven kids. Not one of them comes to me and says, "Mom, I'd be happy to do the dishes for you today." But they have to because that's part of their responsibility. Work is a building block to better things. I didn't see it then. As a parent, I see it now. My children hate it, but they do it because they have no choice. I don't give them the belt. I have other ways to make sure it happens. The ability to work helps us to learn how to deal with the problems that come, and that's what it did for me. It gave me the ability to dig in my heels and say, "How can I make this happen?"

Number two, probably the most important for me were caring and supportive people throughout all of my life. I was fortunate to have such people. A lot of times, it wasn't my parents because they were too busy needing to take care of their own stuff. For me, the first and foremost as a child was my grandma. A lot of us have wonderful grandmas and grandpas. Mine was my Grandma Kahaunaele, who is my mother's mother. Grandma Kahaunaele lived just down the road from us, which made it nice. She was a wonderful, wonderful, quiet Hawaiian woman. She had red hair and white skin. I'm not sure how that happened; it's one of those things they don't tell you about in your family history. She didn't say much. I don't remember her voice, but she had this incredible heart. I remember a couple of things you need to know. Number one is we were "those children." You know what "those children" are? The ones where you as parents say, "I don't want you playing with 'those children.' I don't want you going to 'those people's' house." We were "those children" that nobody wanted around. I don't know if it's because we were different, or because we were always dirty, or because our clothes were always dirty. I don't know why, but we were. That's how I felt. Grandma Kahaunaele never treated me like one of "those children." What you need to understand, however, is she was immaculately clean. Her house was spotless and shiny. She washed and ironed pillowcases, underwear, T-shirts. That's how she was. It was immaculate.

You can imagine what she thought when she saw us coming out of the cane field because we'd cut through the park, cut through the cane field. And if there was water in the irrigation ditches, we'd jump in there and catch toads and tadpoles and whatever else there was. And then we ended up at her house. She must have said, "Oh my golly. Here they come." You know, I would have. I'm a grandma. I can understand this now. If she thought it, she never said it, never said it to me. Not once do I remember her saying to me, "You are so filthy. Go home. I don't want you here." However, what she would do is she would dump us in the outside tub and wash off the red dirt and then let us in the house.

My Grandma Kahaunaele is the only person I remember who would comb my hair. I remember going to school one day and the teacher said to me, "Doesn't anybody ever comb your hair? Doesn't anybody ever wash your face?" I guess I was dirty. Grandma Kahaunaele was the only one who would comb my hair. You know, Hawaiian girls always have long hair, and I had long hair, but it was always tangled, and it was always dirty. I remember sitting in the playground, first grade, and wondering why my head was so itchy. It's because it was so dirty. Back then I'd scratch and scratch. Grandma Kahaunaele was the one who would wash my hair, and she was the only one who would take the tangles out. She would sit me down at her knee and she'd have this giant, yellow comb. She'd patiently take every tangle out of my hair. And for any of you who've had long tangled hair, with a comb going through it, not fun, you know? Your head is yanking as it gets caught, and I'd be crying. She would say, "Almost *pau*, almost *pau*." *Pau* means finished. "Almost done." She would eventually get finished, and I remember feeling clean, and I remember feeling pretty, and I remember feeling like maybe somebody cares for me, even for just a little while.

Grandma Kahaunaele had a wooden leg. When she was a child, a car ran over her toes. The infection grew and grew and grew until they cut her leg off just below her knee. In order to put her wooden leg on, she put [on] about six pairs of socks and then she'd buckle her leg right here. I can still [see] her doing it at the edge of her bed. At night when she would go to bed, she would take off the leg and take off the socks and stand it at the post of her bed. We spent many, many nights at Grandma and Grandpa Kahaunaele's home. When mom was in the institution, that's where we stayed—because my father couldn't handle all of us.

I remember waking up at night with nightmares and crying, and being afraid, looking for someone to care for me. My vision, that I will never forget, is this woman crawling on her hands and knees down the hall to come and make sure that I was okay . . . because she had no leg. She took her leg off. Then, when I was all right and settled and feeling better, she would crawl back to her room. An example, a memory, of caring and support unsurpassed by anything else for me.

I had a fifth-grade math teacher, and I remember she said to me one day, "You are a good-for-nothing Hawaiian and will never amount to anything." Now, as a ten- or eleven-year-old you simply say, "Okay." You take that information and you store it. You store it in the back of your brain. Back then, if you answered back to your teacher, you'd get whacked from the principal. Then you'd go home and get whacked again from your parents. So you just take that information and you store it. At the same time in my life, I had a principal [who] said to me, "You are Hawaiian and you can be anything you choose to be." Each one of these people said this to me once. I remember the tone. I remember the words. I remember everything about both situations.

I think I listened to Ron Martin, my principal. As I thought about this over these last few years, it had nothing to do with being Hawaiian. I'm sure he said to other students, "You are Japanese, and you can be anything you choose to be." "You are Filipino, and you can be anything you choose to be." It had to do with "This youngster needs me today. This youngster needs me to say something today to help her over the hump!" And that's what he did. I will always be grateful for that.

Third thing—first was hard work, [second was] caring and supportive people—that made a difference for me was education. When I was twelve years old, I left Kauai and went to the main island of Oahu because there is a school there for Hawaiian kids. You must be Hawaiian to go to that school—all of the money comes from King Kamehameha. His granddaughter, who had no children of her own, left all of her estate, land, and money to the education of Hawaiian children. So we have the Kamehameha School and I had the privilege of attending at age twelve, seventh grade. Personally I would not send my child away at age twelve. There is too much that goes on in the life of a twelve-year-old. But for us it was one of the best things my parents did. When I asked my mom why she sent us, she said it was cheaper for them. That's the truth. They were struggling. Dad still had his alcohol problem. He was still gambling, all kinds of stuff. So to give us the opportunity to go away and be cared for and get an education was good for them.

At age sixteen, as a junior in high school, I became pregnant. The policy at Kamehameha School at that time was when you're pregnant, you're gone. I was taken to the office of the dean of students; her name was Wynona Reuben. Ms. Reuben was a big, tall lady, and she had a man's voice. And if you were in her office, you were in trouble. I was in her office because I was in trouble, and she basically said, "Well, I'm sorry. You've got to leave." She put me on an airplane back to Kauai to tell my parents. I went home and talked to my mother, who was not happy.

We had to make some decisions. The decision at that time was that I would get married. So at age sixteen, I got married. At age seventeen, I had my first child. We came back to Oahu because that's where my husband-to-be lived, and he [had] just graduated from high school. We went [back] to the Kamehameha School and they said, "Sorry, you're out of here."

So my mother took me to a school in downtown Honolulu. It was a special education school. There's mainstreaming now, but back then there wasn't. It was for "special needs" children of all ages. We walked into this school and it was green and wooden and [had] broken windows that had boards on them. It was, in my perception, not a good place. [It] had children in wheelchairs and babies up to what looked like adults who were [disabled] mentally, physically, emotionally, all kinds. It was terrifying. I looked at that, and in tears I turned to my mom and said, "Mom if this is what a high school diploma means, I don't need it. I cannot do this. I cannot be here." And so we left.

We went back up [to] Wynona Reuben's office. I don't know how or what happened, but I was allowed to go back to school, pregnant and married. It had never happened in this institution before. A few years ago, I wanted to find out what happened, so I called my counselor who was still counseling at that school. I said, "Tom, how come they let me come back?" He said Wynona Reuben called the counseling department—they had been looking at the problem of teenage pregnancy in students—and she said to them: "You know the parent-student program we've been talking about? I want you to push it and I want this student to be the first one in it. She is not a bad student. She just made a mistake."

She was the help. Now in this institution called Kamehameha School, it is not easy to make change. I had teachers who refused to have me in their class because I was pregnant and because I was married. One of "those children" again. "These kinds of students don't belong at Kamehameha." I was not allowed into some of the classes. There were others who were ready for the change. What made the difference here was Wynona Reuben, who was willing to take the risk for kids, to go out on a major limb for them.

The other thing that going away to Kamehameha did for me, it broadened my vision a whole lot. It helped me make some choices that I never knew I could. All around me in my neighborhood was alcoholism and abuse. Uncle Sonny across the way, every day, all day long, he sat on his porch with his bottle of Primo Beer. Uncle Henry next door was a policeman but when he got angry, he would beat his children. I remember one day his littlest son came out of the house with an iron burn on his back because his dad was angry with him. All around me, that's what I saw. In my own home, that's what I saw, and I thought that's the way life has to be. When I went away, I realized that it wasn't the way it had to be. There were people who had fathers who didn't drink. I realized that I could make choices.

It was there, when I was a student at Kamehameha, that I promised myself I would never date or marry anybody who drank. I saw what alcohol did to my mother. It destroyed her. The alcohol also destroyed my father. I remember seeing my father passed out in his urine and vomit. And I refused to have that in my life. I made that choice. That is not something I wanted for me or for my children. And I've been able to keep true to that promise to myself.

I should mention that my teenage husband, eighteen years old at the time [we married], is still my husband of twenty-six years. He's a pretty neat guy. He's a schoolteacher. He's been teaching for twenty-one of those twenty-six years, and it was because of people who cared about us who helped us get through those beginning times. So allowing for choices, participation, and involvement that broadens vision—that was number three.

The fourth thing that made a difference for me—when there was no Grandma Kahaunaele, when there was no Ron Martin, when there was no Wynona Reuben, [or] the many, many others who cared—was that somewhere, someplace down the line, somebody had taught me, "There is somebody greater than us who loves you." And that is my hope and my belief. Whatever that translates for you—a belief in a God, a belief in a religion, a goal, a dream, something that we can hang on to. As adults, we need to give our young people hope and something to hang on to. As young people, we need to find our own."

❏

CHAPTER SEVEN

Troubled Teenagers
Roads to Recovery in Adulthood

At age ten, twenty-five youngsters (M: 14; F: 11) in this cohort needed long-term mental health care (of more than six months' duration). Their emotional problems had been identified through behavior checklists filled out independently by their parents and their teachers and confirmed by diagnostic tests and observations of clinical psychologists and child psychiatrists (Werner and Smith, 1977). Twenty (80%) of these children had conduct problems and displayed overt antisocial behavior. Among the other five were two diagnosed as adjustment reactions to childhood, and one each with a diagnosis of childhood neurosis, schizoid personality, and sociopathic personality.

By age eighteen, the number of individuals with serious mental health problems had grown to seventy youths (M: 23; F: 47). Among them were teenagers who had been sent to the Hawaii State Mental Hospital or the local hospitals on Kauai for mental health reasons or who had been under treatment as outpatients at the Kauai Community Mental Health Center. Their diagnoses ranged from problems of sexual identity to neurotic symptoms, hysteria, severe depressions (including two suicide attempts), obsessive-compulsive disorder, and paranoid, schizoid behavior. Half of the males and one-third of the females in this group also had records of juvenile offenses (Werner and Smith, 1982).

The changing sex ratio in mental disorders from childhood to adolescence that we found on Kauai is supported by national data from first admissions to public and private mental health hospitals, general hospitals, and outpatient clinics. In childhood, boys tend to have higher rates of mental health problems than girls, but by late adolescence, females tend to have higher rates than males. The pertinent literature on childhood and adolescence suggests that boys experience more stress than girls in the first decade of life and are more vulnerable than girls to the effects of biological insults or caregiving deficits in childhood. This trend is reversed by the end of the second decade of life, with females reporting more stressful life events than males, especially when they are confronted with teenage pregnancies and early marriages.

We noted significant differences in exposure to stressful life events between youths with mental health problems in their teens and peers (of the same age and sex) without serious coping problems by age eighteen. Among both sexes, a higher proportion of individuals with mental health problems in adolescence had parents who were alcoholic or psychotic and brothers or sisters who were developmentally disabled. A higher proportion of teenagers with mental health problems had experienced the arrival of a younger sibling before they were two years old and received "below normal" ratings on the two-year developmental examination by the psychologists.

By age ten, the majority of the youths who developed mental health problems in their teens were already having problems in school. In adolescence, a higher proportion of these youngsters had conflict-ridden relationships with their peers and experienced prolonged parental absences due to desertion, separation, or divorce.

For both sexes, a combination of serious learning and behavior problems with a moderate to marked physical handicap by age ten was the most powerful set of predictors of serious mental health problems in adolescence. The predictability of later mental health problems improved considerably from the early to the middle childhood years, reflecting the cumulative effects of biological predisposition and caregiving deficits during the first decade of life. Children who had grown up in chronic poverty were most vulnerable (Werner and Smith, 1977).

TROUBLED YOUTHS IN THEIR EARLY THIRTIES

We were able to obtain follow-up data at ages 31/32 for 81 percent (57/70) of the individuals with mental health problems in their teens (M: 23; F: 34). By the time they had reached their early thirties, more than half of the youths with mental health problems in adolescence had recovered. Nearly half of the men and two-thirds of the women in this group did not have any problems that necessitated the intervention of the courts, the Departments of Health and Mental Health, or the Department of Social Services of the state of Hawaii. The proportions of troubled youths who showed spontaneous recovery in adulthood in this Pacific Asian cohort are identical with those reported by Robins (1978) in her studies of black and Caucasian teenagers in St. Louis and by Magnusson (1988) in his follow-up studies of a contemporary Swedish cohort.

But there were some continuing casualties as well. About half of the troubled teenage boys and a third of the troubled teenage girls encountered problems in making the transition to adulthood. One-third of the men but only 8 percent of the women with mental health problems in their teens required mental health services between ages eighteen and thirty-two. Among them were one male and two females who had previously been diagnosed as schizophrenic and three males who had problems with their sexual identity. One of the males in this group was dismissed from the air force after four months' service.

Nearly half of the men but only 5 percent of the women with mental health problems in their teens had criminal records by age thirty-two. Among them were the majority of children who had been diagnosed as having conduct disorders by age ten. Twenty-two percent of the men with mental health problems in their teens had criminal court records *and* had been admitted to psychiatric care after age eighteen. Among them was an individual who had attempted murder, another who shot and killed a man in a domestic quarrel, and others who had been involved in serious narcotic offenses and repeated car thefts. These men had been referred to psychiatric care by the local courts.

Our findings are similar to those reported by Magnusson (1988) from his longitudinal study of a Swedish cohort born in 1955. In his cohort, as in ours, about a third of the males with onset of psychiatric disorders in their teens remained in psychiatric care as young adults. Among Swedish males with previous mental health problems in their teens, about half of those with criminal records needed psychiatric care when they reached young adulthood.

Our findings, albeit with different ethnic groups in a different geographical and cultural context, are identical and support his plea that psychiatric illness and criminality cannot be effectively studied in isolation from each other. Most vulnerable in our cohort was the small group of teenagers who had both records of mental health problems and records of juvenile offenses by age eighteen. Eleven of the twelve men in this group and six of the thirteen women had two or more coping problems by the time they reached their early thirties. These included broken marriages, criminal records, and/or psychiatric illnesses.

NEW ADMISSIONS TO PSYCHIATRIC CARE AFTER AGE EIGHTEEN

Sixteen individuals in this birth cohort first received psychiatric care after our follow-up at age eighteen. Six (40%) were diagnosed as schizophrenics; two (13%) were diagnosed as suffering from severe depression; three (20%) had marital problems; three (20%) were diagnosed as adjustment reactions to adulthood; and two (13%) were diagnosed as having mental health problems associated with borderline mental retardation.

Men and women were about equally represented among the first admissions to psychiatric care at ages 18–19, 20–24, 25–30, and 30–32. Some 88 percent of the men but only 38 percent of the women in this group had been in need of remedial education by age 10 or had committed some juvenile offenses by age 18. A third of the males but none of the females among the first admissions to psychiatric care between ages 18 and 32 had a parent with a serious mental health problem and/or a criminal record by age 32.

We noted that four of the six individuals diagnosed as schizophrenics and one of the two individuals with affective disorders had been exposed to moderate to severe degrees of perinatal stress at birth. These rates are four to five times higher than for the cohort as a whole. (Only 3 percent of all children born in 1955 had been exposed to severe perinatal complications, and 10 percent had experienced complications of moderate severity.)

Although our sample is small, our findings agree with reports from larger studies with different ethnic groups on the U.S. mainland and in Denmark. Buka, Lipsitt, and Tsuang (1987) reported some preliminary results of a twenty-year prospective investigation of perinatal complications and psychiatric outcomes. Their study cohort consists of 176 singleton births, diagnosed as either "severe toxemia" or "breech delivery," and 176 matched controls, all selected from the Providence, R.I., center of the National Collaborative Project (NCP). Preliminary analyses of their follow-up data at ages 18–24 suggested elevated rates of substance abuse, antisocial personality, and schizophrenia associated with the perinatal complications of breech birth or severe toxemia.

Complementary findings have also been reported from the Copenhagen High Risk Study of the offspring of schizophrenic mothers (Cannon, Mednick, Parnas, Schulsinger, Praestholm, and Vestergaard,

1993). A higher proportion of these offspring had suffered from pregnancy and birth complications than did those who did not become psychotic. In both the Danish and the Kauai longitudinal studies, association between perinatal stress and deviant behavior in adulthood varied by gender, with males being more vulnerable than females.

TROUBLED YOUTHS AT FORTY

We were able to obtain follow-up data at age forty on 82.5 percent of the individuals who had been diagnosed as having serious mental health problems in their childhood and/or youth. Two individuals were deceased. One male (who also had been delinquent in his teens) had died from gunshot wounds in a drug bust; one female, who had been pregnant as a young teenager, had died from (cervical) cancer. A third of the survivors with previous mental health problems had some continuing midlife problems, including difficulties with finding and keeping a job, problems in marital and interpersonal relationships, and problems with substance abuse. There were significant gender differences among those who had "recovered" and those who were still "in trouble."

Of the surviving women who had been diagnosed as having mental health problems in their teens, only about one out of six (N: 4/23) still had serious adaptation problems at age forty. Of the females with mental health problems in adolescence who also had been delinquent, one out of four (N: 2/8) were still "in trouble" at the end of their forth decade of life. Among them were two women who had accumulated a criminal record (for fraud and forgery).

Among the men who had been diagnosed as having mental health problems in their teens, a third (N: 8/24) were still having serious coping problems at age forty. Of the males with mental health problems in adolescence who had also been delinquent, nearly one out of two (N: 6/14) were doing poorly. A third had accumulated criminal records between ages eighteen and forty that included narcotic drug offenses and domestic abuse (against spouse or children), resulting in restraining orders. Individuals who had previously suffered from serious psychoses (one woman with schizophrenia, two females and one male with chronic depression) had continuous problems in midlife.

As a group, both men and women who had had mental health problems in their teens had significantly higher unemployment rates than did their resilient and low-risk peers—about double that of the national average at the time of the forty-year follow-up. Among the men, nearly half (47.1%) were still single at age forty. Fifty percent of the men who were married and had children worried about them—at rates significantly higher than those for their low-risk and resilient peers. The men who had been troubled teenagers also had significantly higher scores on the Anger scale of the EAS Temperament Survey—scores that had increased from ages thirty-two to forty (see Tables 10 and 11 in Appendix I).

At age forty, only a third of the women with previous mental health problems were satisfied with their current work—in contrast to five out of six among their resilient peers (31.3% vs. 84.6%). More than half (53.8%) reported communication problems in their marriages, and only a third (33.3%) considered their spouse to be their friend. Fewer than half were satisfied with their relationships with their siblings, and only one out of four felt in control of both the pleasant and the unpleasant events that happened in her life—dimensions on which they differed significantly from their resilient peers.

A significantly higher proportion of these women worried about their family and a significantly lower proportion was satisfied with life at forty. Overall, women with mental health problems in their teens also scored lower than the resilient women on two of the scales of Psychological Well-Being: Positive Relations with Others and Self-Acceptance. Low scorers on this dimension tend to have few close, trusting relationships with others, feel more often frustrated in interpersonal relationships, and tend to feel dissatisfied with aspects of their selves.

It needs to be stressed, however, that the *majority* (N: 49) of the individuals with mental health problems in adolescence were now in stable relationships and jobs, and were responsible parents and citizens in their community. Looking back at the lives of the troubled youths who had staged a recovery in adulthood and were making a satisfactory adaptation at midlife, we noted a number of protective factors and turning points in their lives that contributed to positive changes in their life trajectories.

PROTECTIVE FACTORS IN THE INDIVIDUAL AND THE FAMILY ENVIRONMENT

The Men

Males with mental health problems whose status improved over time tended to be firstborn or only children whose mothers had a higher level of education than did the mothers of those who still had problems at age forty. They also had grown up in smaller families where there were significantly more positive interactions between the infant and his primary caregiver. By age ten, these boys had significantly higher scores on the PMA IQ and a nonverbal measure of problem-solving ability (PMA reasoning factor) than did troubled youths who still had problems in midlife. They also had better reading skills.

By the time these boys had reached their senior year in high school, they had on the whole a more favorable attitude toward school and more realistic educational and vocational plans beyond high school than did troubled youths who were still having problems in midlife. They also encountered significantly fewer stressful life events in adolescence and in adulthood than did troubled males who had some continuing problems in adulthood, and scored significantly higher on the Activity scale of the EAS Temperament Survey for Adults.

In contrast, the men who were still doing poorly in midlife tended to come more frequently from homes where fathers were alcoholic or mentally ill. Among males whose mental health problems persisted from adolescence to midlife, a higher proportion had also been exposed to moderate–severe perinatal stress.

The Women

Women with mental health problems whose status improved over time had been rated significantly more often as more advanced in physical and intellectual development in pediatric examination at age two than did women who still had problems by age forty. Like the recovered males, they scored significantly higher on the PMA IQ and a nonverbal test of problem-solving skills at age ten, and they had better reading skills by grade four than did females whose trouble persisted into midlife. They also scored significantly higher on the Sociability scale of the EAS Temperament Survey for Adults.

The caregiving style of their mothers had been characterized by more positive interactions in infancy, and they had received more emotional support from family members in childhood than had women whose mental health problems persisted into midlife. In the transition to adulthood, between ages eighteen and thirty-two, women who had recovered from their troubles reported significantly fewer stressful life events than did females whose mental health problems persisted. They also encountered fewer stressful life events and significantly more sources of emotional support in the fourth decade of their lives, including support from a spouse or mate.

A Supportive Spouse or Friend

At both ages thirty-two and forty, the most frequently mentioned sources of emotional support for individuals who had had mental health problems in adolescence but who had recovered in adulthood, was a spouse or a close friend. About half of the women (54%) and nearly two-thirds (64%) of the men who had been troubled teenagers reported that their spouses had helped them most in dealing with difficulties and stresses in their adult lives. Two-thirds of the men and women in this group also relied on the emotional support of close friends.

A marine mechanic who had been painfully shy and stuttered a lot in his teens told us, "I am not much into going out into night clubs or dancing. I like to stay home with my wife. She has given me a positive view of life." A stock clerk who grew up with a rejecting father and turned into an insecure, aggressive teenager in need of psychotherapy added, "Talking things out with my girl friend has made all the difference. She accepts me the way I am."

A welder who had been a troubled youth but was happily married and had two children at age thirty reported, "The most important thing that has happened to me so far in my life is my marriage. I learned how to give fifty-fifty and to talk my problems out with my wife." Ten years later, at age forty, he wrote, "Meeting my wife and marrying her was the most important experience that has helped me make the kind of person I am today."

A woman lawyer who had been diagnosed as having "adjustment reactions of adolescence" at age eighteen, when she was confused about her college plans and had broken up with someone she thought she would marry, looked back in her thirties: "I met the right husband after college. We had good pre-marital counseling and have relied on our faith to guide us. I have learned in my marriage to respect his point of view without requiring him to change into the person I want him to be, and he does the same with me."

"I am living life to the fullest," wrote a woman who at fifteen had been sexually abused by her adopted father and at seventeen had married an abusive husband. In her twenties she had received some counseling in a battered women's center and got a divorce. By thirty-two, she was happily married to a man "with whom I can talk things over and whose company I can enjoy. I got to analyze my life, see things clearer. I like myself now." At forty, she was in charge of housekeeping at a large resort hotel, "thanks to my husband who supported me along the way to where I am today."

Psychotherapy

About a third of the men and women in this cohort who had been identified as having serious mental health problems in adolescence had received some form of mental health care in their teens and twenties. This relatively small proportion was identical with the percentage of youngsters among child guidance referrals who received treatment one or two generations ago—before any widespread federal, state, or local concern for the mental health of America's youth (Robins, 1966).

Among major sources of referral to state-supported mental health care for troubled youths were the courts and other community agencies (37.0%), private physicians and hospitals (22.2%), and family or friends (22.2%). There were relatively few self-referrals (14.8%). About half of the referred individuals received mental health care in an inpatient setting, at local hospitals or in the state hospital in Honolulu; the other half were seen in outpatient clinics on Kauai or the other Hawaiian islands.

Of the third who received publicly funded mental health care, about half (44%) were judged to be "improved" at the time their treatment terminated. Mental health professionals tended to assign this label most often to men and women with the diagnoses of adjustment reactions to adolescence or adulthood and to individuals with marital problems, transitory depressions, and hysterical personality disorders. Among those judged "unchanged" or "undetermined" were individuals with major psychoses (schizophrenia, severe depression) and the "sociopathic" personalities. The fortunate few who had received counseling and were improved expressed less conflict and greater insight in our interviews than did individuals whose condition had remained unchanged or worsened. They also had a more positive self-concept.

A young woman who had received help from mental health professionals in her late teens and early twenties, and then gone on to graduate with a law degree and become a manager of a legal department, wrote,

"I am happy with myself now. I used to worry about achieving my goals and how others regarded me. I know now that I am a good thinker, articulate, rational, and committed, and that I have leadership qualities. I want to be the best attorney I can be." That refrain was echoed by another woman in this cohort who was once considered a "bright but neurotic youngster." She sought counseling after a nervous breakdown precipitated by her decision to leave a graduate theological seminary. She felt then that she had let down her parents and friends. In her thirties, she was a pension analyst, happily married, and expecting a baby. She wrote, "I have learned to get along with others and to make others feel good about themselves."

The men who had improved with the help of counseling were less defensive about their experience than men whose mental health problems persisted. Wrote a bartender in California who was the son of an alcoholic father who had abused him as a child, "In adolescence I found out that my father had an affair, so I got into self abuse, i.e. drugs and alcohol. What psychotherapy and a lot of reading has taught me is that I am responsible for myself, and that I can accept people the way they are. I can't change them unless they want to change, but I can be compassionate with them. I still worry sometimes about whether I will be successful, whether I will ever accept myself fully, and whether I can maintain a healthy relationship, but I am much more confident now."

At both age thirty-two and age forty, fewer than 10 percent of the individuals who had been troubled teenagers rated mental health professionals of *any* kind (psychologists, psychiatrists, social workers) as helpful in times of crisis or stress. In our follow-up studies in early adulthood and midlife, mental health professionals were ranked twelfth among fourteen sources of support, far behind spouses and friends, parents, siblings, members of the extended family, coworkers, teachers, mentors, ministers, and faith and prayer. Only self-help organizations and pets were mentioned by a lower percentage of respondents as helpful in difficult times.

Those who were still having contacts with mental health professionals at age forty seemed to value their medications more than their rehabilitation efforts or psychotherapy. Wrote a woman who had been diagnosed as a paranoid schizophrenic at age twenty, "I am hopeful that Clorazil and new medications will allow me to do more [in the next ten years of my life]." At age forty, she was still unemployed, single, childless, and mostly dissatisfied with her relationship with her partner, who was mentally ill as well. She continued to worry about her health and "who will take care of me when my parents die."

In a more hopeful mood, another woman who suffered from an agitated depression gave credit to Prozac, her psychologist, and her masseuse for the progress she had made in the past three years. But two other women and a male who sought help for depression and anxiety disorders were not satisfied with the effects of medication or therapy. A woman with "obsessive-compulsive" behavior characteristics, who had received counseling since her early twenties, had a more positive attitude. When asked about the experience that had been most important in making her the kind of person she was at age forty, she responded, "I would say *pain*—it has given me insight and the ability to be strong and tough when all else failed. Also God and faith!!"

MEMBERSHIP IN A RELIGIOUS GROUP

A significant minority among the individuals with mental health problems in our cohort (one out of three women, one out of five men) had joined religious denominations that assured them salvation, security, and a sense of mission. Prominent among them were the Jehovah's Witnesses and, to a lesser extent, the Church of Jesus Christ of Latter Day Saints.

Jehovah's Witnesses share a belief that the final battle between Good and Evil will occur in the very near future. The chief duty of faithful Witnesses is to warn nonmembers and to educate them to join their New World Society to escape annihilation in this battle.

The Watchtower Bible Tract Society objects to higher education and psychiatry and instead empowers each of its members to be a minister and missionary to the world. Most Witnesses hold down secular jobs to support themselves and their families, but their main focus is five regular meetings each week in the local Kingdom Hall and an average of eleven hours each month of door-to-door preaching. This schedule almost always mandates withdrawal from secular activities.

The simplicity of the life of most Witnesses is appealing. Many come from limited educational backgrounds. Among the men and women in our cohort who became converts and were active in the Watchtower Society, only one had attended a junior college. Her job as a bookkeeper in a local store was more skilled than those of the other Witnesses, who were housewives, waitresses, carpenters, and janitors. Two of the men worked full-time for the ministry, one as a bookbinder and one as a cabinetmaker. Both had been sent from Kauai to the world headquarters of the Jehovah's Witnesses in Brooklyn and considered their stay there the best period of their lives. One was still working in New York at the time of the forty-year follow-up.

Wrote the cabinetmaker, who was the son of a schizophrenic mother and who had been a slow and withdrawn child when he was seen in the local mental health clinic as a youngster, "I love Hawaii, the place where I was born and raised, and I think I always will, but the best part of my life has been my stay here at the world headquarters of the Watchtower Society. I have learned a lot, not only about my trade, but also about how to deal with people. I have many close friends here."

This view was echoed by a full-time minister back in Hawaii, who was also a doughnut and pizza maker, cashier, and newspaper delivery man: "The best period of my life so far was between 1974 and 1983. I served as a volunteer at the Watchtower Bible Tract Society in Brooklyn, New York." To this man, who was once placed in a class for the educable mentally retarded, the most important things in life had been baptism as one of Jehovah's Witnesses and marriage. What had helped him most in dealing with the difficulties and stresses in his life was "my Bible knowledge and my relationship with God." When we asked him at thirty-two what he most wanted to accomplish in his life, he cheerfully replied, "To live forever on a Paradise Earth according to God's promises in the Bible." What he worried most about, however, was "how to pay the bills, keep the car running, and have food to eat."

At age forty he was still having financial problems. Having lost his job as a result of cutbacks in the economy, he was now self-employed, cheerfully making do with "odd jobs." The lack of steady employment had been stressful for him, but he had not given up his calling. "I and the other Jehovah's Witnesses go door-to-door in our community, talking to people about God's Kingdom and what it will do for mankind," he wrote us. And to our question about his expectations for the next ten years of life, he replied, "The scene of the world changes daily. It would be difficult to rest my hope on anything it has to offer. If I could continue to have a happy united family that would be just fine with me."

The women Witnesses were equally steadfast and devoted. One, who as a teenager had made several suicide attempts, told us at age thirty-two, "What helped most in dealing with the difficulties in my life was prayer and acting upon the examples found in the Bible." Asked at age forty what experience she considered most important in making her the kind of person she was, she replied, "Becoming a Christian and having children of my own."

Perhaps the greatest transformation in this group was that of a young woman who was raped at age fifteen by a friend of her father's. Diagnosed as a "borderline psychotic" (severe depression and paranoia) at age sixteen, she became a drug addict by age seventeen. In her early thirties she was happily married and worked as a bookkeeper, but the main focus of her life was "the five weekly Bible discussion meetings that I attend with my husband. He and I are both dedicated and baptized Jehovah's Witnesses." For her, the most important thing that had happened in her life was "being a student of the Bible and living my life according to Bible standards." At forty, she was an assistant manager and the mother of three accomplished high school students. But she was most proud of her volunteer activities. She wrote, "As one of Jehovah's Witnesses, I use my time off from work to help my neighbors understand the Bible's message."

Equally devoted to their faith were individuals with mental health problems in their youth who had joined the ranks of the Latter Day Saints as young adults. The Mormon Church is very active in missionary work in Hawaii and has many features attractive to young seekers. Its members find a rich spiritual, social, and recreational life in its fellowship. Participation in the priesthood gives each Mormon male a sense of direct involvement in the church.

Mormons also know that their church is interested in their temporal welfare and will come to their aid if they should become ill or unemployed. The extensive church welfare program is one of the chief attractions of Mormonism. Latter Day Saints in good standing (who have contributed 10 percent of their gross income to the church, and another 2–3 percent to the upkeep of their local ward) can count on receiving substantial help in the form of food, clothing, cash, and help in finding a job. Needy Mormons may apply for assistance in case of sickness, unemployment, or other personal or family problems.

Mormons have a dedicated membership, a strong missionary impulse, and a tradition of encouraging large families and higher education. Among the members of this cohort who converted to the Mormon faith were individuals who were, on the average, better educated and more intelligent than those who became Jehovah's Witnesses. They also had more children than their peers. Their commitment to their newfound faith reflected a strong missionary zeal. Wrote a security guard who had needed mental health care as a child, "What I want to accomplish most in my life is to fulfill my Heavenly Father's Plan." The most important thing that had happened in his life so far was "being married for Time and Eternity." What had helped him most in dealing with the difficulties in his life was "being a member of the Church of Jesus Christ of Latter Day Saints, and being able to rely on help from the bishop of the LDS Church."

A baker, who had a mental breakdown when he was in his late teens, considered his membership in the Church of Latter Day Saints to be the experience that had done most to make him the kind of person he was at forty. "I know who I am, where I came from, why I am here and where I am going after this life." Meanwhile he spent some thirty-five hours each week volunteering in a local ward, ministering to the spiritual welfare of its residents. "Knowing that we will be an eternal family" was the most positive aspect of motherhood for a Mormon convert woman, offspring of an alcoholic father and a severely depressed mother. At thirty-two, she had seven children, ranging in age from fourteen to four, and enjoyed her work in the State Department of Education in Honolulu. What she wanted most then was to get a college education and to help her children achieve all they could. At age forty, she had obtained a master's degree, three of her children were attending college, and one was a missionary in Japan. As a much-sought-after speaker, she was bringing a message of hope to many "at risk" kids: "There is somebody greater than us who loves you—that is my belief."

RECOVERY FROM LIFE-THREATENING EXPERIENCES

More than any other group in this cohort, the individuals who had successfully overcome serious mental health problems in their teens had learned positive lessons from serious illnesses and accidents that had struck them or close family members in their twenties and thirties. "After my auto accident my life has changed drastically for the better," wrote a man who had undergone reconstructive surgery after his face had been shattered. "Facing a life threatening illness, and having a near death experience was the most important experience that have helped me make the kind of person I am today," noted another man who had spent eight months in the hospital in his late thirties and had undergone ten operations to repair his intestinal tract. "My mother died after months of pain and suffering; it opened my eyes to the real world," wrote a third.

"Pain, pain, pain—life itself is a teacher," wrote one of the women who managed to go on to graduate school and to become a successful insurance agent after struggling with serious mental health problems in adolescence and young adulthood. "No one is going to pick you up after you fall," noted another. "If you make a mistake, you learn from it," was the motto that guided this woman to a successful adaptation at midlife.

Expectations for the Next Decade of Life

The men who were still struggling with mental health problems at age forty were far less sanguine and articulate about their expectations for their next decade of life than were those who were coping well at midlife. "Don't know!" wrote one man who was spending fifty hours a week watching T.V. (more time than sleeping and working!). "Live it day by day," wrote another who was worried about aging. "I have no expectations at the present moment," confided a third who was still single and childless at age forty. "I am taking every day at a time. As they say, take time and smell the roses!" "Time to me is the essence of life," wrote a fourth male who was barely scraping by on a job with the Public Works Department of the County of Kauai.

The women whose mental health problems had persisted to age forty were equally vague about their expectations for the future: "I haven't really thought that far ahead," wrote one female who had been diagnosed with learning disabilities and mental health problems in the early teens. "I never thought that far along," echoed another. "I hope I can get it together to see at least one dream come true," ventured a third who was a waitress in the same restaurant she had worked in for the past twenty years and whose health was "tremendously affected by people smoking."

These statements stood in stark contrast to the expectations of the men and women who had managed to overcome their troubled teens. "I want to build on what I have achieved so far," wrote a man who was the offspring of alcoholic parents and who had been a troubled youth himself. At age forty, he was a bank examiner and the proud father of two girls. "I want to watch my children enter a successful adulthood." "To become better than what I am today," wrote a member of the Latter Day Saints, whose four children were all enrolled in a center for gifted and talented children.

His expectations were shared by the women who had overcome their mental health problems and who were making a satisfactory adaptation to midlife. "I want to live my life to the fullest, loving and supporting my family, watching my children grow into something that will make you proud," wrote the daughter of alcoholic parents who had overcome her own mental health problems with the "unconditional" support of her spouse. "I am looking forward to my son's graduation and work, and to our daughter's marriage and raising of her children and handling of her job," wrote another woman who once had been a troubled adolescent and now was a capable manager of a local store. "I want to be hopefully still around to see and love my grandchildren," added the assistant manager of a restaurant who had found her calling among the Jehovah's Witnesses. For her, as well as for most of the individuals who once had been troubled teenagers, the words "I hope" had taken the place of "I don't know" when they voiced their expectations for the next stage of life.

In Sum

By age forty, a significant positive shift in life trajectories had taken place in about two out of three of the individuals who had been troubled by mental health problems in their youth. Positive changes in both early adulthood and midlife were more common among the women who had such problems in adolescence than among the men. Only a minority of the troubled youths, especially those with schizophrenia, chronic depressions, and substance abuse problems, were still in need of mental health or rehabilitation services by age forty.

Few in this cohort had availed themselves of professional help—the proportion who did had dropped from a third in early adulthood to less than 10 percent in their fourth decade of life. A significant minority had found instead a sense of stability, security, and coherence by joining conservative religious groups. The most significant turning point for the majority of troubled youths, however, had been meeting and marrying an accepting and supporting spouse.

Individuals who had an active and sociable temperament and good problem-solving and reading skills were more likely to overcome mental health problems than those who elicited less positive responses from their family and the community at large (see Tables 12 and 13 in Appendix I). Overall, the prognosis for youths who were shy or lacked confidence as teenagers was considerably better in adulthood than for youths who had displayed antisocial behavior, or for the offspring of parents who had serious mental health problems or problems with substance abuse *and* who had experienced severe perinatal stress.

CHAPTER EIGHT

Life Trajectories of Delinquent Youths

On the basis of the police and family court records available on Kauai and in the other district courts in Hawaii, we had identified seventy-seven males and twenty-six females in this birth cohort who had been involved in their teens in larceny, burglary, car theft, malicious injury, assault and battery, possession and abuse of drugs, or sexual misconduct (Werner and Smith, 1977). A number of these youths had also repeatedly run away from home, violated curfew regulations, hunted unlawfully, or been truant from school over extended periods of time.

Most of the youths with delinquency records in our cohort had displayed problems in school *before* they were in trouble with the police. By age ten, one out of two had been considered in need of remedial education or special class placement, and one out of five had been in need of mental health services. The combined rates of educational and mental health problems for these children by age ten were twice as high as the rates for the cohort as a whole.

There were also significant differences in exposure to stressful life events between youths with delinquency records and same-sex peers without problems. Among both sexes, a significantly higher proportion of youngsters with delinquency records had been exposed to stressful life events that disrupted their family units, such as serious discord between parents, father absence, parental separation, desertion, or divorce. A higher proportion of males with police and/or family court contacts had been exposed to such stressful life events in childhood, while a higher proportion of females had been exposed to such stress in adolescence. About a third of the delinquent males had fathers with criminal records and substance abuse problems; delinquent females had a high proportion of family members (parents, siblings) with developmental disabilities.

The female delinquents had more multiple problems in the second decade of life than had the male delinquents. By age eighteen, half of the females but only one out of four among the males with delinquency records had serious mental health problems necessitating in- or outpatient treatment. The rate of teenage pregnancies was four times as high among delinquent females as it was among women without delinquency records in this cohort.

For both sexes, predictions of delinquency in adolescence increased from modest correlations at year two to substantial multiple correlation coefficients by year ten. Variables that were predictive of delinquency in girls in adolescence reflected the presence of behavior problems and a need for mental health services in the early elementary grades. In contrast, most boys who were to become delinquent had learning problems and were in need of remedial education (especially in reading) by age ten. Predictions improved when we took into account the family's socioeconomic status (low), the mother's level of education (low), and the presence of a congenital defect (Werner and Smith, 1977).

The Delinquents in Their Early Thirties

We have follow-up data in adulthood on 82.5 percent of the delinquents in the 1955 birth cohort (M: 60; F: 25). These data include everyone who had a record with the criminal, civil, and family courts of the state of Hawaii, the statewide Mental Health Registry, the Department of Health, the Department of Social Services and Housing, the Division of Vocational Rehabilitation, and the U.S. Veterans Administration (for individuals who had enlisted in the armed forces).

Six males with police records had died by age thirty-two—accounting for half of all the male deaths in this cohort since age eighteen. Three men had died in their early twenties—one in a car crash and two from accidental drowning. A fourth, a scuba diver, had an accident when free diving at thirty feet for tourists under a glass-bottom boat off the Kona Coast of the Island of Hawaii. The fifth died from cerebral laceration after receiving a gunshot wound. The sixth casualty was a young man who had suffered from AIDS and who died from respiratory arrest and cryptococcal meningitis at age thirty. As a teenager, he had been involved in car thefts and substance abuse. He joined the U.S. Marines at age eighteen and had received an honorable discharge after one year's service.

Twenty-one individuals (M: 18; F: 3) with delinquency records were among the thirty-one surviving members of the 1955 birth cohort who had criminal records by the time they reached age thirty-two. Most prevalent in young adulthood were violations of narcotic laws, violent crimes (including murder, forcible rape, robbery, and aggravated assault), possession of stolen property, and disorderly conduct. Seventy percent of the males arrested for criminal offenses had a delinquency record, as did 66 percent of the female adult offenders. Such a *retrospective* look at the lives of persons who committed adult offenses may give the impression of a considerable amount of stability in criminal behavior. When we took a *prospective* view, however, we found that only 23 percent of the male delinquents and only 11 percent of the female delinquents in this cohort were convicted for any adult crimes. Most juvenile offenders avoided arrest after reaching adulthood. This was especially true for individuals with only one or two offenses before age eighteen.

Our findings with a Pacific Asian sample on rural Kauai dovetail with those reported from other longitudinal studies of contemporary cohorts of young adults on the U.S. mainland and in Europe. Wolfgang, Thornberry, and Figlio (1987) reported from Philadelphia that only 28 percent of white males who were taken into custody as juveniles were arrested as adults (but for blacks the percentage was 54). A study of a Swedish birth cohort, born the same year as the children of Kauai, found that only a third of the male offenders in childhood and adolescence had any record of adult criminal activity by age twenty-nine (Magnusson, 1988). A follow-up of a birth cohort in Great Britain (Woodsworth, 1979) also noted that more delinquent boys than girls became recidivists.

Characteristics of Persistent Offenders

Three out of four among the small group of juvenile offenders (N: 21) who committed further crimes in adulthood had grown up in chronic poverty as children. Two out of three had PMA IQs below 90. Half came from families broken by desertion, separation, or divorce, and one out of three had a father with a criminal record. Four out of five in this group had been considered in need of remedial education by age ten, before their delinquent careers began. On the average, these persistent offenders had been arrested four times prior to age eighteen.

By age thirty-two, nearly half in this group (45%) had broken marriages. Their divorce rate was twice as high as that for delinquents who did not engage in criminal activity as adults, and three times as high as that for the cohort as a whole. This group also contained the highest proportion of men who were delinquent in child support payments and who had a history of family abuse (i.e., who battered spouses and children). A third of the men had been referred to state mental health agencies for diagnosis and (more rarely) treatment.

With the exception of property crimes there was not much consistency in the type of offenses these individuals committed as juveniles and as adults. Only 20 percent of the individuals convicted on narcotic drug offenses in young adulthood had been arrested for substance abuse as teenagers; only a third who were involved in crimes of violence (assault, rape, attempted murder) between the ages of eighteen and thirty-two had been arrested for assault and battery or malicious injury in adolescence. But nearly two-thirds (63%) of the men and women who were engaged in theft and burglary or car theft in young adulthood had been arrested for larceny, burglary, and/or car theft in their teens as well.

Our findings with this small group of delinquents turned criminals on a Hawaiian island are similar to those reported by Wolfgang and his associates (1987) from a large cohort of Caucasian and black males in Philadelphia; by Farrington (1989) from a cohort of British working-class youth, and by Magnusson (1988) from a cohort of Swedish men born in the same year as our study children.

Farrington (1989, in press) reported that the majority of the sixty-five London boys who were first convicted before their twenty-first birthday and went on to commit further crimes up to age forty came from low-income homes, scored low on intelligence tests in middle childhood, had experienced poor child rearing and a disrupted family life, and had a parent who had been convicted for a crime. These characteristics were quite similar to the backgrounds of the persistent offenders on Kauai.

Wolfgang and his associates (1987) reported from a sample of 975 Philadelphia males (representing 10 percent of the original cohort studied) that serious offenses were committed by a relatively small number of offenders and that males with four or more arrest records before age eighteen had a much higher probability of arrests for adult crimes by age thirty than those with only one or two juvenile offenses. Among the minority of Swedish males whose criminal activities persisted from adolescence to adulthood, about half also had other adjustment problems, such as alcoholism or mental health problems (Magnusson, 1988). The story is the same for the persistent offenders on Kauai.

However, we found significant sex differences between male and female delinquents whose antisocial behavior persisted into adulthood. A higher proportion of female than male delinquents who were engaged in criminal acts in adulthood had congenital defects (M: 14.3%; F: 37.5%), had parents who were alcoholic, mentally ill, or retarded (M: 19%; F: 75.0%), and had siblings with developmental disabilities (M: 4.8%; F: 71.5%). Our numbers are small, but our findings are in agreement with other American and European research reviewed by Widom and Ames (1988), findings that suggest that chronic female offenders may have a greater biological predisposition to antisocial behavior than male offenders. This issue needs to be addressed more systematically in prospective studies of delinquency and crime.

LATECOMERS TO CRIME

Ten individuals (eight men and two women) from this cohort were first arrested for adult crimes after age eighteen, without having had a record of previous juvenile offenses. All but one had been convicted for only one criminal offense before age thirty-two. The exception was a male who was first convicted for first-degree rape at age nineteen and subsequently arrested for assault (at age twenty-six) and terrorist threats and harassment of a public servant (at age twenty-eight). The offenses of the newcomers were similar to those of the persistent offenders, ranging from the most frequent offense, promotion of dangerous drugs, to assault, property crimes, and driving under the influence of alcohol.

The socioeconomic class distribution of the newcomers to crime resembled that of the birth cohort as a whole. Half came from poor homes, the other half from middle-class homes, but like the persistent offenders, 80 percent of the newcomers to crime in young adulthood had been in need of remedial education as early as grade five. Seventy percent had PMA IQs below 90 at age ten and had been considered either slow learners, learning disabled, or borderline mentally retarded. Low intelligence was also one of the few childhood predictors found in the Cambridge Study of Delinquent Development that differentiated the latecomers to crime from the other working-class males who had not committed any juvenile or adult offenses by age thirty-two (Farrington, 1989).

By age forty, one more male delinquent, the seventh, had died a violent death. He became a homicide victim at thirty-eight. But only 4 percent of the former delinquents had committed additional crimes in their thirties: three males had been charged with narcotic drug offenses, theft, and domestic violence; one female, a single mother with no previous criminal record, was found guilty of seven counts of theft and three counts of forgery of welfare checks accumulated in a desperate effort to support her growing family. She was an exception. By the time they had reached age forty, four out of five (81%) among the women with a previous delinquency record were in stable relationships and jobs, and were responsible parents and citizens in their community. The same held true for three out of four (77%) of the male delinquents who had no record of adult crimes.

But there were still some significant problems that the former delinquents encountered when they faced a labor market that had been severely downsized because of a serious economic recession on the island. Some 17 percent of the men and some 12 percent of the women who had been delinquents were unemployed at age forty—rates that were significantly higher than the nondelinquent rates for both the state of Hawaii and the nation as a whole. Men who had once been delinquent had significantly higher scores on the Anger scale of the EAS Temperament Survey for Adults than did their nondelinquent peers ($p < .05$). The women who had been delinquent teenagers scored significantly higher on the Distress scale ($p < .05$).

Major worries for both the men and the women in this group at age forty centered on their precarious financial status. Worries about "job security," "inability to pay bills because of unemployment," "losing my present job," "being unable to support my family," "lack of steady yearly income," and "being able to make it" were more common for the former delinquents at midlife than for *any other* group in this cohort. These worries were often accompanied by the somewhat unrealistic expectations (mostly by former male delinquents) that in the next decade of life they might be able to "become more self-sufficient financially," "pay off the mortgage," "keep finances in check," "be more prosperous," and even have the financial security to "retire" and "go fishing."

Unlike any other group, the majority of the former delinquents, both men and women, considered the period between ages eighteen and twenty-two to be the most satisfying stage of their lives. Very few (7.5%)

preferred their present stage of life. At age forty, they reported a higher proportion of marital problems, chronic discord, and substance abuse than did their peers in the cohort who had not been delinquent.

There were also significant differences between women who had been delinquent in their youth and their peers on three dimensions of the Scales of Psychological Well-Being: Environmental Mastery ($p < .05$), Positive Relationships with Others ($p < .01$), and Self-Acceptance ($p < .01$). At the threshold of midlife, female delinquents reported more difficulties in managing their everyday affairs and felt less capable of changing or improving the context in which they lived. They felt more isolated and frustrated in their interpersonal relationships and were more dissatisfied with themselves and what they had accomplished than were the women who had successfully overcome the odds of poverty and an unstable home environment. They were also less concerned with the discipline of their children.

PROTECTIVE FACTORS AND TURNING POINTS

We noted, however, a number of protective factors and turning points in the lives of the majority of delinquent youths who did *not* go on to a life of adult crimes and who managed to make a satisfactory adaptation at age forty.

Personal Characteristics

Delinquents who did not go on to commit any adult crimes had significantly higher mean scores on the Cattell IQ at age two than did the persistent offenders (96.3 vs. 89.4). They were also significantly more advanced in self-help skills in early childhood (mean social quotient: 117) than were juvenile offenders who later were arrested for adult crimes (mean social quotient: 108).

By age ten, only a small proportion of the desisters (12.7%) were considered in need of mental health services, in contrast to a significant minority (35.7%) of the persistent offenders. A lower proportion of desisters than chronic offenders had been described by their teachers as having temper tantrums and uncontrollable emotions, and as being extremely irritable. Delinquents who did not commit any adult crimes also had significantly higher scores on the Socialization scale of the California Psychological Inventory at age eighteen than did delinquents who became persistent offenders. Similar findings have been reported from the Cambridge Study of Delinquent Development in Great Britain, which followed inner-city boys from ten to forty (Farrington, 1989).

Family

The presence of an intact family unit in childhood, and especially in adolescence, was a major protective factor in the lives of delinquent youths in this birth cohort who did not commit any offenses in adulthood. Only one out of four in this group grew up in a home where either the mother or the father was absent for prolonged periods of times. In striking contrast, five out of six among the delinquents who went on to commit adult crimes came from families in which the same-sex parent was absent for prolonged periods of time during their teens because of separation, desertion, or divorce.

Police and court records also revealed that among the delinquent youths who did not go on to criminal careers, the parents or other elders (grandparents, aunts) were more actively involved in their rehabilitation process than were the parents of persistent offenders. Parents would appear with the youths in court, assist in restitution where it was called for, and attend, with their sons and daughters, the counseling sessions provided by the family court. In some cases, the parents expressed embarrassment and shame over the behavior of their offspring—they felt that they had "lost face."

In contrast, most delinquent youths who went on to become persistent offenders had parents who were too involved in their own emotional and marital problems to cooperate actively with the family court and schools. Some left the island (for Honolulu and the mainland) to remarry and start a new family. Foster home placement and the Hawaii Youth Correctional Facility did not prove to be adequate parent substitutes for the persistent offenders in this group. For some, however, a promising alternative appeared to be enlistment in the military or marriage to a stable spouse.

Military Service

Laub and Sampson (1993) and Elder (1986) have shown that a personal history of disadvantage, poor grades, and self-inadequacy increased the appeal of military service for earlier generations of delinquent youth who joined the armed forces during World War II and the Korean War.

The same can be said for a subgroup of delinquent youths in this birth cohort who had grown up under the shadow of the Vietnam War. By the time they were in high school, the compulsory draft had been eliminated and antimilitary feelings generally ran high in the United States.

Voluntary enlistment in the armed forces, however, remained an attractive alternative for delinquent youths from disadvantaged backgrounds whose mediocre school record might have led to employment problems. This was especially true for a generation that entered the workforce during one of the worst economic recessions in the United States since the Great Depression.

The appeal of military duty for these youths can be linked to the educational and vocational benefits of the G.I. Bill (Elder, 1986, 1999). Educational assistance was extended to any veteran who served on active duty for more than 180 continuous days, any part of which occurred after January 31, 1955, and before January 1, 1977, and who was released under conditions other than dishonorable or who continued on active duty. An eligible veteran, who had served a period of eighteen continuous months or more after January 31, 1955, was entitled to educational assistance for forty-five months. In addition, a veteran pursuing high school training after release from active duty could receive an educational assistance allowance without a charge against his or her basic entitlement. Also, a veteran who had to pursue additional secondary training, such as refresher courses, or make up for deficiencies to qualify for admission to an appropriate educational institution could receive educational assistance without a charge against the basic entitlement.

Twenty-two youths among the delinquents in this birth cohort enlisted in the armed forces—the majority right out of high school. Two-thirds were eighteen years old when they signed up; the others joined between ages twenty and twenty-four. Two-thirds joined the U.S. Army, 14 percent joined the U.S. Air Force, and 10 percent each joined the U.S. Navy and the U.S. Marines. Altogether, delinquent youths accounted for one-third of the voluntary enlistments into military service among members of this birth cohort. Enlistment rates among the individuals with records of juvenile offenses were more than twice as high as the national average (of 14.6%) for persons in their age group at that time (U.S. Bureau of Labor, 1986).

The majority of the men (and one woman enlistee) served for three years or more. They rose from a pay grade of E-1 ($620 per month base pay and free room and board, health care, and commissary privileges) to a pay grade of E-5 ($890 per month base pay and attending privileges).

All received a satisfactory performance rating and an honorable discharge, including the young marine who later died from AIDS.

Military service turned out to be a helpful moratorium for many delinquent youths on Kauai and opened doors to educational and vocational opportunities that were utilized by two-thirds of these veterans. Two among the army volunteers and one in the air force made the military a career and retired after serving twenty years in uniform. One became an army recruiter. Two-thirds of the veterans used their educational benefits to obtain technical training or a college education. Most often they chose a junior college, but there were also some graduates of four-year colleges in this group.

At age 31/32, some men fondly recalled the friends they had made in the military and the opportunities that opened up to them. Wrote a man who was a victim of child abuse, "I learned confidence on the job and how to be responsible." A security guard, who served for three years in the air force, remembered, "The best years of my life were my three years of service in Germany and all the friends I made." "The friends I made in the army have helped me most in life," wrote a former juvenile offender who had become a correctional officer for the state of Hawaii. The army recruiter considered his major mission on the job "to overcome the rejection by the public. I make people aware of what the army has to offer and the changes that have occurred over the years." At age 40, some of the former delinquents considered "going into the armed forces" one of the experiences that had been most important in making them the responsible persons they had become at midlife. They especially appreciated the opportunity for travel that military service provided and the chance to take college-level courses as part of their educational benefits.

Marriage

Investigators in the Cambridge Study of Delinquent Development had noted that former delinquents who married were convicted of fewer crimes than was the case among those who remained single in their twenties (West, 1982). We found a similar trend among the former delinquents in the Kauai Longitudinal Study. By age thirty-two, persistent offenders were more likely to be either single or divorced than were the men and women who refrained from criminal acts as adults. That was true at age forty as well.

The majority of respondents among the former delinquents who had committed no adult crimes considered their spouses to be major sources of help in difficult times. Wrote a communication technician with a record of larceny as a teenager, "My wife has really kept me in line and has contributed to helping me deal with the big decisions in life. She has changed my life for the better and taught me things like being open-minded and looking at people from a more positive perspective." This sentiment was echoed by a fire equipment operator who had a juvenile record of shoplifting and malicious injury: "The most important thing that has happened to me in my life so far is getting married to a great wife. She taught me to stop and think things out before acting."

Several of the men who were rehabilitated juvenile offenders commented on the company and emotional support provided by their wives that had replaced the support of their former male associates. Wrote an electrician with a juvenile record of larceny and repeated traffic violations, "The best time of my life has been after marriage—it is very pleasant to have someone to come home to every night." "Talking to my wife" and "the positive attitude of my wife" were recurrent comments of delinquent males who were happily married and had committed no adult crimes. Looking back at their lives at age forty, they considered "meeting my wife" and "getting married" among the experiences that had been most important in making them the kind of persons they had become at midlife.

The female delinquents who were settled in family life and who had no criminal arrest records as adults relied on their husbands as a major source of emotional support as well. One out of five among these women had had a first marriage (usually as a teenager) that ended in divorce, but each appeared happy with a second relationship. A library aide who had a teenage record as a runaway and shoplifter wrote, "The best years of my life are now. I am content in my marriage. I have a daughter, and, now, in the other half of my life I can teach and watch her grow."

The quality of the relationship and the kind of person chosen as a marriage partner appeared more important for the former youthful delinquents than did the change from single to marital status per se. And, not infrequently, it was a second marriage for both men and women in this group that had a restraining effect on them, rather than a hasty marriage contracted because of a teenage pregnancy or the desire to get away from a dysfunctional family.

Some of the former delinquents stressed the importance of a faith or religious belief they shared with their spouses. A former runaway from a foster home who had been raped at age sixteen and had subsequently become involved in sexual misconduct and narcotic offenses wrote, "My husband and I are both dedicated and baptized Jehovah's Witnesses. We attend four weekly Bible discussions. There we learn how to cope with various problems that confront us daily." A truck driver with a record of juvenile thefts wrote, "Because I changed my whole life style for the better—personally and in my relationship to my wife—she and I can deal with all the stresses in life." "Believing in faith, the Lord, and my wife has made all the difference," commented a plantation worker with a juvenile record of malicious injury. "Becoming a Christian and marrying a Christian was the most important experience in my life," wrote a former juvenile delinquent who, at age forty, was a supervisor in a construction company.

Parenthood

More than half of the persistent male offenders among the former delinquents on Kauai (N: 10/18) had been sued by their wives for child support. More often than not their wages were eventually garnished by order of the court because the men were negligent in their support. In contrast, delinquents who refrained from adult crime expressed a more positive and responsible attitude toward parenthood.

In response to our question "What has been the most important thing that has happened in your life so far?" a factory mechanic exclaimed, "Being a father. My ten-month- old daughter is my first and greatest accomplishment so far." "Seeing my kids grow up and the way they adjust to life makes me feel responsible," wrote a plantation worker. "Understanding their ways of thinking and trying to put them in perspective with life is one of the most difficult things I had to learn about raising children," a fireman added. "Having your child lift you up when you are down has been the most satisfying experience as a father," wrote a warehouse manager. "Watching our kids grow up without being brats, like we were," was the joy of a mother of twins who had accumulated a police record of several offenses by age fifteen. Perhaps the army recruiter captured best a pride in parenthood that was shared by many: "The best period in my life is now. Why? Because I am a father and I know that the cycle of life is starting all over again."

At age forty, when many had teenage sons and daughters in high school, parental pride was sometimes mixed with some concern. An electrician worried about "children that might be turning to the bad way of life—drugs, crime, etc." (his were O.K.), and a woman who once had done drugs herself was now worried about her daughter "when she gets to be a teenager." A local bank examiner and a janitor had other concerns: they worried about whether they might have the money to send their children to college. There was no doubt in their minds that they would do all they could to give their sons and daughters a chance at a better life than they had known in their rebellious adolescence.

In Sum

Most of the delinquent youths in this birth cohort did not go on to adult criminal careers. Three-fourths of the males and 90 percent of the females with records of juvenile offenses avoided arrest on reaching adulthood. This outcome was especially true for those with only one or two offenses before age eighteen.

The majority of the adult crimes in this cohort were committed by a small group of juvenile offenders with an average of four or more arrests before age eighteen. About half in this group had broken marriages and were delinquent in child support payments. The group also included the men who had battered their wives and/or children. The vast majority of these persistent offenders had been in need of remedial education before they began their delinquent careers (by age ten), had been considered troublesome by their teachers and parents, and had grown up in homes where either the mother or the father was absent for prolonged periods of time during adolescence.

In contrast, delinquent youths who did not go on to commit any adult crimes tended to score within the average range of intelligence in early and middle childhood and were not described as troublesome by their teachers or parents when they were in grade school. During their teens, they lived in intact family units in which at least one of their elders provided structure and stability in their lives. Military service, marriage to a stable partner, and parenthood proved to be positive turning points in the adult lives of these crime-resistant juvenile offenders—especially for the men.

But at midlife, in times of economic recession, former delinquents were still vulnerable financially. They had significantly higher rates of unemployment and more worries about supporting themselves and their families than did their nondelinquent peers at age forty. Delinquent males also had less realistic expectations for their future and a higher mortality rate than any other "high-risk" group in this cohort.

❑

CHAPTER NINE

Coping with Learning Disabilities

Among the high-risk children from the 1955 cohort whom we followed to age forty were twenty-two individuals (M: 14; F: 8) who, at age ten, had been considered in need of special services for a learning disability (Werner and Smith, 1977). A panel consisting of a pediatrician, a psychologist, and a public health nurse had made such an assessment on the basis of the combined results of group and individual examinations (psychological and medical), grades, and behavior checklists filled out by teachers and parents independently. They used the following four criteria:

1. Evidence of serious reading problems (i.e., reading more than one grade level below age expectancy) in spite of average (or above average) intelligence as demonstrated by performance on the Wechsler Intelligence Scale for Children (WISC).

2. WISC subtest scores characterized by a great deal of scatter with a significant (more than one standard deviation) discrepancy between verbal and performance IQ.

3. Large number of errors, for age, on the Bender-Gestalt Test.

4. Persistent hyperkinetic symptoms (extremely hyperactive, unable to concentrate, distractible) as judged by teacher, mother, and diagnostic evaluations.

Among these children, the proportion of boys (64%) was nearly twice that of the girls (36%). A high proportion came from homes rated low (50%) and very low (27%) in socioeconomic status; children whose socioeconomic status was middle and upper class were underrepresented (23% vs. 44% in the total cohort).

We carefully matched the LD cases with controls, drawn randomly from the master list of 1955 births, who were of the same gender and came from the same socioeconomic and ethnic background, but who had no learning or behavior problems at age ten. We first examined differences between LD and control cases on selected variables at birth, in infancy, and in early childhood. We then focused on their status at age eighteen, and at ages thirty-two and forty. Finally, we took a look at the links between protective factors and outside sources of support that contributed to a successful adult adaptation for most of the individuals with learning disabilities.

EARLY RISK FACTORS

Children who had a learning disability by age ten had a higher proportion of perinatal complications (10% vs. 0%), low birth weight (14% vs. 4.5%), congenital defects (9% vs. 4.5%), and conditions judged at birth to be related to minimal brain dysfunctions (13% vs. 5%) than control cases of the same gender, socioeconomic status, and ethnic group.

By age one year, a significantly higher proportion of mothers of children who were later to become learning disabled rated their infants as "not affectionate," "not cuddly," "not good-natured," and as "fretful," compared with control mothers. In turn, more mothers of children who later developed learning disabilities were themselves rated as "erratic" and "worrisome" by public health nurses and social workers who observed them in their interactions with their babies at home.

By age two, children who later became learning disabled were characterized by psychologists during developmental examinations significantly more often as "awkward," "distractible," "fearful," "restless," "slow," or "withdrawn" than were toddlers in the control group. Their mothers were more often characterized as "careless," "indifferent," or "overprotective." There was also a significant difference between children who later developed learning disabilities and controls on the Cattell Infant Intelligence Scale (Cattell, 1940). Their mean Cattell IQ was in the "slow learner" range (88); that of the control children was in the normal range (100). Independently of the psychological examination, pediatricians rated a higher proportion of children with learning disabilities as "below normal" in physical development at age two (24% vs. 0% in the control group). Thus, it appears that both pediatric and psychological screening in early childhood did identify a significant proportion of youngsters who later had serious learning problems in school.

Contact with Community Agencies during Adolescence

In the span between ages ten and eighteen, more than four-fifths of the youths diagnosed as having learning disabilities at age ten had some contact with community agencies. This rate exceeded that of any other "at-risk" group. It was nine times as high as that of controls matched by age, gender, socioeconomic status, and ethnicity, and nearly three times as high as that of the total cohort of 1955 births.

Differences between LDs and controls were highly significant for *total* agency contacts, for contacts with the Department of Education's Office of Guidance and Special Services, and for contacts with the high school counselors. Youths with learning disabilities also had more contacts with the Department of Health's Division of Public Health Nursing, and with the police.

One out of three youngsters with learning disabilities (36%) was seen by the Department of Education's Special Services and their high school counselors because of poor school attendance and truancy. Only one was actually placed in a special learning center and work-study program, but the others received individual attention in regular classes, had curriculum adjustments, had speech therapy, or saw a professional counselor.

One out of five was seen for diagnosis by the Department of Health, Division of Public Health Nursing. It confirmed the presence of organic damage and a learning disability, but took no further action except for referrals to other agencies. The Division of Mental Health saw three individuals with learning disabilities for diagnostic purposes (neurotic symptoms and problems with sexual identity). Two received psychotherapy and one received drug therapy.

The most frequent contacts outside the school system for youths with learning disabilities were with the judiciary system. Twenty-seven percent, nearly twice the rate for the total 1955 cohort, had contacts with the police; half of these were repeated contacts that led to referral to the family court. Reasons included car accidents, malicious injury, larceny, burglary, running away from home, repeated truancy, curfew violations, and trespassing and unlawful hunting—generally a record of repetitive, impulsive, antisocial behavior. Actions taken by the judiciary system included placement on probation, detention in the Hawaii Youth Correctional Facility, placement in the Job Corps, and, in one case, placement in the Hawaii State Mental Hospital.

TEST RESULTS AT AGE EIGHTEEN

Results on the group tests of scholastic aptitude and academic achievement taken in grade twelve confirmed a picture of continued poor scholastic performance and serious underachievement for youngsters diagnosed as having a learning disability in grade five. There were significant differences between the LDs and control cases on all subtest and total scores of the School and College Ability Test (SCAT, 1966), with the most pronounced difference on the verbal scale, and on all subtest scores of the Sequential Test of Educational Progress (STEP, 1966), with the most pronounced difference in reading and writing achievement. Persistent visual-motor problems were noticed as well. While there was some improvement in Bender-Gestalt scores for all but two of the thirteen individuals for whom we were able to obtain scores at age eighteen, the results continued to indicate serious perceptual-motor problems.

On the threshold of adulthood, youths who had been diagnosed as having a learning disability at age ten also scored significantly lower than control cases on measures of self-assurance and interpersonal adequacy, socialization and responsibility, achievement potential, and intellectual efficiency. At age eighteen, they had significantly lower scores than the control cases on the following dimensions of the California Psychological Inventory (CPI): *Sociability* (identifies persons of outgoing, sociable, participative temperament); *Self-acceptance* (assesses factors such as a sense of personal worth, self-acceptance, and capacity for independent thinking and action); *Socialization* (indicates the degree of social maturity, integrity, and rectitude the person has attained); *Responsibility* (identifies persons of conscientious, responsible, and dependable disposition); *Tolerance* (identifies persons with permissive, accepting, and nonjudgmental social beliefs and attitudes); *Commonality* (indicates the degree to which a person's responses correspond to the modal, or common, pattern established by the inventory); *Achievement via Independence* (identifies those factors of interest and motivation that facilitate achievement in a setting where autonomy and independence are positive behaviors); and *Intellectual Efficiency* (indicates the adequacy and effectiveness with which a person uses his or her intellectual resources).

Noteworthy also was a highly significant difference between youths with learning disabilities and control groups on the Novicki Locus of

Control Scale. The learning-disabled youngsters scored significantly higher in the *external* direction (mean 18) than the control group (mean 12), and believed more strongly that events were beyond their control and happened to them as a result of fate.

INTERVIEW RESULTS AT AGE EIGHTEEN

At age eighteen, we were able to reach 90 percent of the youngsters who had been diagnosed as having a learning disability at age ten and the same proportion of control cases. Both interview ratings (made by the psychologist at the end of the interview without any reference to other follow-up data, based on the total story and the youth's behavior) and specific answers to interview questions yielded a pretty dismal picture for these youths that extended over many areas of their young lives, including their plans for the future: "Maybe I'll try to go to college, any kind of college, as long as it is a place for learning." "I might go to school . . . not sure . . . but just enough to get a good job." "I just want to get out of school now." "The way I think is that if you just pass, it's OK."

As for their social life, in and out of school, and their view of parental support and understanding, these were typical comments: "We don't do much as a family, I'm afraid—we are only together if it's time for worries or when we eat." "My mother? She is nervous and overwrought, I guess that's about it." "When I was little they spanked me a lot when I did things wrong. . . . Now they scold me a lot, but don't spank anymore because they think I'm old enough to understand what's right and what's wrong." "My father? He's not that close to me. I don't know why but in the whole family I'm the only one he doesn't like—at least he acts that way. He always hassles and scolds me." "My mother understands me pretty good but my father—I doubt it—he's still got his old ways."

Questioned as to how people liked him, one youth with a learning disability said: "Not much. I'm slow." He described himself as "kind of shy." And when asked what he wanted most out of life, he shook his head: "I haven't thought of it." Another told us: "I like to be closer to myself since I am all alone all the time anyway. My family and friends go out but I stay home."

Had we concluded our follow-up of the individuals with learning disabilities at age eighteen, at the threshold of adulthood, we would have come up with an overwhelmingly negative prognosis for their lives. Only one of four learning-disabled children identified by age ten had improved by age eighteen; the few lucky ones who did gave credit to the sustained emotional support of family members, peer friends, and elders who had bolstered their self-esteem. In contrast, most of the learning-disabled teenagers considered intervention by counselors, mental health professionals, and special education teachers "of little help."

ADULT ADAPTATION OF INDIVIDUALS
WITH LEARNING DISABILITIES

During early and middle adulthood, we were able to obtain interview data about their work, family, and social life, an assessment of their state of health and psychological well-being, and community records (from the courts, the state department of health, and vocational rehabilitation agencies) on 82 percent (N: 18) of the learning-disabled individuals in this cohort. By age thirty-two, the life course of most adults diagnosed as learning disabled in childhood had considerably improved. Less than 10 percent had criminal records or persistent mental health problems—in contrast to 27 percent with delinquency records and 32 percent with serious mental health problems in adolescence. Their marriage and divorce rates were similar to those of the 1955 cohort as a whole, as were their employment records. None were unemployed or relied on welfare payments. The majority worked in service jobs or as skilled technicians.

One-half of the individuals with learning disabilities had obtained additional education after high school, either in a technical school or in a community college. One-fourth of the individuals with learning disabilities worried about their work and reported stress-related health problems, but the majority were satisfied with their job performance, their social relationships, and their marriages.

Two men and two women had persistent coping problems in their early thirties. The two men, both of whom were offspring of alcoholic fathers, had a criminal record. The two women, both of whom had had mental health problems at ages ten and eighteen, were still struggling with psychiatric problems in early adulthood. But three out of four among the adults with learning disabilities were judged to have made a successful adaptation to the demands of work, marriage, and social life at age thirty-two.

Eight years later, at age forty, the same proportion, three out of four, among the individuals with learning disabilities had made a satisfactory adaptation to midlife. Despite a downturn in the local economy in the aftermath of Hurricane INIKI, no one who was actively seeking work in this group was unemployed. Most men worked as skilled workers or technicians in the construction industry. Most women worked in service jobs in local hotels and restaurants, or as providers of health care. Two of the women were full-time homemakers. They were among the few learning-disabled individuals who still had persistent mental health (and marital) problems at age forty. "I am still experienc[ing]," wrote a single mother with a teenage son who received limited welfare benefits, when asked about her expectations for the next decade of life; "I haven't really thought that far ahead." The other, a mother of four children, who had been physically abused by her husband, was scarred by that experience: "I taught [thought] my husban[d] was everything to me," she wrote on her questionnaire, "I taught [thought] that I couldn't find nobody for myself. Now whatever he says about another woman or [when] he trys to make me jelouse, I just don't care. I'm very cold. I don't worry about him and make him wonder about me." She hoped, in the next ten years of her life, "To enjoy every moment with my kids; to keep busy, not worrying."

In contrast, the expectations of the majority of the learning-disabled individuals who had made a satisfactory adaptation to midlife were best summarized by the comment made by an occupational therapist assistant, who could draw on the emotional support of her husband, parents, friends, and coworkers: "I want to excel," she wrote. "I want to make the right choices for my life."

Protective Factors and Turning Points

Several clusters of protective factors appeared in her interview and in the records of the other learning-disabled men and women who were satisfied with their job, marriage, children, and social life at age forty and who were free of any major health or psychiatric problems (Werner, 1993, 1999):

1. Temperamental characteristics that had helped these individuals to elicit positive responses from a variety of caring persons: parents, teachers, friends, spouses, and coworkers.

2. Special skills and talents and the motivation to use efficiently whatever abilities they had; realistic educational and vocational plans; and regular chores and domestic responsibilities assumed as children and teenagers.

3. Characteristics and caregiving styles of the parents, especially mothers, who nurtured self-esteem in their children, and structures and rules in the household that gave these individuals a sense of security.

4. Supportive adults who fostered trust and acted as gatekeepers for the future. Among these "surrogate" parents were teachers, elder mentors, youth leaders, and members of church groups.

5. Openings or opportunities at major life transitions—from high school to the workplace, from single to married status and parenthood—that set the majority of individuals with learning disabilities on the path to a successful adult adaptation.

It needs to be kept in mind that the individuals whose lives we have followed from birth to adulthood came from a more disadvantaged background than children who are clients of psychotherapists or of private centers for educational therapy. They went to public schools at a time when there were fewer provisions for the early education of learning-disabled children in the United States than there are today. Truly, the "odds were against them," yet with few exceptions they have grown into responsible adults who hold down a steady job, have stable marriages, and are caring parents.

There are only a handful of other studies in the literature that have focused on protective factors in the lives of individuals with learning disabilities who have made a successful transition into adulthood (Brooks, 1994; Miller, 1996). Some of the key factors that enabled them to "overcome the odds" included self-understanding and acceptance, realistic goal setting, and perseverance, as well as supportive adults in their family and/or community. Spekman, Goldberg, and Herman (1992) found that, in early adulthood, successful men and women with learning disabilities expressed a strong sense of being in control of their fate. They believed that they were not passive victims of their disabilities, but agents capable of changing their lives. They were able to "dose challenges" for themselves and had developed effective strategies for coping and reducing stress. They also sought, accepted, and appreciated the support and counsel provided by members of their family and/or community.

Reiff, Gerber, and Ginsberg (1997) identified a nearly identical set of factors in their study of learning-disabled adults who "exceeded expectations." Their model of success focused on the individuals' ability to take control—a set of conscious decisions to take charge of their lives, to adapt to changing circumstances, and to move ahead. A realistic goal orientation, persistence, and "learned creativity" (i.e., reliance on special talents and skills they had developed to cope with their learning disabilities) enabled these men and women to attain a remarkable degree of personal, social, and vocational success. Rogan and Hartman (1990) and Vogel, Hruby, and Adelman (1993) reported that such compensatory strategies and high-achievement motivation were related to both educational and employment success in college students with learning disabilities.

Hechtman (1991) reviewed the evidence on long-term outcomes of children with attention deficit/hyperactive disorder (ADHD) and noted that individuals with positive outcomes in adulthood shared a number of protective factors that we also found in our own follow-up study of successful men and women with learning disabilities. They tended to have higher initial IQ scores and lower initial scores on hyperactivity and distractibility, had the ability to tolerate frustration, and grew up in a home environment that fostered emotional stability in the child.

In addition to these personal qualities within the individual that served a protective function, a support network within the family and community enhanced the likelihood of successful outcomes. Successful adults with learning disabilities and ADHD actively sought and utilized the advice and support of family members, teachers, friends, employers, or coworkers. They purposefully selected their mentors and sought help from a supportive spouse.

In Sum

Our follow-up study on Kauai—together with a handful of other reports on the adult lives of individuals with learning disabilities from the Midwest and the East and West Coast of the United States and Canada— informs us that a substantial number (but by no means all!) were enjoying satisfying, successful, and meaningful lives in their thirties and forties. They alert us to the need to look beyond the horizons of special education to ways in which we can provide a continuum of services that reduce the likelihood of negative chain reactions associated with a learning disability, promote self-esteem and efficacy, and offer second chances in later life, in the transition to work, marriage, and parenthood.

❏

CHAPTER TEN

Risk Factors and Protective Factors
What Matters over Time?

When our study began, the American public had become aware of the risks of pregnancy and birth complications. President John F. Kennedy's family had revealed the existence of a mentally retarded sister; the Nobel laureate Pearl S. Buck had written about her child "who never grew," and Vice President Hubert Humphrey had told the nation about his grandson who was afflicted with Down's Syndrome. We have a recurrence of such concerns today—as ever smaller low-birth-weight babies leave the intensive care units of American hospitals and enter the ranks of children with developmental disabilities (Werner, 1999).

There is a lesson from our study that bears remembering: the impact of perinatal complications tends to diminish with time, and the developmental outcomes of virtually every biological risk condition become more and more dependent on the quality of the rearing environment. Pre- and perinatal complications in our longitudinal study were consistently related to serious impairment of physical and psychological development in childhood, adolescence, and adulthood *only* when they were combined with chronic poverty, parental psychopathology, or *persistently* poor rearing conditions—*unless* there was serious central nervous system damage.

Outcomes by Age Two

Of the infants in our cohort who died before the two-year follow-up, more than three-fourths (77%) were from the small group (N: 23) that had been exposed to severe perinatal complications. Four-fifths (80%) of the deaths among the boys up to age two, and two-thirds (67%) of the deaths among the girls, were due to severe complications. Among the surviving study children, the incidence of perinatal complications by degree of severity was approximately the same for boys and girls.

At age two, there was a direct relationship between severity of perinatal stress and the proportion of children rated "below normal" in physical status by the pediatricians: 11 percent of those with no perinatal complications, 23 percent of those with moderate perinatal complications, and 36 percent of those with severe perinatal complications were classified in this category. The latter had major congenital defects, requiring long-term specialized care.

As perinatal stress increased in severity, the proportion of children considered "below normal" in intellectual status also increased. The proportion of children with Cattell IQs under 85 more than doubled when we compared the children with no perinatal complications with those who had undergone severe complications.

The effects of perinatal stress on intellectual status by age two were greater among children who grew up in poor, unstable households than among children whose parents were better off economically. Toddlers who had experienced severe perinatal stress but lived in stable middle-class families did nearly as well on developmental tests of sensorimotor and verbal skills as toddlers who had experienced no such stress (mean IQ: 95 vs. mean IQ: 102). The most impaired were toddlers who had been exposed to *both* severe perinatal stress *and* a poor, unstable home environment (mean IQ: 61).

Outcomes by Age Ten

By age ten, differences found between children with various degrees of perinatal complications and those without perinatal stress were less pronounced than at age two and centered on a small group of survivors of severe perinatal stress. The strongest associations were between degree of perinatal stress and the proportion of children at age ten who required educational placement in special classes and/or who had serious physi-

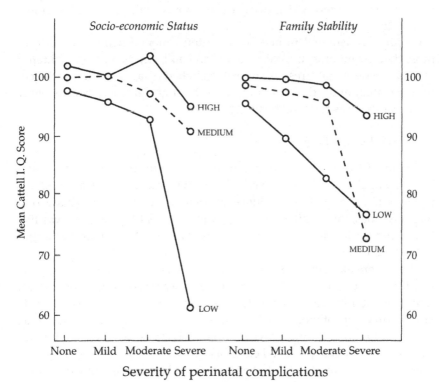

Measures of environment

Figure 2. Mean Cattell IQ scores at age 2 by severity of perinatal complications, socio-economic status, and family stability: 1955 birth cohort, Kauai

cal handicaps (predominantly defects of the central nervous system and musculoskeletal system, and problems with vision, hearing, and speech). Among the mentally retarded at age ten, for instance, the incidence of moderate perinatal stress was twice as high as in the total birth cohort; the incidence of severe perinatal stress was ten times as high.

At age ten, perinatal stress accounted for much less of the variance in PMA IQ scores than the quality of the home environment. The children *with* severe perinatal stress who had grown up in homes rated "high" in educational stimulation did not differ significantly from children *without* perinatal stress who were raised in homes with "high" ratings in educational stimulation. Both groups achieved above-average PMA IQ scores (mean: 114 vs. mean: 115). Much larger was the difference between PMA IQs of children with severe perinatal stress coming from homes rated "high" in educational stimulation (mean: 114) and children with severe perinatal stress who had grown up in homes with "low" educational stimulation (mean: 92).

Children considered in need of long-term mental health services (of more than six months duration) at age ten had twice as high an incidence of *moderate* perinatal stress as controls matched by age, gender, socioeconomic status, and ethnicity, and twice as high an incidence of *severe* perinatal stress as the total birth cohort.

Outcomes by Age Eighteen

Four out of five of the small group who had survived *severe* perinatal stress by age two still had behavior, learning, and/or physical problems in late adolescence. The incidence of mental retardation in this group was ten times, the incidence of serious mental health problems was five times, and the incidence of physical handicaps was two times that found in the total cohort.

There were also some residual effects of *moderate* perinatal stress: The incidence of serious mental health problems was three times as high, and that of mental retardation and teenage pregnancies was twice as high, among survivors of moderate perinatal stress as in the cohort as a whole. It should be pointed out, however, that in contrast to youths who had suffered from severe perinatal complications, the majority of individuals who had been subjected to moderate perinatal stress were free of serious physical, learning, or behavior problems by age eighteen.

Outcomes by Age Forty

By age forty, only the small group of survivors of severe perinatal stress differed significantly from their peers in the proportion of self-reported health problems (50% vs. 21%), mental retardation (29% vs. 3%), need for vocational rehabilitation (29% vs. 3%), physical handicaps (14.5% vs. 6%), and mortality rates between eighteen and forty (9.5% vs. 2.3%) (see Table 14 in Appendix I).

Among those who had died during that period were two individuals who had been diagnosed as mildly mentally retarded (MMR) when they were ten years old. Both had been small for their gestational age—a risk factor that has been found in British studies to be strongly associated with heart disease and hypertension in adulthood (Barker, 1997).

Follow-up data at ages 32 and 40 on seventeen surviving MMRs (of whom 75% had grown up in poverty) show that only 25 percent of the women and 30 percent of the men in this group managed to make a satisfactory midlife adaptation. The quality of their adaptation was related to their level of intelligence. The majority with poor adaptation (at work and in family life) at age 40 had IQ scores at age 10 that were significantly lower than the scores of those with "adequate to good" adaptation (mean IQ: 55 vs. mean IQ: 68). Personality characteristics also appeared to make a difference, such as dependability, good social skills, a likable, "easygoing" temperament, as well as the financial and emotional support of parents and siblings.

There were five individuals with persistent mental health problems at age forty who had been subjected to the interacting influence of genetic risk (they were offspring of schizophrenic parents) *and* moderate to severe perinatal stress. Similar findings from the Danish high-risk studies of offspring of schizophrenics with a history of obstetric complications suggest the possibility of structural brain abnormalities in these cases (Cannon et al., 1993).

PARENTAL PSYCHOPATHOLOGY

Alcohol abuse and alcohol dependence are the two most prevalent and deleterious psychiatric disorders in the United States and in Europe (Grant, 2000; Rutter and Smith, 1995). A report on U.S. children, based on the 1992 National Longitudinal Alcohol Epidemiologic Survey, estimates that approximately one out of four children (some 28 million) lived in households where one or more adults had abused or been dependent on alcohol at some time before the children reached age eighteen. This extraordinary number (that exceeds the number of children in poverty in the United States) defines one of today's major public health problems.

Our data suggest that a lifetime exposure to parental alcoholism (from early childhood up to age eighteen) was a major risk factor that had a strong association with poor adaptation at age forty for the men in our cohort, especially if they lived in a household with an alcoholic father. Associations between maternal alcoholism and poor midlife adaptation were significant as well. Mental health problems of the mother (other than alcoholism), for example schizophrenia or chronic depression, also showed a modest association with poor midlife adaptation for the males.

For the women, there were significant associations between parental psychopathology in adolescence and their own midlife adaptation. By age forty, daughters of fathers who had a history of lifetime abuse of alcohol reported less satisfaction with their present state of life, and more frequent alcohol abuse themselves.

The negative associations between chronic parental alcohol abuse and/or mental illness and quality of adult adaptation were more pronounced for the sons than for the daughters—a finding that has also been reported by Rydelius (1981) from his follow-up study of the offspring of alcoholic fathers in Sweden, and by Mednick and his associates (1984) from their longitudinal studies of the offspring of schizophrenic mothers in Denmark.

LINKS BETWEEN STRESSFUL LIFE EVENTS AND ADULT COPING PROBLEMS

Figures 3 and 4 show stressful life events in childhood, adolescence, and young adulthood that were linked directly to coping problems at age 40.

For both men and women, there were negative associations between the following variables and quality of adaptation by age 40: low family income during early childhood (birth–2); need for remedial education by age 10; problems in school during the teen years; and number of contacts with public health clinics for a range of adolescent health problems, including cardiac, neurologic and orthopedic problems, and problems with vision, hearing and speech.

For the men, there were also negative associations between the following variables and quality of adaptation at age 40: number of children in the family by age 10, and substance abuse between ages 18 and 40.

For the women, there were negative associations between the following life events and quality of adaptation at age 40: birth of a younger sibling before age 2; serious childhood illnesses between birth and age 2; death of a sibling before age 10; need for long-term mental health care by age 10; mother and father in conflict during adolescence; problems in the relationship with parents during the teen years; financial problems during adolescence; and a record of delinquency and mental health problems by age 18.

PATTERNS OF STRESSORS LINKED TO POOR ADAPTATIONS AT AGE FORTY

So far, we have presented associations between single stressors in childhood, adolescence, and young adulthood and quality of adaptation at age forty. An examination of patterns of stressful life events, however,

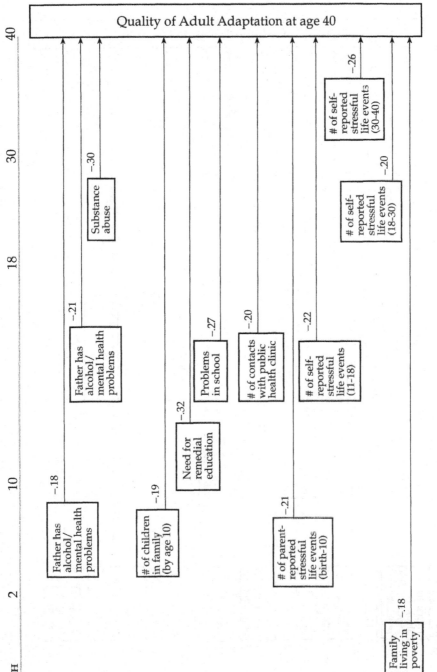

Figure 3. Correlation coefficients linking stressful life events to quality of adult adaptation at age 40: Males

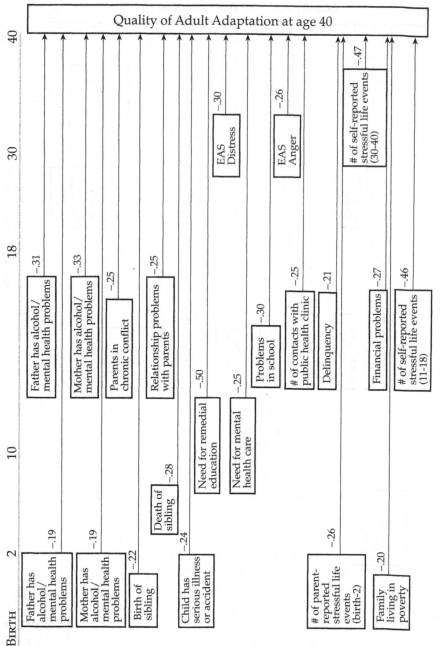

Figure 4. Correlation coefficients linking stressful life events to quality of adult adaptation at age 40: Females

may enable us to predict outcomes better than does the correlation of any single adverse event. Discriminant function analysis allows us to examine the pattern of weights of sets of stressors that predict membership in a given group (i.e., poor vs. good adaptation). It can be used with continuous as well as dichotomous variables (Norusis, 1985). (See Tables 15 and 16 in Appendix I.)

The Men

When we entered the variables that had a significant negative correlation with adaptation ratings at age 40 for the men into a discriminant function analysis, we were able to correctly classify 83 percent of the males with poor adaptation and 75 percent of the males with good to adequate adaptation in midlife (canonical correlation = .68; $p < .0002$). When we examine the pattern of the standardized canonical correlation coefficients for the males, we see that some stressful life events tend to contribute more weight to the function than others. Among stressors making the greatest (negative) contributions to outcome at age 40 were the number of stressful life events experienced in the first decade of life; need for remedial education by age 10; exposure to a father with alcohol and/or mental health problems in (early) childhood and adolescence; self-reported problems with substance abuse between ages 18 and 40; and the number of stressful life events encountered by the male in the fourth decade of life.

The Women

When we entered all the variables that had a significant negative correlation with adaptation ratings at age 40 for the women into a discriminant function analysis, we were able to correctly classify 64 percent of the females with poor adaptation and 94 percent of the females with good to adequate adaptation at midlife (canonical correlation = .72; $p < .0001$).

The pattern of standardized canonical coefficients that discriminated between the women with and without poor outcomes at age 40 was somewhat different from that of the men. Among the variables making the greatest (negative) contribution to outcome at age 40 were serious illnesses and accidents suffered between birth and age 2; death of a sibling between ages 2 and 10; need for mental health care by age 10; exposure to a father with alcohol or mental health problems in adolescence; conflicts in relationship with the mother; and number of referrals to public health clinics for chronic health problems during the teen years.

The women appeared more vulnerable—across time—to the long-term effects of illnesses in early childhood and adolescence, to the loss of sustained attention by their mother, and to conflict-ridden relationships in their families. The men appeared more vulnerable to the long-term effects of parental psychopathology (alcoholism and mental illness), and reported more problems with substance abuse than the women in the third and fourth decade of life.

With few exceptions, the variables that showed strong associations with poor outcomes at age forty had also predicted serious coping problems at age thirty-two (Werner and Smith, 1992). The exceptions were serious illnesses in early childhood and health problems in adolescence whose negative long-term effects (especially for the poor) were beginning to show up at the threshold of midlife. The same trend has been documented by the British Medical Research Council in a systematic search of the archives and records offices of the health departments in England and Wales (Barker, 1997; Hertzman, 1994).

But the previous chapters have shown that men and women who were exposed to potent risk factors in childhood were not predestined to reach midlife with a sense of failure and beset by major coping problems. Not every member of a "high-risk" group was doomed to be one of life's losers. At each developmental stage, there were opportunities for protective factors to buffer the negative impact of risk factors. We will now take a look at the individual dispositions and sources of support in the family and community that contributed to the resilience and/or recovery of the high-risk children and youths in this cohort. Most of the protective factors in childhood and adolescence that were associated with positive outcomes at age forty had also been predictors of successful adaptation at age thirty-two (Werner and Smith, 1992).

Protective Factors within the Individual

During the developmental examinations at age 2, independent observers (psychologists and pediatricians) used more adjectives denoting a positive social orientation for high-risk children who grew into adults without any major coping problems than for individuals who were having problems at age 40. Observers described a higher proportion of these youngsters as "agreeable," "cheerful," "friendly," "responsive," "self-confident," and "sociable," in contrast to their high-risk peers who later developed problems, and who were more often characterized as "anxious," "bashful," "fearful," "suspicious," or "withdrawn" in their response to strangers at age 2. They also performed better on developmental tests of language and motor development (as measured by the Cattell Infant Intelligence Scale) and were more advanced in self-help skills (as measured by the Vineland Social Maturity Scale)—especially the females.

Among the high-risk individuals who succeeded against the odds, there was a significant positive association between the PMA IQ, a (nonverbal) measure of problem-solving skills at age 10 (PMA reasoning factor), and successful adaptation at 40. By grade four, these children also had higher scores on the STEP reading achievement test than did their high-risk peers who had coping problems in adulthood.

By the time they graduated from high school (at age 18), these same individuals had higher expectations for their future accomplishments than did the high-risk youths who developed problems in midlife. They also had more realistic educational and vocational plans.

There was a strong positive association between their scores on the CPI scales measuring Socialization and Intellectual Efficiency at age 18 and the quality of their adaptation at age 40. Teenagers who had attained a high degree of social maturity, were resourceful, and put their intellect and talents to good use by the time they graduated from high school had a better chance of managing a successful transition into adulthood and midlife than those who had scored lower on these scales at age 18. The high-risk women who were doing well at age 40 also had higher scores on the Responsibility scale at age 18. They tended to be conscientious and dependable.

A potent protective factor among the high-risk individuals who grew into a successful adulthood was a faith that life made sense, that the odds could be overcome. The men and women who made successful transitions into adulthood and midlife had a more internal locus of control at age 18 than their peers who developed coping problems at age 40. They expressed a strong belief that they could control their fate by their own actions.

By age 32, the successful men rated themselves higher on the Activity and Sociability scales of the EAS Temperament Survey than the men who developed coping problems by age 40. The women who succeeded against the odds had lower Anger and Distress scores than the women with coping problems at age 40.

By age 40, the high-risk men and women who had made a successful transition to midlife scored significantly higher than their peers on five out of six dimensions of the Scales of Psychological Well-Being: Environmental Mastery, Personal Growth, Positive Relations with Others, Purpose in Life, and Self-acceptance (but *not* autonomy). For both men and women, scores on the Self-acceptance scale had the highest correlation with the independent ratings of quality of adaptation at age 40.

PROTECTIVE FACTORS WITHIN THE FAMILY

High-risk individuals who coped well by the time they had reached age 40 tended to come from families with fewer than four children, with a space of more than two years between siblings. They tended to have mothers who were older and better educated than the mothers of individuals who had persistent coping problems in adulthood—especially the men.

For the women, there was a positive association between the proportion of positive adjectives used to describe their mothers' caregiving style with their daughters at ages 1 and 2, and quality of adaptation at age 40. Mothers whose daughters developed into adults without coping problems tended to be more responsive to their toddlers' needs than were the mothers whose offspring developed problems in adulthood. They were more often described by independent observers as "affectionate," "kind," and as "taking things in stride."

Mothers who were gainfully and steadily employed during the time their children were between 2 and 10 years old tended to have daughters who coped well at age 40. Another important protective factor was the emotional support provided by other members of the family (grandmothers, older siblings) during early and middle childhood. For men who later succeeded against the odds, the degree of educational stimulation provided during early and middle childhood was positively correlated with quality of adaptation at age 40.

For high-risk women, there was a positive association between their feelings of security as part of their family at age 18 and the quality of their adaptation at age 40. Both the men and the women in turn relied on their spouses as major sources of emotional support in the third and fourth decades of life.

Protective Factors in the Community

The presence of caring adults outside the family with whom the youngster liked to associate in childhood and adolescence was an important protective factor for high-risk individuals who made a successful transition into adulthood and midlife. Among these surrogate parents were grandparents, uncles, aunts, neighbors, parents of boy- or girlfriends, youth leaders, ministers, and members of church groups.

Caring teachers and elder mentors also played a crucial role in the lives of high-risk boys and girls who made a successful transition into adulthood and midlife. Once they entered the world of work, coworkers and bosses became major sources of emotional support for the women. So did friends. The number of informal sources of support available to the individuals in the third and fourth decades of life correlated positively with their quality of adaptation at age 40.

Predictors of Satisfaction with Work at Age Forty

Let us now turn to an examination of the protective factors in the work lives of the men and women in this cohort who had surmounted adversities in their childhood and youth and who rated themselves as successful and satisfied with their accomplishments at age 40 (see Tables 17 and 18 in Appendix I).

The Men

High-risk males who liked their jobs and were satisfied with their vocational accomplishments at age 40 had mothers with more education than the men who were dissatisfied with their work. They also had encountered fewer problems in school and fewer stressful life events in adolescence. At age 32, they had higher scores on the Activity scale of the EAS Temperament Survey; and at age 40, they scored significantly higher on two of the Scales of Psychological Well-Being: Purpose in Life and Self-acceptance. Substance abuse, on the other hand, had a strong negative

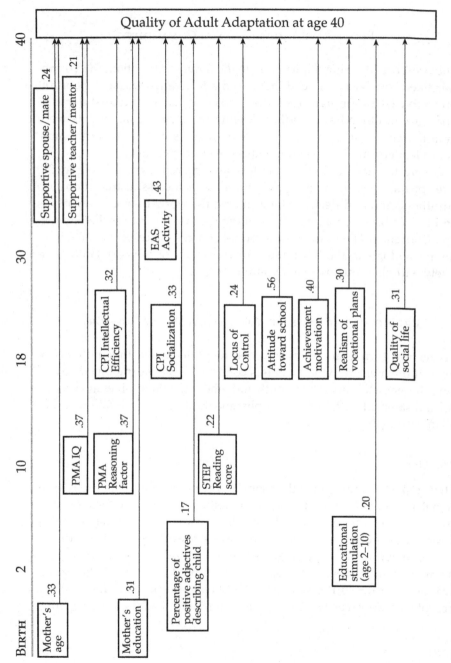

Figure 5. Correlation coefficients linking protective factors to quality of adult adaptation at age 40: Males

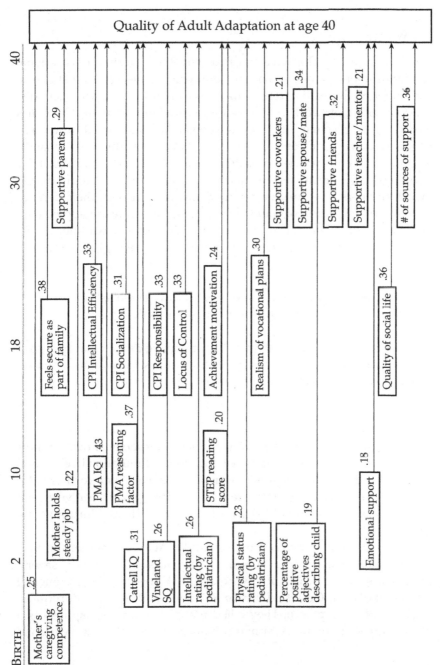

Figure 6. Correlation coefficients linking protective factors to quality of adult adaptation at age 40: Females

association with work satisfaction and vocational accomplishments ($r = -.47$) for the men.

The Women

High-risk females who were satisfied with their work and vocational accomplishments at age 40 had higher scores on the PMA IQ at age 10 and on the STEP reading test at grade four than women who were dissatisfied with their work. At age 18, they scored higher on the CPI scales measuring Intellectual Efficiency, Responsibility, and Socialization, i.e., they were more resourceful, dependable, and conscientious as teenagers than the women who were dissatisfied with their work at age 40. They also professed a greater feeling of security as part of their family during their teen years ($r = .49$), and reported less conflict with their parents, fewer problems in school, and fewer stressful life events in adolescence and adulthood. Paternal alcoholism (in adolescence) was negatively associated with the daughter's work satisfaction at age 40 ($r = -.30$).

PREDICTORS OF SATISFACTION WITH INTERPERSONAL RELATIONSHIPS AT AGE FORTY

We now turn to an examination of the protective factors that had positive associations with satisfactory relationships with parents, spouses, children, and friends at age 40 (see Tables 19 and 20 in Appendix I).

The Men

High-risk men who were satisfied with their interpersonal relationships at age 40 had been exposed to more educational stimulation in early and middle childhood than men who were dissatisfied at age 40. They also had a more favorable attitude toward school during their teen years and more satisfactory relationships with family and friends during young adulthood.

At age 32, they had scored higher on the Activity Scale of the EAS Temperament Survey, and at age 40 they scored higher on several dimensions of the Scales of Psychological Well-Being: Environmental Mastery, Personal Growth, Positive Relations with Others, Purpose in Life, and Self-acceptance. They relied more often on their spouse as a major source of emotional support than did high-risk males who had trouble making lasting and caring commitments. Paternal alcoholism (in adolescence) was negatively associated with the quality of their interpersonal relationships at age 40 ($r = -.33$); self-acceptance was positively correlated ($r = .45$).

The Women

For the high-risk women, a feeling of security as part of their family at age 18 was the most powerful predictor of satisfactory interpersonal relationships at age 40 ($r = .66$). The proportion of positive adjectives used by observers in the home to characterize the caregiving style of their mothers with their infant daughters (at ages 1 and 2) also had positive association with the women's satisfaction with their interpersonal relationships at age 40—as did the quality of their social life at age 18.

At age 40, women who were satisfied with their interpersonal relationships turned more often to their spouses, parents, friends, and coworkers as sources of emotional support and expressed less fear and distress on the EAS Temperament Survey than did women who were dissatisfied with their interpersonal relationships. They also scored higher than the dissatisfied women on all dimensions of the Scales of Psychological Well-Being (except for autonomy).

PREDICTORS OF A POSITIVE SELF-EVALUATION AT AGE FORTY

We close this section with an examination of variables that were associated with a positive self-evaluation at age 40 (see Tables 21 and 22 in Appendix I).

The Men

Among the best predictors of a positive self-evaluation at age 40 for the men was their mother's educational level and their scores on the activity scale of the EAS Temperament Survey at age 32. Men who rated themselves more positively at age 40 had been exposed to more educational stimulation in their family in childhood, had scored higher on the Primary Mental Abilities Test (PMA IQ) at age 10, and had attained a high degree of social maturity by age 18. They reported better relationships with family and friends by age 32 and fewer stressful life events between ages 30 and 40 than did men who had a poor self-evaluation. They also scored lower on the Distress and Fear scales of the EAS Temperament Survey at age 40. The best predictor of a positive self-evaluation for these men was their score on the Self-acceptance scale ($r = 54$).

The Women

Among the best predictors of a positive self-evaluation for the women at age 40 was their fathers' level of education, their feeling of security as part of their family at age 18, and the emotional support they received from their spouse or mate. The proportion of positive adjectives used by observers to characterize their mothers' caregiving style (at ages 1 and 2) had modest positive associations with the daughters' self-evaluation at age 40.

Women with a positive self-evaluation at age 40 had higher scores on the CPI scales measuring Socialization, Intellectual Efficiency, and Responsibility and higher ratings on the quality of their social life at age 18 than did women who were critical of themselves at age 40. They also scored significantly lower on the Distress, Anger, and Fear scales of the EAS Temperament Survey at ages 32 and 40. The best predictor of a positive self-evaluation at age 40 for the women was their score on the Self-acceptance scale ($r = .60$).

DISCRIMINANT FUNCTION ANALYSES

So far, we have looked at links between single protective factors in childhood, adolescence, and young adulthood and the quality of adaptation of high-risk men and women at age 40. We now present a set of predictors that maximally differentiated between individuals with a successful midlife adaptation and those with serious coping problems at age 40 (see Table 23 in Appendix I).

The High-Risk Men

We combined some thirty-six variables (from early and middle childhood, adolescence, and young adulthood) in a discriminant function analysis that enabled us to correctly identify 84 percent of the high-risk males *without* coping problems at age 40, and 83 percent of the males *with* coping problems (canonical correlation = .70; p < .01). When we examined the pattern of the standardized canonical coefficients that discriminated between men who made a successful adaptation to midlife and men who had a record of problems on the job, problems in interpersonal relations, and a poor self-evaluation, we noted about a dozen variables that tended to contribute the most weight to this discriminant function.

Among these variables were the age of the mother at the time her son was born; ratings of her caregiving skills when the boy was an infant; ratings of the toddler's social orientation and physical status at age 2; ratings of the emotional support available to the child between ages 2 and 10; the number of adults and children in the household by age 10; ratings of the teenager's attitude toward school; the realism of his educational and vocational plans and his score on the CPI scale of Intellectual Efficiency at age 18; and his Activity score on the EAS Temperament Survey.

The High-Risk Women

When we combined the same variables for the high-risk women, we correctly identified 83 percent of the females who had made a successful adaptation at age 40, and 81 percent who had serious coping problems (canonical correlation = .70; p < .05). Among the variables that contributed the most weight to the discriminant function for the women were the toddler's scores on developmental tests of cognitive development (Cattell IQ) and social maturity (Vineland SQ) as well as ratings of her physical status at age 2; ratings of her social orientation and the mother's positive interactions with her daughter at age 2; ratings of the emotional support and educational stimulation provided for the child in the home between ages 2 and 10; and the number of adults available to her as caregivers by age 10.

The PMA IQ and scores on a test of reasoning skills at age 10; scores on the CPI scales measuring Intellectual Efficiency, Responsibility, and Socialization; ratings of a (favorable) attitude toward school and the realism of educational and vocational plans at age 18 also contributed significantly to the discriminant function for the high-risk women. So did the number of sources of emotional support they relied upon between ages 30 and 40. Protective factors within the individual tended to make a greater impact on the quality of adaptation at age 40 for the high-risk women than for the high-risk men—a trend we had also observed at our previous follow-up at age 30 (Werner and Smith, 1992).

CHAPTER ELEVEN

❑

Paths to Successful Adult Adaptation

One of the major objectives of our follow-up studies in adulthood was to document how a chain of protective factors, linked across time, afforded individuals an escape from the adversities they had encountered in their formative years. We did so in a series of latent variable path analyses (Lohmöller, 1984). The path diagrams for the models that accounted for most of the variance in the quality of midlife adaptation for the high-risk men and women can be found in Appendix I, together with the path coefficients and the latent variable correlations (see Tables 25–28).*

These path models represent a pattern of temporal relationships at six points of the development cycle (from birth to age forty) that illustrate the complexity of the phenomenon of resilience—the *process* that leads to positive adaptation within a context of adversity. They show how a series of protective factors *within* the individual and *outside* sources of support and stress are linked together, in childhood, adolescence, and young adulthood, and how these variables, in turn, predict the quality of adaptation and psychological well-being at midlife. They also point to multiple opportunities for intervention—strategies designed to reduce the negative impact of stress, to enhance competence and self-efficacy, and to provide emotional support for youngsters who grow up in difficult circumstances.

---

* The path coefficient multiplied by the latent variable correlation serves as an estimate of the variance that *each* variable contributes to the *total* variance of the outcome measures.

The protective factors that correlated with adult adaptation at age forty in our study could be grouped into several (theoretical) constructs called "latent variables" or LVs. Among these latent variables were several clusters of manifest (observable) variables that represented characteristics of the individual (see Table 24 in Appendix I):

Autonomy and social maturity, a cluster of variables that included the Cattell IQ, the Vineland SQ, and a count of adjectives describing the child's positive social orientation, checked by independent observers during the developmental examinations at age 2.

Scholastic competence, a cluster of variables that included the PMA IQ and scores on a practical problem-solving test (PMA-R) and on the STEP reading test at age 10.

Self-efficacy, a cluster of variables that included scores on the CPI scales measuring Intellectual Efficiency and Responsibility; scores on the Locus of Control scale, and ratings of achievement motivation and realism of educational and vocational plans at age 18.

Temperament, a variable that included scores on the Activity and Distress scales of the EAS Temperament Survey at age 32.

Health status in childhood, adolescence, and adulthood, a variable that included a count of serious illnesses and accidents reported by the individual or his caregivers and the number of referrals to health care providers.

Among the latent variables that characterized the caregiving environment were:

Maternal competence, represented by a cluster of variables that included the mother's age and years of schooling (for the males), and the proportion of positive interactions with her child, checked independently by observers in the home at age 1, and during the developmental examinations at age 2 (for the females).

Sources of emotional support (ages 2–10), a variable that included ratings of the quality of emotional support provided to the child by the extended family, and the number of adults and children in the household by age 10.

Sources of emotional support (ages 11–18), a variable that included ratings of the quality of the teenager's social life and of his/her feelings of security as part of the family.

Sources of emotional support (ages 30–40), a variable that included the number of persons the individual turned to in times of crises, such as a spouse or mate, parents, siblings, members of the extended family, friends, teachers or mentors, coworkers or boss, ministers, mental health professionals.

Number of stressful life events reported in childhood, adolescence, and adulthood.

When we examined the links between protective factors within the individual and outside sources of support or stress, we noted that the men and women who made a successful adaptation at midlife had relied on sources of support within their family and community that *increased* their competencies and efficacy, *decreased* the number of stressful life events they subsequently encountered, and *opened up* new opportunities for them.

The protective processes that fostered resilience in the face of adversity manifested themselves early in life. We noted that—across a span of several decades—maternal competence was positively related to their offspring's adaptation in adulthood, at ages 32 and 40. Girls whose mothers interacted in a predominantly positive way with their infant daughters were more autonomous and socially mature at age two and more competent at age 10. They also attracted more emotional support in childhood and adolescence, and experienced fewer stressful life events in each decade of life than did the daughters of mothers who were less competent caregivers. Males with more competent mothers were more successful in school at age 10, more resourceful and efficacious at age 18, and relied upon more sources of emotional support in adulthood than did the sons of mothers who were less competent caregivers.

For both boys and girls, there was a positive association between autonomy and social maturity at age 2 and scholastic competence at age 10. Boys who were more autonomous as toddlers had fewer health problems in childhood and adolescence and encountered fewer stressful life events in the first decade of life. Girls who were more socially mature as toddlers had fewer health problems in each decade of life and fewer serious coping problems by age 40.

For both males and females, there was a positive association between the emotional support they received in childhood, their scholastic competence at age 10, and the quality of their adaptation at age 40. Individuals who could count on more sources of emotional support in childhood encountered fewer stressful life events than those who had little emotional support.

Scholastic competence at age 10, in turn, was positively linked to self-efficacy and the ability to make realistic plans at age 18. Males with higher scholastic competence at age 10 had fewer health problems in adolescence and higher activity scores on the EAS Temperament Survey at age 32. They also availed themselves of more sources of emotional support in adulthood. Females with higher scholastic competence at age 10 attracted more sources of emotional support in their teens. For both boys and girls, the emotional support they received in adolescence from their family and friends was positively linked to their self-efficacy and ability to make realistic plans at age 18.

Men and women who were resourceful and realistic in their educational and vocational plans at age 18 received higher scores on the Scales of Psychological Well-Being at age 40. Their temperament was related to the quality of adaptation at age 40 as well. Men who scored higher on the Activity scale of the EAS Temperament Survey at age 32 coped better at age 40 than did men with lower activity scores. Women with higher Distress scores at age 32 had more health problems and lower scores on the Scales of Psychological Well-Being at age 40.

For both men and women, there was a positive association between quality of adaptation at age 32 and age 40, and between quality of adaptation at age 40 and psychological well-being. Individuals who relied on more sources of emotional support during the fourth decade of their lives coped more successfully at age 40 than those who could count on little help in times of crisis.

The individuals' health status also made a significant impact on the quality of adaptation at age 40. Health problems in childhood (between birth and age 2 for females; between birth and age 10 for males) and health problems in adulthood (between ages 30 and 40) were *both* linked to coping problems at age 40. In each decade, men and women who encountered more stressful life events also had more health problems.

In Sum

The mother's competence and the emotional support available to the youngsters in childhood were positively linked to the quality of their adaptation at age forty, as was the individual's health status, competencies, self-efficacy, and ability to make realistic plans. Many high-risk youths who did well despite formidable childhood adversities, and others who recovered after a troubled adolescence, left their homes and community, sought environments they found more compatible, and took advantage of new opportunities that opened up for them.

We noted, however, that protective factors within the individual (such as autonomy, social maturity, scholastic competence, an internal locus of control, and psychological well-being) tended to make a greater impact on the quality of adult adaptation among the high-risk females than among the high-risk males. The negative impact of poor planning, a low activity level, and chronic substance abuse was more pronounced for the men than for the women by the time they reached midlife.

When we compare our findings with those of other longitudinal studies involving individuals from different generations who lived in different social and geographic contexts, we are encouraged by the fact that many of the protective factors and processes that acted as buffers against adversity among the men and women on Kauai have also been found in urban areas in the United States—in Boston, Baltimore, and Berkeley (Clausen, 1993; Elder, 1999; Furstenberg, 1999; Vaillant, 1993). They are also being replicated in longitudinal studies in Europe—in Great Britain, Germany, and Sweden, to name but a few (Cederblad, 1996; Opp, Fingerle, and Freytag, 1999; Rutter, 1996).

Our findings, together with the research reviewed in the first chapter, suggest that a number of potent protective factors, such as the mother's caregiving competence, the child's autonomy, social maturity, scholastic competence, and self-efficacy, and emotional support from members of the extended family and friends, have a more generalized effect on the life course of vulnerable children and youth than do specific risk factors or stressful life events. They appear in the life histories of individuals from different ethnic groups (Asian, black, Caucasian) and different regions in the United States and Europe, and in countries with different social policies toward children. They were noted among the children of yesteryear, notably the children of the Great Depression, and among members of today's "baby boom" generation. They represent a common core of individual dispositions and sources of support that contribute to successful adaptation in adulthood—especially for youngsters who were reared under adverse conditions. They matter over time. They foster hope!

❏

CHAPTER TWELVE

Lessons from the Journey to Midlife

The fragment of life, however typical, is not the sample of an even web. . . . Latent powers may find the long awaited opportunity; a past error may ure a grand retrieval.
> George Eliot (Marian Evans Cross), *Middlemarch* (1871/72)

For those of us who are stubborn enough to undertake a longitudinal study that spans four decades of life, there is the risk of being peridocially rediscovered by the national news media. An article, entitled "Invincible Kids," that reported on our study when the children of Kauai had reached age forty told the readers that we had been "looking for trouble in paradise" (Shapiro, 1996). In reality, our findings cannot be so easily condensed in catchy newspaper headlines.

Like the Fiddler on the Roof, we will have to qualify the lessons we learned from our study in ways that do not fit into a single sound bite, but that reflect more accurately the evidence that has emerged from observations, tests, and interviews at six stages of the human life cycle: infancy, early and middle childhood, late adolescence, young adulthood, and midlife. This evidence has also been corroborated by findings from a handful of other studies of past and present generations in the United Sates and Europe.

Some of the conclusions we draw from our findings may remind the reader of Tevye's famous refrain: "On the one hand"—"on the other hand." But that refrain distinguishes the developmental researcher from the skillful writer of media headlines that catch the attention of taxpaying citizens and elected politicians, of "grassroots" activists, special interest groups and lobbies, and of the makers of social policy. The task of building a bridge between these diverse ways of communicating the meaning of scientific data that deal with human behavior is a daunting one, but it is one of the issues that we need to address if the findings of developmental scientists are to be appropriately used for the making of sound public policy.

GETTING TO MIDLIFE WITHOUT THE CRISIS

What lessons, then, *did* we learn when we "looked for trouble in paradise"? Most of all, they were lessons that taught us a great deal of respect for the self-righting tendencies in human nature and for the capacity of *most* individuals who grew up in adverse circumstances to make a successful adaptation in adulthood. In the previous chapters we have illustrated the process of resilience and recovery at work in the lives of men and women whose journeys to midlife took different paths, but who arrived at a similar destination.

"Being forty" turned out to be a milestone that brought satisfaction to the overwhelming majority of the members of this cohort. They told us of significant improvements in their accomplishments at work, in their interpersonal relationships, their contributions to their community, and their satisfaction with life—in comparison with previous decades. Only a small minority had been confronted with the "midlife crises" and the "little deaths of first adulthood" that dot the "new map of adult life" presented to us by popular authors (Sheehy, 1995).

Our data agree with the preliminary findings of the MacArthur Survey of Midlife Development, whose participants are a nationally representative sample of men and women from the U.S. mainland. Although the individuals in our study were less affluent than the "average" participant in the MIDUS survey and were coping with repeated cycles of economic hardships and natural disasters, a clear majority—some 60 percent of the men and some 70 percent of the women—felt satisfied with their lives at age forty.

With few exceptions, they had made a successful transition into the stage of generativity in which the needs of others—both the younger and the older generation—were of foremost concern to them. The satisfaction and challenges of midlife seemed to far outweigh their worries about health, finances, and their children's future. For most women, age forty held the promise of new opportunities for personal growth and challenges outside the home; for most men, it was a time for a renewed commitment to their families.

Continuities in Life Trajectories

Among the members of our study cohort were men and women who had been exposed to a combination of potent biological and psychosocial risk factors early on in their lives. They had experienced perinatal stress, grown up in poverty, been reared by parents who had not graduated from high school, and lived in a family environment troubled by chronic discord and parental psychopathology.

Yet one out of three in this group had not developed any behavior or learning problems in school. As they reached the threshold of adulthood they had realistic educational and vocational goals and expectations and expressed a strong desire to improve themselves. Their very existence had challenged the prevailing myth that being a member of a "high-risk" group meant being doomed to be one of life's losers.

At age forty, at a time of serious economic recession and high unemployment on the island, none were unemployed, none had been in trouble with the law, and none had to rely on social services. Their divorce rates, mortality rates, and rates of serious health problems were significantly lower at midlife than those of their same-sex peers in the cohort. Their educational and vocational accomplishments were equal to or had exceeded those of the "low-risk" children (the majority in the cohort) who had grown up in financially secure and stable home environments.

The Recovery of Most Troubled Teenagers

One of the most striking findings of our two follow-ups in adulthood, at ages thirty-two and forty, was that most of the high-risk youths who did develop serious coping problems in adolescence had staged a recovery by the time they reached midlife. This was true for the majority of the troubled teens, but more so for the women than for the men.

Overall, troubled teenagers had a slightly higher mortality rate by age forty than did the cohort as a whole, but the majority of the survivors had no serious adaptation problems by the time they reached midlife. They were in stable marriages and jobs, were satisfied with their relationships with their spouses and teenage children, and were responsible citizens in their community.

Several turning points led to lasting shifts in the direction of life trajectories among the men and women in our cohort. They have also been noted in other longitudinal studies that have followed children and adolescents into early adult life, in both the United States and Great Britain (Rutter, 1996). In previous chapters (6–9) we have examined some of the alterations in life circumstances that led to positive changes in the behavior of many of the troubled teenagers. These changes took place after they left high school, and without the benefit of planned interventions by professional "experts."

One of the most important lessons we learned from our follow-ups at ages 31/32 and 40 was that the *opening of opportunities* in the third and fourth decade of life led to major turning points among the overwhelming majority of the teenage mothers, the delinquent boys, and individuals who had struggled with mental health problems and/or learning disabilities in their teens. Among the most potent forces for positive change for these high-risk youths in adulthood were continuing education at community colleges; educational and vocational skills acquired during service in the armed forces; marriage to a stable partner; conversion to a religion that demanded active participation in a "community of faith"; recovery from a life-threatening illness or accident; and—to a much lesser extent—psychotherapy.

Attendance at community colleges and enlistment in the armed forces were also associated with geographical moves for many of the former delinquents and for the teenage mothers. Both settings provided them with opportunities to obtain educational, vocational, and social skills that made it possible for them to move out of chronic poverty or welfare dependence and to enter a competitive job market. Their newly acquired competence gave them a sense of pride and was rewarded over time by repeated promotions. Such turning points also had effects that "carried forward" to their children. Both the teenage mothers and the former delinquents who had made use of the educational opportunities available to them in adulthood were eager to see their own sons and daughters succeed in school. Many took great pride in telling us, at age forty, that their offspring were now attending college.

Marriage to a stable partner, whom they considered a close friend, was another important turning point for many men and women who had had a troubled childhood or adolescence. Often it was a happy second marriage—after a hastily or impulsively contracted first marriage had ended in divorce. Such marriages provided the once troubled partner with a steady source of emotional support, and with the opportunity to have a caring person who acted as a sounding board, shared their concerns, and bolstered their self-esteem.

Conversion to a religious faith that provided structure, a sense of community, and the assurance of salvation was an important turning point in the lives of a significant minority of men and women who had been troubled teenagers—most of them sons and daughters of alcoholics who had been abused as children and who had struggled with mental health problems and substance abuse problems of their own. Many of them shared their newly found faith with their marriage partners and were deeply committed to the religious education of their children and to spreading the gospel of good will through charitable works in their community.

Some troubled individuals who had struggled with mental health problems in their teens reported a different kind of epiphany that turned their lives around as they approached the fourth decade of life. They had experienced a prolonged and painful bout with a life-threatening illness or an accident that immobilized them for months in a hospital bed. Paradoxically, a brush with death forced them to come to grips with the lives they had led (and sometimes squandered) and to consider the opportunities they would seize when they recovered.

Formal psychotherapy had worked with only a few troubled individuals (some 5%) in this cohort who tended to be better educated and were of a more introspective bent. The majority relied on the rehabilitative effect of medication that relieved anxiety rather than on "talk therapy" that provided insight. The men and women in this cohort consistently ranked mental health professionals (whether psychiatrists, psychologists, or social workers) much lower than the counsel and advice given by spouses, friends, members of the extended family, teachers, mentors, coworkers, members of church groups, or ministers. Their low opinion of the effectiveness of professional help did not improve from the second to the third and fourth decade of life. This finding taught us a lesson in humility!

We also noted that the troubled teenagers who made use of informal opportunities that opened up for them in their twenties and thirties, and whose life trajectories subsequently took a positive turn, differed in significant ways from those who did not make use of such opportunities: They were more intelligent, active, and sociable, and they had been exposed to more positive interactions with their primary caregivers during infancy and early childhood than were youths whose coping problems persisted into midlife.

CORRELATES OF MAJOR COPING PROBLEMS IN MIDLIFE

Many of the lessons we learned on the journey from birth to midlife have been positive: Most men and women in this cohort managed to make a successful transition to early adulthood and midlife—including the majority who had been exposed to major adversities in childhood. Likewise, most troubled teenagers staged a recovery in the third and fourth decade of life by making use of "naturally" occurring opportunities and support systems in their community—without the benefit of any formal intervention programs.

These are the hopeful lessons! But we also need to look at the darker side of life: At each of our follow-up studies in adulthood, at ages 31/32 and at age 40, some one out of six individuals in this cohort were doing poorly. These were men and women who struggled with chronic financial problems and were unable to find or keep steady jobs, who were enmeshed in conflict with their families and neighbors, and who did not think very highly of themselves.

Most but not all of these individuals had grown up in childhood poverty. Most but not all had been in need of remedial education before age ten. Most but not all had become troubled teenagers, with a combined record of delinquencies and mental health problems. A few had grown up in better educated and more affluent families and had been considered at "low risk" for developing problems in childhood, but could not cope with the "hassles" of daily life and setbacks in the economy in adulthood (see Chapter 4). A few had been among the resilient individuals who had successfully coped with major adversities in childhood and adolescence, but who had developed mental health and substance abuse problems in their late twenties and thirties (see Chapter 5).

What they tended to have in common was a familial history of alcoholism and/or mental illness that exacted an increasing price from them as they grew older. This was especially true for the men. A lifetime exposure to parental alcoholism (from birth to age eighteen) was the risk factor with the strongest association with poor adaptation at age forty, especially if the boy had lived in poverty, in a household with an alcoholic father. Associations between maternal alcoholism and poor midlife adaptation for the males were less pronounced—and maternal alcoholism was less prevalent than paternal substance abuse. Substance abuse had a strong negative association with the men's work satisfaction and accomplishments and with the quality of their interpersonal relationships with parents, spouses, children, and friends at age forty.

Females tended to be especially negatively affected if their fathers had alcohol problems when the daughters were teenagers. By age forty, they tended to have more problems at work, were less satisfied with their present state of life, and had more substance abuse problems of their own than did women who had not grown up in homes where the father had been an alcoholic. At age forty, one out of eight women and one out of five men reported substance abuse problems of their own (rates that had *doubled* since age thirty).

Though the prevalence of parental psychoses was much smaller (some 2%), they too were beginning to take a toll on the adult offspring in the third and fourth decade of life. Maternal mental illness showed a modest negative association with the offspring's adaptation at age forty. Offspring of schizophrenics who had also been exposed to obstetric complications suffered from chronic mental health problems in midlife, showing the interactive effects of genetic risk and perinatal stress.

A third group with major coping problems that persisted into midlife were survivors of severe perinatal trauma (some 3%) and individuals who had been born small for gestational age. Those born into poverty and to mothers who had abused alcohol had a greater risk of developing neurological problems. Most of the mentally retarded with poor work records who remained dependent on the support of rehabilitation agencies and members of the extended family belonged in this group. The mentally retarded and those born small for gestational age also had higher incidences of serious health problems (including serious depressions) and higher mortality rates in the third and fourth decades of life than was the norm for men and women their age.

With few exceptions, the variables that showed strong associations with poor outcomes at age forty had also predicted serious coping problems at age thirty-two (Werner and Smith, 1992). The exceptions were serious illnesses in early childhood and health problems in adolescence, whose negative long-term effects (especially for the poor) were beginning to show up at age forty.

There was also an increase in self-reported health problems from age thirty to age forty, including high blood pressure, back and joint problems, asthma, anxiety, and depression, which were linked to coping problems at age forty. Men and women who had encountered more stressful life events in childhood and adulthood reported more health problems as they entered midlife.

THE ROOTS OF RESILIENCE

The chain of protective factors that enabled most men and women to overcome multiple adversities in their formative years and to navigate a successful transition into midlife had many links. They included the individual's biological makeup (an intact central nervous system and good health), psychological dispositions (cognitive skills, temperament, and self-efficacy), and the sources of emotional support he or she could rely upon at each stage of the life cycle.

The lessons we learned from an examination of the process that linked each of these protective buffers together over time were twofold: *first*, the extraordinary importance of the (early) childhood years in laying the foundation for resilience, and *second*, the possibilities for recovery at later stages in development that were available to most individuals who seized the opportunities offered to them by naturally occurring support systems in the community.

When we compared our findings with the results of other longitudinal studies of children and youths from other generations (notably the children of the Great Depression) and from countries (notably Great Britain, Denmark, and Sweden) that have social policies for families and children different from those of the United States, we were encouraged by the fact that the protective factors and processes that acted as buffers against adversity among the men and women in our study had also made a positive impact in earlier generations, in different geographical settings, and in populations that came from different ethnic and socioeconomic backgrounds.

Our findings at age forty reinforce the impression we had at age thirty, that cohort effects (a favorite topic of skeptics in longitudinal research!) may influence the *definition* and *prevalence* of what one considers a developmental risk more than the *process* by which individual men and women cope with adversity (Werner and Smith, 1992).

Our findings suggest that the protective factors that foster resilience and the process of recovery may have a more generalized effect on the quality of adaptation than specific risk factors or stressful life events. The buffering processes that shape resilience have now been demonstrated in children of all races and in a variety of contexts in the United States and in Europe. They are the hallmark of "successful" children, whether they grow up in favorable or unfavorable environments (Masten and Coatsworth, 1998)—but they *do* have a stronger predictive power in the lives of those who are especially challenged by adversity. They seem like the ingredients of the much beloved CARE package that helped the child survivors of World War II find their way when their world had fallen apart (Werner, 2000b).

We were impressed by the long-term effects of parental education and maternal competence on the quality of adaptation of their offspring at midlife—especially for children of the poor. We noted the importance of a caregiver's sensitivity and responsiveness to the infant's needs that led to a foundation of trust, a basic ingredient in the process of recovery in adulthood. We documented the importance of good health in (early) childhood as a buffer against the ill effects of stressful life events and adversities in later life.

We recognized the importance of good reading and reasoning skills in grade school, of a positive attitude toward education and of realistic vocational plans in high school, and of an internal locus of control, a faith that one can shape one's fate by one's own actions. Equally powerful as predictors of successful adaptation were temperamental characteristics such as activity level, sociability, and emotionality that have shown a fair amount of stability from early childhood to adulthood (Kagan, 1994).

Individual dispositions and competencies were also strongly related to the number of stressful life events encountered and reported at each developmental stage. Children who had displayed a greater amount of autonomy and social maturity at age two reported fewer stressful life events by age ten. Individuals with higher scholastic competence at age ten reported fewer stressful life events in adolescence. Men and women who displayed a higher degree of self-efficacy and planfulness in their teens reported fewer stressful life events in their thirties and forties—even though they had grown up in poverty and trying family circumstances.

What mattered along the way was the emotional support of members of the extended family, of peers, and of caring adults outside the home, especially teachers and mentors who became positive role models. Many of the men and women on Kauai who managed to successfully "beat the odds" sought out the people and opportunities that led to positive turnarounds in their lives. Their individual dispositions led them to select or construct environments that, in turn, reinforced and sustained their active, outgoing dispositions and rewarded their competencies. In many ways, individuals made their own environments, picked their own niches (Rutter et al., 1995; Scarr, 1992).

GENDER DIFFERENCES

Ours is one of the few longitudinal studies of past and present generations that included a substantial number of women as well as men and followed both from birth to midlife. At each stage of the life cycle, beginning in infancy, more males than females perished. In childhood and adolescence more boys than girls developed serious learning and behavior problems. In contrast, more girls than boys were among the "resilient" individuals who did not succumb to the negative effects of major biological and psychosocial risk factors in their formative years. Even among the high-risk youths who became troubled teenagers, more women than men managed to make a successful transition into adulthood and midlife.

A number of factors seem to combine to make life generally more difficult for males than females, especially if they grow up in adversity.

Biological Factors

The X chromosome contains at least one hundred important genes other than those specifically related to reproduction. The female has two of these genes (and 4–5% more chromosome material) compared with the hemizygous male, and may be able to marshal more resistance to external hazards of development. As one biologist has put it, the genes on the X chromosome fly without a copilot in men (Ridley, 1999). These differences may be more likely to reveal themselves when the organism is stressed.

The other possibility involves the tendency for a mother without a Y chromosomal gene to be sensitized to gene products of the Y chromosome and to provoke a reaction from her immune system, thus creating a relatively unhealthy prenatal environment for the male fetus. This might produce neurological damage prenatally and contribute to the greater incidence of behavior disorders, learning disabilities, and mental retardation observed in males in childhood that do not substantially improve over time.

We also know that there are dramatic sex differences in brain growth and in the areas in which brain activity occurs. Young girls are more verbal than young boys and tend to have fewer problems with reading, a skill that is essential for successful adaptation in adulthood in our culture. The male hormone, testosterone, correlates with aggression (hence there tend to be more violent crimes among males), but it also suppresses the immune system. When stressed by life events, especially those over which they cannot exert control, males tend to become more vulnerable to infection, cancer, and coronary diseases than females. In humans, as in many species, males catch more diseases and have higher mortality rates than females—as we saw in our cohort, especially among the delinquents and the mentally retarded.

Psychosocial Factors

The women in our cohort tended to have a wider range of educational and occupational options than did women in previous generations. A higher proportion went to college and a higher proportion were in managerial and professional positions than among the women who were participants in the longitudinal studies of past generations (Clausen, 1993; Terman and Oden, 1959; Vaillant, 1993). They also had more control of their reproductive lives and could more easily leave a marriage that was "irretrievably broken." They could even choose to enter the armed forces in peacetime to further their educational and vocational goals and to affect a geographic move that took them away from a poor or dysfunctional home environment.

From the time they entered the labor market, there were also dramatic changes in the island economy (and in the U.S. economy in general) that made it possible for the women in this cohort to become self-supporting adults, not dependent on a male breadwinner—even if they were divorced and had children of their own. The island shifted from an economy that was primarily agriculture based to an economy that was service and tourist oriented. Even during repeated recessions, more women than men were able to find and keep jobs, especially if they were not highly skilled.

On the whole, women tended to also make use of more informal sources of emotional support than the men. When they faced stressful life events and adversities, they were more prone to turn to women friends and coworkers. In fact, being part of the workforce gave women more access to persons they could turn to when the going "got rough."

Men were more reluctant to share their problems with other males (whom they were apt to perceive as potential competitors). If depressed, men were more inclined than women to turn to alcohol to ease their pain—a temporary "solution" that, over the decades, only increased the likelihood of additional problems in the workplace and in interpersonal relationships.

In Sum

Throughout this study, there were large individual difference among "high-risk" individuals in their responses to both negative and positive circumstances in their lives. The very fact of individual variations in coping skills among the men and women who lived in adverse conditions suggests that educational, rehabilitation, or therapeutic programs designed to improve their conditions will have variable effects, depending upon the dispositions and competencies of the participants in such programs. That is an issue that needs to be carefully addressed in strategies for intervention, whether their aim is to decrease risks and increase resilience in the formative years, or to foster the process of recovery from a troubled childhood or youth in the adult years.

Implications for Social Policy and Social Action

Like most of the "first-generation" studies of resilience, our study has focused on *naturally* occurring phenomena that make it possible for individuals to succeed despite overwhelming odds. Many "second-generation" studies of prevention and intervention now under way represent efforts to learn from *deliberate* attempts to alter the course of development in so-called high-risk children and youth in a positive direction (Masten and Coatsworth, 1998). In the United States, these efforts, though commendable, take place in a social policy vacuum, for unlike the countries that make up the European Union, we do not yet have a national commitment to create universal policies to benefit children and families.

We have shown that many of the potent risk and protective factors that have a lasting impact on adaptation in adulthood can be identified in (early) childhood: The quality of the mother-infant interaction, the spacing of her children, the health status of the young child, reading skills and scholastic competence in the early grades, *all* are important protective factors that equip us to weather adversities, both in our formative years and in adulthood.

Yet, in a country where the majority of mothers with infants are now in the labor force and where nearly half of the fourth grade students and more than one-fourth of the eighth graders score below basic reading level, we have no universal policies for (paid) parental leave, no universal access to high-quality child care programs and early childhood education, no universal health care or insurance for our children, and no national standards or accountability for the teaching of reading in our schools. In comparison with the countries that make up the European Union, we spend considerably more money in trying to "fix" serious coping problems (for example in the construction of jails) than in preventing them!

Strategies for Intervention: "Bottom Up" versus "Top Down"

State legislators and local educational agencies appear more attuned to the needs of families and children than does the federal government. Though our study was conducted far away from the center of political power in Washington, D.C., it has, over the years, made an impact on social policy in Hawaii and California—slowly and incrementally, and happily on a bipartisan basis. It began with changes in the delivery of services for children in the state of Hawaii. Thanks to the efforts of many concerned people—members of the Teamsters Union, mental health professionals and volunteers—several community action and educational programs for high-risk youngsters have been established on Kauai since our study began. The modest royalties from our books support their work. Partly as a result of our findings, the legislature of the state of Hawaii has funded special mental health teams to provide services for troubled children and youths. In addition, the State Health Department established the Kauai Children's Services, a one-door-coordinated effort to enhance child development and to provide services for youngsters with developmental disabilities and rehabilitation in a single facility.

In California during the period of welfare-to-work reform, our findings were utilized by the State Department of Social Services and the Governor's Bipartisan Advisory Committee to plan services for children that would buffer the negative impact of the repeal of the Aid for Families with Dependent Children Program (AFDC) and facilitate the transition to Temporary Assistance for Needy Families (TANF).

Some of our graduate students obtained grants from the David and Lucille Packard Foundation to brief new legislators in the California assembly and senate on issues concerning children and the risk and protective factors that have significant influences on their lives. Since there are term limits in California, this gave our students an opportunity during each legislative session to educate the assembly members and senators who were newcomers to social policy making in California.

Toward the end of our forty-year follow-up, the Consortium of Social Science Associates in Washington, D.C., arranged a congressional breakfast seminar that focused on the topic of "fostering resilience in kids." It drew participants from the nation's legislative body and generated interest in the fiscal support of grassroots programs such as elder mentors, Big Brothers/Big Sisters, and 4-H whose positive impact on the lives of high-risk youngsters we had documented (Werner, Randolph, and Masten, 1996).

In the meantime, all over the country a flurry of prevention and intervention projects have evolved that aim to reduce risk factors and to enhance competence in the lives of youngsters who face major adversities, especially children who are born and spend their early childhood years in poverty (Brooks-Gunn and Duncan, 1997). Irrespective of economic conditions, their numbers have not decreased in the past decade, but have increased in some states of the union, like California, home to one out of eight children in the nation.

In *Within Our Reach: Breaking the Cycle of Disadvantage,* Schorr (1988) has isolated a set of common characteristics of programs that have successfully prevented poor outcomes for children who grew up in high-risk families. Such programs typically offer a broad spectrum of health, education, and family support services, cross professional boundaries, and view the child in the context of the family and the family in the context of the community. They provide children with sustained access to competent and caring adults, both professionals and volunteers, who teach them problem-solving skills, enhance their communication skills and self-esteem, and provide positive role models for them.

David Hawkins (2000) and his associates at the Seattle Social Development Project have published a comprehensive research guide to "what works" in Creating Communities That Care, an overview of effective prevention programs. Marc Freedman (1999) in *Prime Time* offers a compelling discussion of the merits of intergenerational programs, such as the Foster Grandparent Program, the Experience Corps, and the "Troops to Teachers" Program. Preliminary evaluations of these programs have shown a positive effect on the well-being of the older individuals, mostly retirees, who participate in them and on the youngsters they serve, whether they are infants and toddlers with developmental disabilities, preschoolers in Head Start projects; "inner city" children with reading problems, or potential school dropouts, such as teenage mothers and juvenile offenders in detention homes.

The positive effects of one-to-one mentoring on the lives of teens has also been demonstrated in a nationwide evaluation study by the Philadelphia-based Public/Private Ventures (P/PV), a policy research organization. In 1995, Big Brothers/Big Sisters operated all across the country and maintained 75,000 active matches between adult volunteers and children. On average, the adult-youth pairs met for three to four hours, three times a month, for at least a year. Researchers from P/PV examined 959 ten- to sixteen-year-olds who had applied to Big Brothers/Big Sisters programs in 1992 and 1993. Over 60 percent of the sample youths were boys; more than half were minorities, mainly black. Almost all lived with a single parent. Over 80 percent came from poor households, 40 percent from homes with a history of substance abuse, and nearly 30 percent from homes with a history of serious domestic violence. Half of these youths were randomly assigned to a group for which Big Brother/Big Sister matches were made. The other half were assigned to waiting lists.

The results were striking. The addition of a Big Brother or Big Sister to a youngster's life for one year cut first-time drug use by 46 percent, lowered school absenteeism by 52 percent, and reduced violent behavior by 33 percent. Participants in the Big Brothers/Big Sisters program were significantly less likely to start using alcohol, less likely to assault someone, more likely to do well in school, and much more likely to relate well to friends and family. These effects held across races, for both boys and girls (Tierney and Grossman, 1996).

Limits to Deliberate Social Intervention

Most intervention programs that have been based on findings from studies of resilience have focused on preschool and school-age children. Few so far have addressed the potential for recovery in adults, in settings such as churches, community colleges, hospitals, and the military, which opened up opportunities for many individuals in our study who had problems in adolescence but who turned their lives around in their twenties, thirties, and early forties.

Unfortunately, the most effective demonstration programs in the United States serve only a fragment of "at risk" youth and their families. Even Head Start, the only nationwide program for young children who live in poverty—now in its fourth decade of existence—reaches only forty percent of those who are eligible. We really do not know how selection effects (who gets in, who gets left out) ultimately influence the reported outcomes for these programs.

We found in our study, for example, that troubled youths who had grown up in poverty, but who were socially and intellectual competent, profited more from naturally occurring opportunities that opened up for them in adulthood than those who were less active, sociable, and intelligent. These individuals also had more competent caregivers in their family in early childhood than men and women who did not utilize the resources available to them in their community when they became adults.

Sandra Scarr (1992) has alerted us to the fact that it is not easy to intervene deliberately in children's lives to change their development unless their environments are outside the normal species range. We know how to rescue children from extremely bad circumstances and to return them to normal developmental pathways—but only within the limits of their own heritable characteristics, such as intelligence, temperament (activity, sociability), psychobiologic reactivity (cardiac and immunologic responses under stress), and susceptibility to familial alcoholism or psychoses (Barr, Boyce, and Zeltzer, 1994; Ridley, 1999).

We make this point not to discourage any of the "competence enhancement" programs (Masten and Coatsworth, 1998) and "strength building policies" (Leadbeater, 2000) that have been promulgated by professional experts, but simply to make a plea for humility when it comes to introducing these programs to a community that cares, to concerned parents, members of the local school boards, or to potential volunteers who want to help young people.

A sobering lesson from Europe is contained in a book entitled *Psychosocial Disorders in Young People: Time Trends and Their Causes*, which documents the general increase in living standards and the reduction of social inequities through deliberate social policies in the member countries of the European Union (Rutter and Smith, 1995). Since World War II, improved living conditions have been associated with a falling infant mortality (and low birth weight) rate, marked improvements in physical health, and a rising life expectancy.

In contrast, there have not been parallel trends for reduction in the psychopathological disorders of youth. Instead, suicide rates, rates of depressive disorders, and, especially, drug and alcohol problems have gone up. Even in a country as socially committed as Sweden, with free pre- and postnatal health care, paid parental leave for *both* parents, subsidized day care, education and housing for *all* its children and youth, some 28 percent of the youngsters living in urban families in Stockholm are considered "at risk" because of chronic alcoholism in one or both parents—percentages that are nearly identical to those reported in the United States (Grant, 2000; Werner and Johnson, 1999).

HOPE FOR THE FUTURE: PROGRESS IN UNDERSTANDING THE HUMAN GENOME

Knowing our present limits in the realm of deliberate social intervention does not mean we should despair. In the year 2000 a consortium of private and public researchers provided us with a first view of the "book of life"—the map of the human genome. Deciphering this map and putting that knowledge to beneficial use will be the work of generations to come, but even today we have a glimpse of what can be accomplished in preventing the devastating impact of genetic disorders that, unchecked, used to lead to debilitating neurological damage. Pearl Buck's child "who never grew" (in Chapter 10) suffered from phenylketonuria (PKU), an enzyme deficiency that, unrecognized and untreated at the time, led to severe mental retardation in her little girl. Now, each newborn is screened to see if he or she is a carrier of PKU, and all those afflicted with the disorder can be effectively treated with a special diet that prevents the buildup of damaging toxins in a child's brain. Here is just one example of what we might be able to accomplish with targeted intervention once we know the genetic base of conditions that lead to chronic psychopathology—including alcoholism and the major psychoses.

As in the case of PKU or dyslexia (a familial reading disorder), our increasing genetic knowledge will ultimately allow us to remedy genetic defects with mostly nongenetic interventions, whether they are medical, nutritional, or educational. The knowledge of the heritability of individual dispositions that help us to overcome adversity and the fact that genetic influences can express themselves later in life should not lead us to the conclusion that *heritability* is *immutability*. But we need to recognize that the environment a child experiences is as much a consequence of his or her genes as it is of external factors (Ridley, 1999).

Research on risk and resilience must pay more attention to the testing of hypotheses about causal relationships by making use of behavior genetic strategies. Many stressful experiences, such as parental discord, parental mental illness, substance abuse, or divorce, impinge differently on different siblings in the same family. Thus, we need to look more carefully at the contributions of shared versus nonshared family environments to the vulnerability and resilience of high-risk children (Rende and Plomin, 1993).

Ultimately, the most powerful tests of hypotheses about protective factors and resilience may come from intergenerational studies of siblings in high-risk families who *differ* in developmental outcomes and from evaluation studies of intervention programs whose objective is to *change* the course of development in individuals who have been exposed to potent biological and/or psychosocial risk factors. Both types of studies should have high priority for research in the decades to come.

Future research on risk and resilience needs to acquire a cross-cultural perspective as well that focuses on children of the developing world and on immigrant children from these countries who in their daily lives are confronted with many biological and psychosocial risk factors that increase their vulnerability far beyond that of their peers who were born in affluent industrialized countries. We need to know more about individual dispositions and sources of support that transcend cultural boundaries and operate effectively in a variety of high-risk contexts.

Last but not least, there is an urgent need to study the process of resilience and recovery in later life. We have seen examples of positive changes in later years among Terman's gifted children and the Harvard graduates studied by Vaillant (1977, 1993), and among the children of the Great Depression who were followed into their sixties and seventies (Clausen, 1993; Elder, 1999). Most of these individuals were well educated and had achieved a measure of financial security by the time they reached middle age. They also lived in a historical period when educational and occupational opportunities were more accessible to men than to women.

It remains to be seen how well the "ordinary" keiki o ka aina—the children of Kauai—will manage the losses that come with the aging process and the new opportunities that are available to them, for they can count on longer and healthier lives than previous generations. Having witnessed their capacity to overcome great odds when they were young, we are hopeful that the decades to come will be a time of continued personal growth and generativity for them.

For—

> To embrace one possibility after another—that is surely the basic instinct. . . . If the whole world of the living has to turn on the single point of remaining alive, that pointed endurance is the poetry of hope . . .
>
> Barbara Kingsolver, *High Tide in Tucson* (1995)

Appendixes

Appendix I

Table 1. Kauai Longitudinal Study: 1955 birth cohort by ethnicity and socio-economic status (SES)

		% in each SES category		
Ethnic group	% of cohort	High (1,2)	Middle (3)	Low (4,5)
Japanese	33.7	14.3	54.3	31.3
Part Hawaiian	22.9	2.0	31.3	66.7
Filipino	17.9	2.6	15.7	81.7
Ethnic mixtures	16.8	5.7	26.7	67.6
Portuguese	6.5	7.1	33.3	59.5
Anglo-Caucasians	2.5	76.5	23.5	0

Table 2. Survey results at age 40, by gender

Topics	Males %	Females %
Marital status at age 40	(N: 184)	(N: 195)
Single, never married	19.0	9.2**
First marriage	38.6	61.0**
Divorced, remarried	11.4	10.8
Divorced, not remarried	31.0	19.1**
Widowed	0.9	1.3

Table 2. Continued

Topics	Males %	Females %
Present employment	(N: 144)	(N: 180)
Service worker	11.3	9.4
Skilled technician	29.6	5.6**
Sales, clerical, secretarial	3.5	20.0**
Managerial, administration	24.6	30.6
Teacher, counselor, nurse	4.2	17.2**
Professional (doctor, lawyer)	4.9	3.9
Artist, writer, designer	3.5	2.8
Agricultural worker	2.8	0
Full-time homemaker	0	9.4**
Unemployed	11.3	5.0**
Work satisfaction	(N: 144)	(N: 180)
Mostly satisfied	64.6	69.6
Somewhat satisfied/dissatisfied	30.1	30.4
Mostly dissatisfied	5.3	0
Satisfaction with marriage or current relationship	(N: 184)	(N: 195)
Mostly satisfied	72.2	77.9
Ambivalent/dissatisfied	27.8	22.1
Difficult/stressful relationship	(N: 71)	(N: 117)
Financial worries	33.8	29.9
Problems with communication	8.5	14.5
Problems with others outside family	1.4	12.8**
Problems with children	21.1	21.4
Living situation	5.6	9.4
Personal differences	29.6	32.5
Lack of commitment	5.6	4.3
Physical/mental illness	2.8	6.8
Balance of work, home, relationship	19.7	15.4
If divorced, problems leading to breakup	(N: 57)	(N: 37)
Too young when married	5.6	7.1
Personal differences between self and spouse	38.9	50.0**
Lack of time together	16.7	7.1
Financial difficulties	11.1	17.9
Substance abuse	22.2	17.9
Lack of commitment/trust/fidelity	27.8	35.7
Children	(N: 149)	(N: 177)
None	35.6	21.2*
1	15.8	11.4
2	22.6	36.4
3	16.4	20.7
4	8.2	7.6
5	0.7	1.6
6	0	0
7	0.7	1.1
Relationship with children	(N: 77)	(N: 119)
Mostly satisfied	86.3	88.5
Somewhat satisfied	12.5	12.3
Dissatisfied	1.3	0

Table 2. Continued

Topics	Males %	Females %
Children's schooling	(N: 77)	(N: 119)
Children in preschool	57.4	75.7**
Children in special services	10.6	16.7
Children in gifted programs	5.3	4.9
Sources of satisfaction as parent	(N: 77)	(N: 119)
Watching children grow	93.4	87.1
Encourages responsibility in self	10.5	6.9
Shared affection	10.5	27.6**
Difficulties/stresses of raising children	(N: 77)	(N: 119)
Financial demands	7.1	14.0
Balance of responsibilities	27.1	30.7
Discipline	22.9	18.4
Teaching children (morals)	17.1	14.9
Child's independence	15.7	21.1
Negative outside influences	15.7	22.8
Child's illnesses/injury	7.1	7.0
Expectations for children	(N: 77)	(N: 119)
Good health	5.2	7.6
Happiness/satisfaction	32.8	47.1*
Achievement	54.7	67.2
Good education	33.8	35.3
Good values	27.3	44.5**
Raised children differently from own childhood	(N: 57)	(N: 100)
Children have more materially	19.0	22.0
Less strict with our children	29.3	25.0
Better communication	36.2	57.0**
Different values	12.1	15.0
Different contexts	17.2	17.0
Status of Parents	(N: 118)	(N: 152)
Father still living	73.9	70.5
Mother still living	85.6	86.2
Parents dependent on S	(N: 110)	(N: 143)
parent(s) live(s) with S or need(s) some financial help	18.8	13.4
Parent(s) somewhat emotionally dependent on S	27.3	33.8
Parents completely independent	53.9	64.1
S dependent on parents	(N: 118)	(N: 152)
Still living with parents	17.1	4.9*
Needs some financial help	11.7	10.5
Somewhat emotionally dependent	30.6	28.7
Completely independent	61.3	67.8
Relationship with father	(N: 90),	(N: 112)
Mostly satisfied	77.8	77.7
Mixed/dissatisfied	22.2	22.3
Relationship with mother	(N: 102)	(N: 134)
Mostly satisfied	81.4	79.1
Mixed/dissatisfied	18.6	20.9
Relationship with siblings	(N: 118)	(N: 152)
Mostly satisfied	69.0	64.9

Table 2. Continued

Topics	Males %	Females %
Somewhat satisfied/dissatisfied	28.4	31.1
Mostly dissatisfied	2.6	4.0
Positive aspects of relationship with siblings	(N: 118)	(N: 152)
Financial support	20.3	11.8*
Emotional support	58.5	71.7**
Shared interests, activities	70.3	66.0
Models, shared values	46.5	43.1
Providers of child care	18.8	21.5
None: does not maintain contact with siblings	3.0	4.2
Positive aspects of friendship	(N: 118)	(N: 152)
Financial support	8.5	5.3
Emotional support	70.9	90.7**
Shared interests	92.3	84.7
Models, shared values	51.3	59.3
Providers of child care	8.5	17.3
Can't think of any	2.6	3.3
Considers spouse a friend	62.6	59.3
Satisfaction with allotment of time	(N: 118)	(N: 152)
Satisfied	78.6	75.0
Dissatisfied	21.4	25.0
Regularly involved in volunteer activities	(N: 118)	(N: 152)
Church activities	30.0	45.3*
Athletic activities	40.0	22.6*
Support groups	3.3	1.9
Military activities (reserve duty)	3.3	1.9
Community organizations	26.7	35.2
Children's/school groups	26.7	29.6
Most important to S at this time	(N: 118)	(N: 152)
Independence	7.7	10.6
Achievement	9.4	10.6
Social change	12.8	6.6
Family commitment	45.3	41.1
Financial security	29.9	34.7
Creative pursuits	2.6	4.7
General health problems	(N: 118)	(N: 152)
None reported	80.8	77.2
High blood pressure	4.8	4.9
Asthma	2.7	3.8
Allergies	1.4	2.2
Back problems	3.4	2.2
Joint problems	2.1	0
High cholesterol	1.4	0
Serious depression	(N: 118)	(N: 152)
Never	35.0	27.2
Yes, once or twice	57.3	68.2
Yes, frequently	7.7	4.6
Symptoms occurring over past year	(N: 118)	(N: 152)

Table 2. Continued

Topics	Males %	Females %
Frequent headaches	9.4	27.0**
Dizziness	8.5	12.5
Trouble sleeping	29.1	36.8
Tiring easily	22.2	43.4**
Constant worry and anxiety	29.1	32.2
Trouble concentrating	19.7	11.8
Stomach ulcers	4.3	5.3
Chronic constipation	3.4	4.6
Poor appetite	4.3	3.3
Gaining weight	28.2	43.4**
Health maintenance	(N: 118)	(N: 152)
Does nothing special	16.1	19.1
Gave up smoking or drinking	26.3	15.8
Diet	40.7	59.2**
Has massages, sees chiropractor	13.6	12.5
Exercises regularly	69.3	53.3**
Takes hormones, PROZAC	0	3.9
Does yoga or meditates	4.2	8.6
Personal strong points	(N: 109)	(N: 148)
Physical characteristics	3.7	2.7
Personality traits	64.2	64.2
Intellectual abilities	32.1	39.9
Special talents	5.5	7.4
Values	23.9	33.8*
Personal habits	44.0	56.8*
Personal weak points	(N: 100)	(N: 144)
Physical characteristics	6.0	4.9
Personality traits	37.0	45.8
Intellectual abilities	19.0	11.8
Values	1.0	5.6
Personal habits	58.6	71.5*
Worries	(N: 113)	(N: 151)
Finances	47.8	51.3
Spouse, mate	10.6	11.8
Children	27.4	46.7**
Work	22.1	12.5
Friends	1.8	2.0
Social issues/future	17.7	30.3*
Family (extended)	17.7	15.2
Health issues	21.2	28.9
Control over good/pleasant things	(N: 118)	(N: 152)
Almost no control	0.8	1.3
Mostly not under my control	6.8	6.6
About half the time under my control	31.4	34.2
Mostly under my control	50.0	48.0
Almost total control	11.0	9.9
Control over bad/unpleasant things	(N: 118)	(N: 152)

Table 2. Continued

Topics	Males %	Females %
Almost no control	3.4	5.9
Mostly not under my control	21.2	27.6
About half the time under may control	35.6	26.3
Mostly under my control	34.7	36.2
Almost total control	5.1	3.9
Sources of help during stressful/difficult times	(N: 118)	(N: 152)
Spouse/mate	63.6	69.7
Parents	52.5	61.8
Siblings	33.1	46.7*
Other family members	25.4	26.3
Friends	70.3	73.0
Neighbors	8.5	6.6
Teachers, mentors	12.7	8.6
Coworkers/boss	28.8	33.6
Minister/faith/prayers	17.8	28.9*
Mental health professionals	5.1	11.2
Self-help organizations	5.1	7.2
Nobody; did it myself	7.6	5.3
Important experiences that have shaped S	(N: 111)	(N: 140)
Love from others	24.3	23.6
Positive upbringing	26.1	26.4
Starting a family	19.8	28.6
Personal abilities	21.6	17.9
Difficulty/adversity overcome	27.9	44.3**
Learning/education	20.7	21.4
Work	18.0	20.0
Leaving Kauai	12.6	20.0
Faith, idealism, social activism	12.6	10.0
Self-rating at age 40	(N: 118)	(N: 152)
Happy, delighted	17.8	24.3
Mostly satisfied	43.2	47.4
Mixed	36.4	26.2
Mostly dissatisfied	1.7	2.0
Unhappy	0.8	0
Expectations for future	(N: 107)	(N: 147)
Self-fulfillment/development	53.3	56.5
Improve close relationships	11.2	12.2
Marriage	18.7	23.8
Children	29.0	52.4**
Career/job/monetary success	54.2	69.4**
Social concerns	0.9	1.4

*$P < .05$.
**$P < .01$.

Table 3. Stressful life events between ages 30 and 40, by gender

	Males (N: 118) %	Females (N: 152) %
Change in residence	59.0	62.5
Loss of home	11.1	9.9
Marriage	28.2	27.0
Remarriage	12.0	14.5
Pregnancy	0	36.2
Birth of a child	38.5	34.9
Adoption of a child	3.4	2.0
Change in employment	56.4	57.9
Promotion	49.6	44.7
Loss of job	24.8	16.4
Trouble with boss	23.1	23.7
Financial problems	41.9	46.7
Marital problems and separation	28.2	37.5
Marital reconciliation	6.0	8.6
Divorce	16.2	17.1
Breakup of long-term relationship	19.7	14.5
Chronic family discord	3.4	13.2*
Trouble with in-laws	5.1	17.8*
Personal illness or injury	27.4	28.9
Physical abuse	0.9	7.2
Mental health problem(s)	3.4	7.9
Problems with substance abuse (alcohol, drugs)	20.5	12.5*
Serious or chronic illness of mother	18.8	10.5
Serious or chronic illness of father	19.7	25.7
Serious or chronic illness of spouse	5.1	3.9
Serious illness or disability of child(ren)	7.6	4.6
Mother alcoholic or mentally ill	2.6	1.3
Father alcoholic or mentally ill	2.6	6.6
Spouse alcoholic or mentally ill	1.7	3.3
Death of mother	6.8	8.6
Death of father	14.5	18.4
Death of spouse	0.9	1.3
Death of child	0.9	0.7
Death of sibling (brother or sister)	2.6	6.6
Natural disaster (hurricane, earthquake, floods)	85.5	80.3
Retirement	0.9	0
Mean N of stressful life events reported	6.7	7.3
SD	3.6	4.1

*P < .05.

Table 4. Significant differences between risk groups: males at age 40

| | Low risk | High risk | |
| | No problems at age 18 (N: 50) % | Resilient at age 18 (N: 15) % | Troubled at age 18 (N: 53) % |
Topics			
Employment			
Unemployed	10.2	0.0	16.9*
Difficult, stressful relationship			
Balance of work, home, relationship	26.7**	0.0	19.4
Problems leading to divorce			
Lack of commitment/trust/fidelity	10.0	0.0	66.7**
No children by age 40	42.6*	15.8	34.8
Satisfaction of being parent			
Shared affection	3.4	30.8**	8.8
Difficulty of being parent			
Balance of responsibilities	21.4	58.3**	20.0
Expectation for children			
Happiness/satisfaction	40.0*	7.7	29.4
Achievement	50.0	46.2	73.5*
Own parent			
Lives with or is financially dependent on son	28.6*	11.1	11.1
Relationship with father			
Mostly satisfied	73.0	50.0	90.2**
Mixed/mostly dissatisfied	27.0	50.0	9.8**
Friends			
Considers spouse a friend	60.5	76.9*	60.8
Most important goal at age 40			
Family commitment	30.0	66.7**	53.8
Worries at age 40			
Family	10.2	42.9**	18.0
Sources of help during difficult times			
Friends	82.0**	53.3	64.2
Teachers, mentors	10.0	40.0**	7.5
Coworkers/boss	24.0	60.0**	24.5
Important factors that helped shape life			
Love from others	31.3	28.6	16.3*
Personal abilities	12.5	50.0**	22.4
Expectations for future			
Improve close relationships	6.5	28.6*	10.6

$*P < .05.$
$**P < .01.$

Table 5. Significant differences between risk groups: females at age 40

| | Low risk | High risk | |
| | No problems at age 18 (N: 83) % | Resilient at age 18 (N: 26) % | Troubled at age 18 (N: 43) % |
Topics			
Employment			
Unemployed	3.1	0.0	11.5*
Work satisfaction			
Mostly satisfied	71.6	84.6	56.1**
Mixed/mostly dissatisfied	28.4	15.4	43.9**
Problems leading to divorce			
Lack of commitment/trust/fidelity	38.9	0.0**	33.3*
Expectations for children			
Happiness/satisfaction	38.1	35.0	16.7*
Positive aspects of relationship with siblings			
Providers of child care	19.5	38.5**	14.6*
Friends			
Considers spouse a friend	64.1	69.2	43.9**
Satisfaction with allotment of time			
Satisfied	77.4	88.0	62.8**
Dissatisfied	22.6	12.0	37.2**
Most important at age 40			
Family commitment	34.6	50.0	27.9**
Symptoms occurring over past year			
Frequent headaches	20.5	26.9	39.5*
Constant worry and anxiety	25.3	26.9	48.8*
Unpleasant things			
Mostly under my control	36.1	53.8*	25.6
Sources of help during difficult times			
Spouse	78.3	69.2	53.5**
Expectations for future			
Self-fulfillment	48.8*	61.5	68.3
Career success	77.5	73.1	51.2**

*$P < .05$.
**$P < .01$.

Table 6. Means and standard deviations on the EAS Temperament Survey for Adults and the Scales of Psychological Well-Being: males at age 40

	Low risk		High risk			
			Resilient		Troubled teens	
	(N: 50)		(N: 15)		(N: 53)	
	Mean	SD	Mean	SD	Mean	SD
EAS Temperament Survey						
Distress	2.12	.82	2.05	.76	2.19	.90
Fear	2.15	.66	2.12	.77	2.07	.66
Anger	2.34	.66	2.19	.82	2.59	.72
Activity	3.04	.77	3.30	.58	3.06	.77
Sociability	3.32	.61	2.87	.96	3.24	.70
Scales of Psychological Well-Being						
Autonomy	4.75	.75	5.00	.96	4.70	.90
Environmental mastery	4.65	.75	4.66	1.15	4.67	.80
Personal growth	5.23	.68	5.18	.80	5.18	.77
Positive relations with others	4.61	1.03	4.44	1.09	4.74	.78
Purpose in life	4.72	.86	4.87	.87	4.78	.83
Self-acceptance	4.81	.97	4.76	.94	4.89	.78

Table 7. Means and standard deviations on the EAS Temperament Survey for Adults and the Scales of Psychological Well-Being: females at age 40

	Low risk		High risk			
			Resilient		Troubled teens	
	(N: 83)		(N: 26)		(N: 43)	
	Mean	SD	Mean	SD	Mean	SD
EAS Temperament Survey						
Distress	2.18	.79	2.02	.75	2.40	.92
Fear	2.30	.68	2.43	.84	2.42	.92
Anger	2.49	.79	2.51	.86	2.68	.85
Activity	3.20	.70	2.94	.74	3.17	.72
Sociability	3.60	.76	3.53	.72	3.38	.78
Scales of Psychological Well-Being						
Autonomy	4.69	.80	4.82	.87	4.93	.67
Environmental mastery	4.66	.89	4.86	.66	4.51	1.08
Personal growth	5.08	.71	5.23	.65	5.22	.80
Positive relationship with others	4.93	.93	5.14	.82	4.47	1.24
Purpose in life	4.70	.89	4.79	.91	4.42	.93
Self-acceptance	4.96	.84	5.18	.67	4.73	1.12

Table 8. Proportion of individuals with coping problems at age 40, by risk group and gender

Risk group		Males %	Females %
Teenage pregnancies	(F: 28)	0	8.7
Mental health problems	(M: 23; F: 47)	33.3	17.4
Delinquents	(M: 77; F: 26)	23.4	19.0
Learning disabled	(M: 14; F: 8)	16.7	40.0
Mentally retarded	(M: 15; F: 10)	71.4	75.0

Table 9. Significant differences at age 40 between resilient females and teenage mothers

	Resilient F (N: 33) %	Teenage mothers (N: 21) %
Unemployed	0	11.8*
Concern with children's discipline	36.8	0*
Sibling provides child care	38.5	7.1*
Future goal: independence	3.8	35.7**
Worries about finances	61.5	21.4*
Worries about family	0	21.4**

** P < .05.
* P < .01.

At age 40, there were also significant differences between resilient F and F who had been teenage mothers on two of the Scales of Psychological Well-Being: Positive Relations with others ($p < .05$) and Self-acceptance ($p < .05$).

Table 10. Significant differences at age 40 between resilient males and males with mental health problems in their teens

	Resilient M (N: 24) %	M with mental health problems in teens (N: 17) %
Unemployed	0	11.8*
Childless at age 40	15.8	47.1*
Difficulty in balancing home and work responsibilities	58.3	0**
Weak points: personality	76.9	22.2*
Worries about children	7.1	50.0*
Personal ability has shaped fate	50.0	10.0*
Never been seriously depressed	21.4	33.3*

** P < .05.
* P < .01.

At age 40, there was also a significant difference between resilient males and males with mental health problems in their teens on the EAS Temperament scale Anger ($p < .05$).

Table 11. Significant differences at age 40 between resilient females and females with mental health problems in their teens

	Resilient F (N: 33) %	F with mental health problems in teens (N: 21) %
Unemployed	0	9.5*
Mostly satisfied with work	84.6	31.3*
Spouse is friend	69.2	33.3*
Communication problems in marriage	14.3	53.8*
Satisfied with sibling relationships	76.9	44.4*
Has mostly control over good events	69.2	27.8**
Has mostly control over bad events	57.6	27.8*
Satisfied with use of time	88.0	55.6*
Worries about family	0	27.8**
Satisfied with life at age 40	80.8	50.0*

$**P < .05.$
$*P < .01.$

At age 40, there were also significant differences between resilient females and females with mental health problems in their teens on two of the Scales of Psychological Well-Being: Positive Relations with Others ($p < .01$) and Self-acceptance ($p < .05$).

Table 12. Significant differences between "troubled" teenage males *with* and *without* coping problems at age 40

Variables	P
Perinatal stress (for M with mental health problems)	<.10
Paternal psychopathology (including substance abuse)	<.05
Maternal education level	<.05
Percentage of positive adjectives describing caregiver in infancy	<.05
Number of children in family by age 10	<.01
PMA IQ at age 10	<.01
PMA reasoning factor at age 10	<.01
STEP reading score at age 10	<.05
Number of stressful life events reported between ages 11 and 18	<.001
Overall attitude toward school in senior year (age 18)	<.001
Realism of educational/vocational plans beyond high school	<.05
Number of stressful life events reported between ages 18 and 30	<.05
EAS Temperament Survey: Activity (age 32)	<.001
Number of stressful life events reported between ages 30 and 40	<.05

Table 13. Significant differences between "troubled" teenage females *with* and *without* coping problems at age 40

Variables	P
Physical status at age 2	<.05
Intellectual status at age 2	<.05
Percentage of positive adjectives describing caregiver in infancy	<.01
Rating of emotional support (ages 2–10)	<.01
PMA IQ at age 10	<.01
STEP reading score at age 10	<.05
Mother absent prolonged periods (ages 10–18)	<.01
Number of stressful life events reported between ages 18 and 30	<.01
EAS Temperament Survey: Sociability (age 32)	<.01
Number of stressful life events reported between ages 30 and 40	<.01
Number of sources of support available between ages 30 and 40	<.01

Table 14. Long-term problems among individuals with perinatal complications

Problems	Total cohort (N: 698) %	Moderate Perinatal Stress (N: 69) %	Severe Perinatal Stress (N: 14) %
Physical handicaps	6.0	6.0	14.5
Mental retardation	3.0	6.0	29.0
Learning disabilities	3.0	7.5	0
Mental health problems	3.0	9.0	14.5
Teenage pregnancies (F)	6.0	14.0	0
Delinquency record by age 18	15.0	17.0	21.5
Criminal record (ages 18–40)	4.4	7.2	0
Need for vocational rehabilitation	2.6	2.9	29.0
Self-reported health problems (at age 40)	21.2	26.3	50.0

Table 15. Stressors: standardized canonical discriminant function coefficients for high-risk males *with* and *without* serious coping problems at age 40 (N: 108)

Stressors	
Mother has alcohol or mental health problems (ages 0–2)	.01
Father has alcohol or mental health problems (ages 0–2)	.21
Number of parent-reported stressful life events (ages 0–10)	.72
Number of children in family by age 10	.06
Need for remedial education by age 10	.35
Father has alcohol or mental health problems (ages 11–18)	.18
Problems in school (ages 11–18)	.16
Number of contacts with public health clinics (ages 11–18)	.13
Number of self-reported stressful life events (ages 11–18)	.08
Problems with substance abuse (ages 18–30)	.20
Number of self-reported stressful life events (ages 18–30)	.11
Problems with substance abuse (ages 30–40)	.38
Number of self-reported stressful life events (ages 30–40)	.44

Table 16. Stressors: standardized canonical discriminant function coefficients for high-risk females *with* and *without* coping problems at age 40 (N: 94)

Stressors	
Mother has alcohol or mental health problems (ages 0–2)	.29
Father has alcohol or mental health problems (ages 0–2)	.15
Birth of a sibling before F is 2 years old	.11
Child has serious illness or accident (ages 0–2)	.33
Number of parent-reported stressful life events (ages 0–2)	.01
Death of a sibling (ages 2–10)	.57
Need for remedial education by age 10	.07
Need for mental health care by age 10	.52
Mother has alcohol or mental health problems (ages 11–18)	.01
Father has alcohol or mental health problems (ages 11–18)	.66
Parents in conflict (ages 11–18)	.15
Problems in relationship with mother (ages 11–18)	.43
Problems in relationship with father (ages 11–18)	.20
Problems in school (ages 11–18)	.04
Number of referrals to public health clinics (ages 11–18)	.39
Delinquency record (ages 11–18)	.03
Number of self-reported stressful life events (ages 11–18)	.12
EAS Temperament Survey: Distress (age 32)	.15

Table 17. Predictors of satisfaction with work: males at age 40 (N: 108)

Variables	r
Mother's educational status	.40
Number of children by age 10	−.26
Problems in school (ages 11–18)	−.26
Number of stressful life events (ages 11–18)	−.38
Substance abuse (ages 18–32)	−.47
EAS Temperament Survey: Activity (age 32)	.31
Number of stressful life events (ages 30–40)	−.41

Table 18. Predictors of satisfaction with work: females at age 40 (N: 94)

Variables	r
PMA IQ at age 10	.43
PMA reasoning factor (age 10)	.42
STEP reading score (age 10)	.26
Problems in school (ages 11–18)	−.42
Problems with parents (ages 11–18)	−.39
Mother absent prolonged periods (ages 11–18)	−.42
Father is alcoholic (ages 11–18)	−.30
Parents in conflict (ages 11–18)	−.30
Feeling of security as part of family (age 18)	.49
Delinquent by age 18	−.30
Mental health problems by age 18	−.33
CPI scale: Intellectual efficiency (age 18)	.24
CPI scale: Responsibility (age 18)	.25
CPI scale: Socialization (age 18)	.31
EAS Temperament Survey: Distress (age 32)	−.29
Number of sources of support (ages 30–40)	.29
Number of stressful life events (ages 30–40)	−.38

Table 19. Predictors of satisfaction with interpersonal relationships: males at age 40 (N: 108)

Variables	r
Rating of educational stimulation (ages 2–10)	.33
Father is alcoholic (ages 11–18)	−.33
Positive attitude toward school (age 18)	.39
EAS Temperament Survey: Activity (age 32)	.37
Positive relationship with family and friends (age 32)	.41
Spouse is major source of emotional support (ages 30–40)	.36

Table 20. Predictors of satisfaction with interpersonal relationships: females at age 40 (N: 94)

Variables	*r*
Predominantly positive mother/daughter interactions (age 1)	.28
Predominantly positive caregiver/child interactions (age 2)	.25
Activity level (ages 1–2)	.23
Mother absent prolonged periods (ages 11–18)	−.35
Problems in relationship with father (ages 11–18)	−.26
Quality of social life (age 18)	.37
Feeling of security as part of family (age 18)	.66
Number of stressful life events (ages 30–40)	−.25
Number of sources of support (ages 30–40)	.39
Spouse is major source of emotional support (ages 30–40)	.46

Table 21. Predictors of positive self-evaluation: males at age 40 (N: 108)

Variables	*r*
Mother's educational level	.49
Educational stimulation (ages 2–10)	.29
PMA IQ (age 10)	.29
CPI scale: Socialization (age 18)	.26
Substance abuse (ages 18–32)	−.39
EAS Temperament Survey: Activity (age 32)	.48
Positive relationship with family/friends (age 32)	.24
Number of stressful life events (ages 30–40)	−.28

Table 22. Predictors of positive self-evaluation: females at age 40 (N: 94)

Variables	*r*
Father's educational level	.44
Predominantly positive mother/daughter interactions (age 1)	.25
Predominantly positive caregiver/child interactions (age 2)	.31
Problems in relationship with mother (ages 11–18)	−.24
Problems in relationship with father (ages 11–18)	−.38
Number of stressful life events (ages 11–18)	−.36
Delinquent by age 18	−.25
Mental health problems by age 18	−.34
CPI scale: Intellectual efficiency (age 18)	.31
CPI scale: Responsibility (age 18)	.30
CPI scale: Socialization (age 18)	.34
Quality of social life (age 18)	.36
Feeling of security as part of family (age 18)	.51
Number of stressful life events (ages 30–40)	−.51
Spouse is major source of emotional support (ages 30–40)	.39

Table 23. Protective factors: standardized canonical discriminant function coefficients for high-risk males and females

Variables	High-risk M (N: 108)	High-risk F (N: 94)
Mother's age at birth of child	.42	.17
Number of stressful life events (ages 0–2)	−.16	−.14
Percentage of positive adjectives describing mother (age 1)	.14	.18
Attention given to baby (age 1)	.15	.07
Baby good-natured (age 1)	.30	.13
Cattell IQ (age 2)	.02	.52
Vineland SQ (age 2)	.01	.35
Percentage of positive adjectives describing infant (age 2)	.35	.40
Percentage of positive adjectives describing caregiver (age 2)	.21	.39
Pediatrician's rating of child's physical status (age 2)	.22	.06
Mother held steady job between ages 2 and 10	.43	.08
Number of adults living in household—not parents	.32	.34
Birth order	.03	.01
Number of children living in household by age 10	−.30	.01
Number of stressful life events (ages 2–10)	−.27	−.19
Rating of educational stimulation (ages 2–10)	.05	.39
Rating of emotional support (ages 2–10)	.19	.54
PMA IQ (age 10)	.12	.57
PMA reasoning factor (age 10)	.11	.52
STEP reading score (grade 4)	.09	.13
Number of stressful life events (ages 11–18)	−.13	−.07
CPI scale: Responsibility (ages 17/18)	.06	.83
CPI scale: Socialization	.12	.23
CPI scale: Intellectual efficiency (ages 17/18)	.19	.34
Novicki Locus of Control score (ages 17/18)	.05	.11
Overall attitude toward school (ages 17/18)	.55	.60
Achievement motivation (ages 17/18)	.15	.03
Realism of educational/vocational plans (ages 17/18)	.31	.43
Quality of social life (ages 17/18)	.06	.40
Number of stressful life events (ages 18–30)	−.09	−.01
Number of sources of support (ages 18–30)	.18	.11
EAS Temperament Survey: Distress (ages 31/32)	−.01	−.47
EAS Temperament Survey: Activity (ages 31/32)	.66	.04
EAS Temperament Survey: Sociability (ages 31/32)	.07	.16
Number of stressful life events (ages 30–40)	−.24	−.81
Number of sources of support (ages 30–40)	.15	.67

Table 24. Protective factors: loading patterns of latent variables (LVs) for high-risk males and females

Manifest variables linked to latent variables (LVs)	High-risk males (N: 108)	High-risk females (N: 94)
LV 1: *Maternal competence*		
Mother's age	.94	
Mother's education	.25	
Proportion of positive interactions with child at age 1		.76
Proportion of positive interactions with child at age 2		.90
LV 2: *Toddler's autonomy and social maturity* (age 2)		
Cattell IQ	.93	.86
Vineland SQ	.90	.83
Proportion of positive adjectives describing child	.65	.74
LV 3: *Sources of emotional support* (ages 2–10)		
Rating of emotional support (ages 2–10)	.75	.73
Number of adults living in household by age 10	.38	.64
Number of children in family by age 10	.69	
Mother has steady employment (ages 2–10)		.50
LV 4: *Health* (ages 0–10)		
Illnesses, accidents (ages 0–10)	.73	.78
Number of health problems by age 10	.88	
Pediatrician's rating of physical status (age 2)		.81
LV 5: *Number of stressful life events* (ages 0–10)	1.00	1.00
LV 6: *Child's scholastic competence* (age 10)		
PMA IQ	.94	.94
PMA reasoning factor	.88	.92
STEP reading score	.66	
Need for remedial education	−.77	−.81
LV 7: *Sources of emotional support* (ages 11–18)		
Ratings of quality of social life	.80	.89
Rating of feeling of security as part of family	.78	.84
LV 8: *Health* (ages 11–18)		
Number of contacts with public health clinics	1.00	1.00
LV 9: *Number of stressful life events* (ages 11–18)	1.00	1.00
LV 10: *Self-efficacy* (age 18)		
Responsibility	.63	.84
Locus of Control	.62	.85
Realism of educational/vocational plans	.51	.80
Achievement motivation	.45	
Intellectual efficiency		.33
LV 11: *Health* (ages 18–32)		
Number of personal illnesses and/or accidents	.68	.68
Problems with substance abuse	.71	.81
LV 12: *Temperament* (age 32)		
Activity	1.00	
Distress		1.00
LV 13: *Rating of adaptation* (age 32)	1.00	1.00
LV 14: *Number of sources of emotional support* (ages 32–40)	1.00	1.00
LV 15: *Health* (ages 32–40)		
Number of personal illnesses and/or accidents	.74	.64
Problems with substance abuse	.84	.89
LV 16: *Number of stressful life events* (ages 32–40)	1.00	1.00
LV 17: *Scales of Psychological Well-Being* (age 40)		
Environmental mastery	.80	.83
Personal growth	.62	.72
Positive relations with others	.48	.79
Purpose in life	.60	.66
Self-acceptance	.84	.87
LV 18: *Rating of adaptation* (age 40)	1.00	1.00

Table 25. Path coefficient matrix for high-risk males (N: 108)

LV	1	2	3	4	5	6	7	8	9	10	11	12	13	14	15	16	17	18
1	0	0	0	0	0	0	0	0	0	0	0	0	0	0	0	0	0	0
2	9	0	0	0	0	0	0	0	0	0	0	0	0	0	0	0	0	0
3	-5	-7	0	0	0	0	0	0	0	0	0	0	0	0	0	0	0	0
4	-1	-20	-14	0	0	0	0	0	0	0	0	0	0	0	0	0	0	0
5	-11	20	28	21	0	0	0	0	0	0	0	0	0	0	0	0	0	0
6	12	34	-31	-8	0	0	0	0	0	0	0	0	0	0	0	0	0	0
7	-1	-1	17	-1	-8	2	0	0	0	0	0	0	0	0	0	0	0	0
8	1	-13	-1	43	0	-19	-9	0	0	0	0	0	0	0	0	0	0	0
9	9	-13	22	-11	25	5	24	15	0	0	0	0	0	0	0	0	0	0
10	-20	9	13	-10	-16	-27	23	4	6	0	0	0	0	0	0	0	0	0
11	-12	-5	0	0	23	6	3	-1	8	11	0	0	0	0	0	0	0	0
12	7	-6	-7	-1	12	24	-3	0	-2	8	-12	0	0	0	0	0	0	0
13	25	-4	-10	26	4	29	-3	-14	-8	-4	-13	-14	0	0	0	0	0	0
14	-30	-9	6	-8	19	21	2	13	-26	-1	5	9	1	0	0	0	0	0
15	0	20	0	-10	-8	-9	-5	13	13	8	41	-3	11	9	0	0	0	0
16	-9	-2	3	-5	4	-2	-7	9	2	-6	8	-4	13	5	59	0	0	0
17	13	6	0	-33	2	10	-6	17	1	-25	-9	30	0	2	9	-11	0	0
18	19	1	-9	-14	22	3	-2	-5	-2	-7	0	23	42	10	-19	-6	7	0

Table 26. Path coefficient matrix for high-risk females (N: 94)

LV	1	2	3	4	5	6	7	8	9	10	11	12	13	14	15	16	17	18
1	0	0	0	0	0	0	0	0	0	0	0	0	0	0	0	0	0	0
2	49	0	0	0	0	0	0	0	0	0	0	0	0	0	0	0	0	0
3	47	3	0	0	0	0	0	0	0	0	0	0	0	0	0	0	0	0
4	1	16	16	0	0	0	0	0	0	0	0	0	0	0	0	0	0	0
5	22	2	12	4	0	0	0	0	0	0	0	0	0	0	0	0	0	0
6	17	25	27	16	−6	0	0	0	0	0	0	0	0	0	0	0	0	0
7	19	−4	11	−2	13	15	0	0	0	0	0	0	0	0	0	0	0	0
8	6	15	28	28	14	−6	0	0	0	0	0	0	0	0	0	0	0	0
9	16	6	21	13	−6	−2	12	3	0	0	0	0	0	0	0	0	0	0
10	−6	0	9	1	7	40	23	14	37	0	0	0	0	0	0	0	0	0
11	13	9	12	7	7	−3	5	−2	10	−9	0	0	0	0	0	0	0	0
12	5	9	−2	14	18	−1	3	−2	10	−5	14	0	0	0	0	0	0	0
13	31	1	23	33	16	44	−9	14	24	10	−3	21	0	0	0	0	0	0
14	12	7	1	9	−8	−7	15	2	4	5	14	16	26	0	0	0	0	0
15	42	15	16	−9	21	15	12	14	4	0	27	22	−7	2	0	0	0	0
16	18	9	−1	7	−4	10	6	1	11	0	5	−8	24	19	41	0	0	0
17	35	18	31	0	10	−8	3	18	2	13	−4	19	24	18	3	−6	0	0
18	10	16	−7	36	9	18	−2	11	11	−6	−1	6	36	10	26	−8	30	0

Table 27. LV correlation matrix for high-risk males (N: 108)

	1	2	3	4	5	6	7	8	9	10	11	12	13	14	15	16	17	18
1	100																	
2	9	100																
3	-6	-8	100															
4	-2	-19	-13	100														
5	-11	13	25	14	100													
6	17	39	-33	-11	-6	100												
7	-1	0	15	-5	-3	-3	100											
8	-5	-28	0	48	5	-28	-10	100										
9	4	-11	32	-3	26	-11	26	10	100									
10	-23	-7	25	-12	-8	-32	3	14	3	100								
11	-17	-2	10	2	24	-3	8	15	1	12	100							
12	9	6	-12	-1	3	22	-4	-5	-5	-5	-11	100						
13	22	10	-26	20	-4	34	-10	-17	-9	-26	-17	-2	100					
14	-31	0	-2	1	16	12	-5	-19	5	-2	10	10	-1	100				
15	-8	12	7	-6	8	-5	2	14	7	14	41	-9	-4	8	100			
16	-14	3	6	0	13	-5	-9	8	12	2	33	-12	6	14	64	100		
17	25	16	-11	-25	-2	28	-14	-4	-6	-30	-17	36	5	2	-5	-11	100	
18	32	17	-23	-5	14	38	-12	-20	-20	-34	-20	33	49	8	-27	-19	31	100

Table 28. LV correlation matrix for high-risk females (N: 94)

	1	2	3	4	5	6	7	8	9	10	11	12	13	14	15	16	17	18
1	100																	
2	49	100																
3	-45	-20	100															
4	-14	-19	19	100														
5	-27	-11	22	9	100													
6	45	43	-44	-29	-21	100												
7	-20	-16	2	-7	-18	-7	100											
8	-17	-24	33	3	36	-4	5	100										
9	-23	-6	25	36	-6	1	15	8	100									
10	16	14	-9	-6	-1	3	-34	3	-42	100								
11	-7	1	-6	7	7	-5	7	-4	-6	-7	100							
12	-1	6	2	13	17	-5	4	-1	9	-9	16	100						
13	8	8	-36	13	-22	40	-12	-18	-31	17	-2	-24	100					
14	16	15	-12	14	-11	13	-19	-2	-11	11	13	11	25	100				
15	-22	4	-6	-6	-13	4	21	7	12	-9	32	25	-5	4	100			
16	-21	4	9	1	-5	16	16	10	23	-10	21	13	-19	13	51	100		
17	16	-3	6	4	1	-12	-4	-11	-14	17	-9	-22	23	19	-20	-18	100	
18	29	26	-28	-29	-3	46	-23	-25	-30	24	-13	-19	51	22	-32	-32	42	100

Table 29. Latent variables (LVs) ranked by proportion of variance contributed to total variance in quality of adaptation at age 40, by gender

	Rank order	
LV	Males	Females
Maternal competence	5	1
Toddler's autonomy/social maturity	6	7
Sources of emotional support (ages 2–10)	3	2
Health (ages 0–10)	2	6
Number of parent-reported stressful life events (ages 0–10)	8	16
Child's scholastic competence (age 10)	4	3
Sources of emotional support (ages 11–18)	11	10
Health (ages 11–18)	14	13
Number of self-reported stressful life events (ages 11–18)	13	5
Self-efficacy (age 18)	12	12
Health (ages 18–32)	10	9
Temperament (age 32)	9	8
Rating of quality of adaptation (age 32)	7	11
Sources of emotional support (ages 30–40)	15	15
Health (ages 30–40)	1	4
Number of self-reported stressful life events (ages 30–40)	16	14

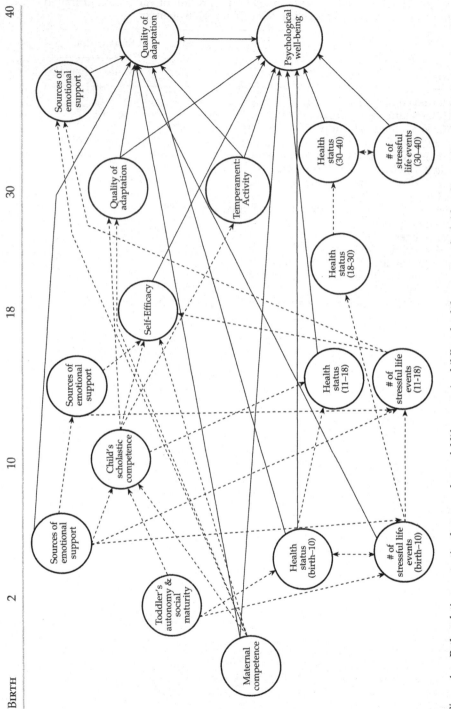

Figure A-1. Paths relating protective factors and stressful life events in childhood, adolescence, and adulthood to quality of adaptation and psychological well-being at age 40: high-risk males

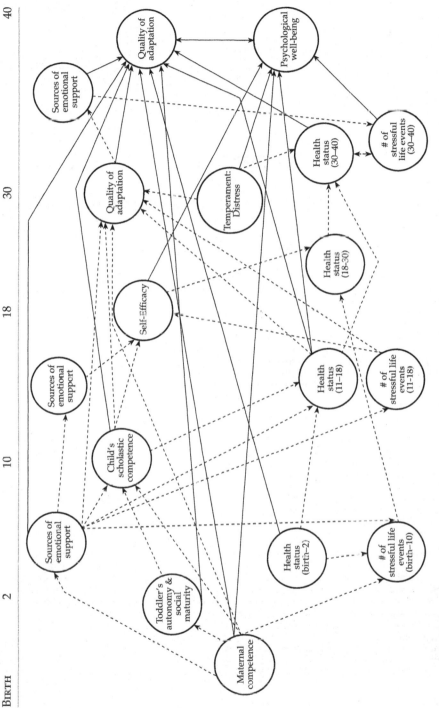

Figure A-2. Paths relating protective factors and stressful life events in childhood, adolescence, and adulthood to quality of adaptation and psychological well-being at age 40: high-risk females

❑

Appendix II

Mild (Score 1)	Moderate (Score 2)	Severe (Score 3)
Mild: preeclampsia, essential hypertension, renal insufficiency or anemia; controlled diabetes or hypothyroidism; positive Wasserman and no treatment; acute genitourinary infection third trimester; untreated pelvic tumor producing dystocia; treated asthma	Marked: preeclampsia, essential hypertension, renal insufficiency or anemia; diabetes under poor control; decompensated cardiovascular disease requiring treatment; untreated thyroid dysfunction; confirmed rubella first trimester; nonobstetrical surgery: general anesthesia, abdominal incision or hypotension	Eclampsia; renal or diabetic coma; treated pelvic tumor
Vaginal bleeding second or third trimester; placental infarct; marginal placenta previa; premature rupture of membranes; amnionitis; abnormal fetal heart rate; meconium-stained amniotic fluid (exclude if breech); confirmed polyhydramnios	Vaginal bleeding with cramping; central placenta previa; partial placenta abruptio; *placental* or cord anomalies	Complete placenta abruptio; congenital syphilis of the newborn
Rapid, forceful, or prolonged unproductive labor; frank breech or persistent occiput posterior; twins; elective cesarean section; low forceps with complications; cord prolapsed or twisted and oxygen administered to newborn	Chin, face, brow, or footling presentation; emergency cesarean section; manual or forceps rotation, midforceps or high forceps or breech and oxygen administered under 5 minutes	Transverse lie; emergency cesarean section; manual rotation, midforceps or high forceps or breech extraction and oxygen administered 5 minutes or more

Mild (Score 1)	Moderate (Score 2)	Severe (Score 3)
Breathing delayed 1–3 minutes; intermittent central cyanosis and oxygen administered under 1 minute; cry weak or abnormal; bradycardia	Breathing delayed 3–5 minutes; gasping; intermittent central cyanosis and oxygen administered over 1 minute; cry delayed 5–15 minutes	Breathing delayed over 5 minutes; no respiratory effort; persistent cyanosis and oxygen administered continuously; cry delayed over 15 minutes
Birth injury excluding central nervous system; jaundice; hemorrhagic disease mild; pneumonia, rate of respiration under 40 and oxygen administered intermittently; birth weight 1,800–2,500 grams and oxygen administered intermittently or incubator or other special care; oral antibiotic to newborn; abnormal tone or Moro reflex; irritability	Major birth injury and temporary central nervous system involvement; spasms; pneumonia, rate of respiration over 40 and oxygen administered intermittently; apnea and oxygen administered intermittently or resuscitation under 5 minutes; *birth weight* 1,800–2,500 grams, fair suck and oxygen administered or incubator; antibiotics administered intravenously; cry absent	Major birth injury and persistent central nervous system involvement; exchange transfusion; seizure; hyaline membrane disease; pneumonia, rate of respiration over 60 and oxygen administered continuously, resuscitation over 5 minutes; *birth weight* under 1,800 grams and oxygen administered or special feeding; meningitis; absent Moro reflex

DIMENSIONS OF PSYCHOLOGICAL WELL-BEING*

Self-acceptance
   High scorer: Possesses a positive attitude toward the self; acknowledges and accepts multiple aspects of self including good and bad qualities; feels positive about past life.
   Low scorer: Feels dissatisfied with self; is disappointed with what has occurred in past life; is troubled about certain personal qualities; wishes to be different from what he or she is.
Positive relations with others
   High scorer: Has warm, satisfying, trusting relationships with others; is concerned about the welfare of others; capable of strong empathy, affection, and intimacy; understands give and take of human relationships.
   Low scorer: Has few close, trusting relationships with others; finds it difficult to be warm, open, and concerned about others; is isolated and frustrated in interpersonal relationships; not willing to make compromises to sustain important ties with others.

* From Ryff and Singer (1996:17).

Autonomy

High scorer: Is self-determined and independent; able to resist social pressures to think and act in certain ways; regulates behavior from within; evaluates self by personal standards.

Low scorer: Is concerned about the expectations and evaluations of others; relies on judgments of others to make important decisions; conforms to social pressures to think and act in certain ways.

Environmental mastery

High scorer: Has a sense of mastery and competence in managing the environment; controls complex array of external activities; makes effective use of surrounding opportunities; able to choose or create contexts suitable to personal needs and values.

Low scorer: Has difficulty managing everyday affairs; feels unable to change or improve surrounding context; is unaware of surrounding opportunities; lacks sense of control over external world.

Purpose in life

High scorer: Has goals in life and a sense of directedness; feels there is meaning to present and past life; holds beliefs that give life purpose; has aims and objectives for living.

Low scorer: Lacks a sense of meaning in life; has few goals or aims; lacks sense of direction; does not see purpose of past life; has no outlook or beliefs that give life meaning.

Personal growth

High scorer: Has a feeling of continued development; sees self as growing and expanding; is open to new experiences; has sense of realizing his or her potential; sees improvement in self and behavior over time; is changing in ways that reflect more self-knowledge and effectiveness.

Low scorer: Has a sense of personal stagnation; lacks sense of improvement or expansion over time; feels bored and uninterested in life; feels unable to develop new attitudes or behaviors.

SCORING SYSTEM FOR RATINGS OF ADULT ADAPTATION AT AGE FORTY

Fourteen items were included in the ratings of the quality of adaptation. They dealt with accomplishments and satisfaction at work and/or school, with the quality of the individual's interpersonal relationships with family and friends, and with the individual's well-being and satisfaction with life. The ratings were based on both the individual's own assessment and community records (from the courts, the Department of Health and Mental Health, and the Department of Social Services, Division of Vocational Rehabilitation).

In the *work/school* area, 1 point was assigned if the individual was either employed or a (full-time) student; 2 points were assigned if she or he was currently unemployed and not pursuing any additional training. Satisfaction with current employment (or student status) was rated on a 3-point scale, ranging from 1-(mostly) satisfied, to 2-ambivalent, to 3-(mostly) dissatisfied. The range of scores in this area was from 2 (best score) to 5 (worst score).

In the area of *interpersonal relationships*, 1 point was assigned if the individual was married, remarried, or widowed; 2 points were assigned if he or she was divorced (once or several times) and not presently remarried, or had no committed relationships as a single person. The quality of the marital relationship, and of relationships with children, mother, father, and siblings, was rated on a 3-point scale, ranging from 1-(very) satisfied, to 2-ambivalent, to 3-(very) dissatisfied. The individual was assigned 1 point if he or she reported having two or more friends, 2 points if he or she had one friend, and 3 points if he or she did not have any friends. One point each was allocated for criminal records, such as spouse or child abuse, narcotic offenses, assault rape, and attempted murder. The range of scores in this area was from 7 (best score) to 15 (worst score).

In the *self-evaluation*, 1 point was assigned if the individual was free of any debilitating health or mental health problems, 2 points were assigned if the individual reported occasional bouts with psychosomatic symptoms and chronic anxiety, and 3 points were assigned if there was any evidence of debilitating emotional problems (such as chronic substance abuse, severe depression, schizophrenia) from self-reports or from the reports of health or mental health agencies. One point was assigned if the individual could count on two or more sources of emotional support (spouse, friends, kith or kin), 2 points were assigned if she or he relied exclusively on one person for such support, and 3 points were assigned if the individual did not have any outside sources of emotional support. The individual's satisfaction with his/her present state of life was scored on a 5-point scale, ranging from 1-happy/delighted, to 2-mostly satisfied, to 3-ambivalent, to 4-mostly dissatisfied, to 5-unhappy. The range of scores in this area was from 3 (best score) to 10 (worst score).

Total scores for this cohort ranged from 12 to 28. Those with *good* adaptation had scores that ranged from 12 to 17; those with *adequate* adaptation had scores that ranged from 18 to 22; total scores ranging from 23 to 28 defined the *poor* outcomes, i.e., individuals with multiple coping problems at age forty.

❏

REFERENCES

Aldwin, C. M. (1994). *Stress, Coping, and Development: An Integrative Perspective.* New York: Guilford.

Alwin, D. F. (1994). Aging, personality, and social change: The stability of individual differences over the adult life span. *Life Span Development and Behavior* 12:135–85.

Anthony, E. J. (1987). Children at high risk for psychosis growing up successfully. In E. J. Anthony and B. J. Cohler (eds.), *The Invulnerable Child*, 147–84. New York: Guilford.

Anthony, E. J., and Cohler, B. J., eds. (1987). *The Invulnerable Child.* New York: Guilford.

Antonovsky, A. (1987). *Unravelling the Mystery of Health: How People Manage Stress and Stay Well.* San Francisco: Jossey-Bass.

Bandura, A. (1997). *Self-Efficacy: The Exercise of Control.* New York: W. H. Freeman.

Barker, D. J. P. (1997). The fetal origins of coronary heart disease. *Acta Paediatrica* 86, supplement no. 422, 78–82.

Barr, R. G., Boyce, T., and Zeltzer, L. K. (1994). The stress-illness association in children: A perspective from the biobehavioral interface. In R. J. Haggerty, L. R. Sherrod, N. Garmezy, and M. Rutter (eds.), *Stress, Risk and Resilience in Children and Adolescents*, 182–224. New York: Cambridge University Press.

Besharov, D. J. (1999, July 14). Asking more from matrimony. *New York Times.*

Bleuler, M. (1984). Different forms of childhood stress and patterns of adult psychiatric outcome. In N. S. Watt, E. J. Anthony, L. C. Wynne, and J. E. Rolf (eds.), *Children at Risk for Schizophrenia: A Longitudinal Perspective*, 537–42. New York: Cambridge University Press.

Brooks, R. B. (1994). Children at risk: Fostering resilience and hope. *American Journal of Orthopsychiatry* 64:545–53.

Brooks-Gunn, J., and Duncan, G. J. (1997, summer/fall). The effects of poverty on children. *The Future of Children*, 55–71.

Brown, B. (1999). Optimizing expression of the common human genome for child development. *Current Direction in Psychological Science* 8 (2):37–41.

Buka, T. S., Lipsitt, L. P., and Tsuang, M. Y. (1987). *Birth complications and psychological deviancy: A 25-year prospective study.* Poster presentation at the Ninth Biennial Meeting of the International Society for the Study of Behavioral Development, Tokyo.

Buss, S. H., and Plomin, R. (1984). *Temperament: Early Developing Traits.* Hillsdale, N.J.: Earlbaum.

Cannon, T. D., Mednick, S. A., Parnas, J., Schulsinger, F., Praestholm, J., and Vestergaard, A. (1993). Developmental brain abnormalities in the offspring of schizophrenic mothers: Contributions of genetic and perinatal factors. *Archives of General Psychiatry* 50:551–64.

Caspi, A., Bem, D. J., and Elder, G. H., Jr. (1989). Continuities and consequences of interactional styles across the life course. *Journal of Personality* 57:375–406.

Cattell, P. (1940). *The Measurement of Intelligence of Infants.* New York: Psychological Corporation.

Cederblad, M. (1996). The children of the Lundby Study as adults: A salutogenic perspective. *European Child and Adolescent Psychiatry* 5:38–43.

Cederblad, M., Dahlin, L., Hagnell, O., and Hansson, K. (1994). Salutogenic childhood factors reported by middle-aged individuals: Follow-up of the children of the Lundby Study grown up in families experiencing three or more childhood psychiatric risk factors. *European Archives of Psychiatry and Clinical Neurology* 244:1–11.

Cederblad, M., Dahlin, L., Hagnell, O., and Hansson, K. (1995). Coping with life span crises in a group at risk of mental and behavioral disorders from the Lundby Study. *Acta Psychiatrica Scandinavica* 91:322–30.

Clausen, J. A. (1993). *American lives: Looking Back at the Children of the Great Depression.* New York: Free Press.

Clausen, J. A. (1995). Gender, context, and turning points in adult lives. In P. Moen, G. H. Elder Jr., and K. Lüscher (eds.), *Examining Lives in Context: Perspectives on the Ecology of Human Development*, 365–89. Washington, D.C.: American Psychological Association.

Cohler, B. J. (1987). Adversity, resilience, and the study of lives. In E. J. Anthony and B. J. Cohler (eds.), *The Invulnerable Child*, 363–74. New York: Guilford.

Communities that Care: Preventive Strategies. A Research Guide to What Works. (2000). Seattle, Wash.: Developmental Research and Programs, Inc.

Dalianis, M. K. (1994). *Early Trauma and Adult Resiliency: A Midlife Follow-up Study of Young Children Whose Mothers Were Political Prisoners during the Greek Civil War*. Stockholm: Karolinska Institute.

Doll, E. A. (1953). *Measurement of Social Competence*. Minneapolis: Educational Testing Bureau.

Eichorn, D. H., Clausen, J. A., Haan, N., Honzik, M. P., and Mussen, P. H. (eds.). (1981). *Present and Past in Middle Life*. New York: Academic Press.

Elder, G. H., Jr. (1986). Military times and turning points in men's lives. *Developmental Psychology* 22:233–45.

Elder, G. H., Jr. (1999). *Children of the Great Depression*. Boulder, Colo.: Westview Press.

Elder, G. H., Jr., Caspi, A., and Van Nguyen, T. (1985). Resourceful and vulnerable children: Family influences in hard times. In R. Silbereisen and H. Eyferth (eds.), *Development in Context*. Berlin: Springer.

Erikson, E. H. (1959). *Identity and the Life Cycle*. New York: International Universities Press.

Farrington, D. P. (1989). Long-term predictions of offending and other life time outcomes. In H. Wegener, F. Loesel, and J. Haisch (eds.), *Criminal Behavior and the Justice System*, 26–29. New York: Springer.

Farrington, D. P. (in press). Psychosocial predictors of adult antisocial personality and adult convictions. *Behavioral Sciences and the Law*.

Felsman, J. K., and Vaillant, G. E. (1987). Resilient children as adults: A forty year study. In E. J. Anthony and B. J. Cohler (eds.), *The Invulnerable Child*, 289–314. New York: Guilford.

Fiske, M., and Chiriboga, D. (1990). *Change and Continuity in Life*. San Francisco: Jossey-Bass.

Freedman, M. (1999). *Prime Time*. New York: Public Affairs.

Furstenberg, F. F., Jr. (1999). How it takes thirty years to do a study. Paper presented at Radcliffe College, Murray Research Center Conference "Landmark Studies of the Twentieth Century," Cambridge, Mass., April 23.

Furstenberg, F. F., Jr., Brooks-Gunn, J., and Morgan, S. P. (1987). *Adolescent Mothers in Later Life*. New York: Cambridge University Press.

Glueck, S., and Glueck, E. (1968). *Delinquents and Non-delinquents in Perspective*. Cambridge: Harvard University Press.

Gonsalves, A. M. (1982). Follow-up of teenage mothers at 26: A longitudinal study on the island of Kauai. Master's thesis, University of California, Davis.

Gough, H. (1969). *California Psychological Inventory Manual* (rev. ed.). Palo Alto, Calif.: Consulting Press.

Grant, B. F. (2000). Estimates of US children exposed to alcohol abuse and dependence in the family. *American Journal of Public Health* 90:112–15.

Havighurst, R. J. (1972). *Developmental Tasks and Education*. 3d. ed. New York: David McKay.

Hawaii State Department of Labor and Industrial Relations. (1998). *Labor Force Information for Affirmative Action Programs*. Honolulu.

Hawkins, J. D. (2000, March). Creating communities that care: Progress and prospects. Paper presented at the 32d Banff International Conference on Behavioral Science, Banff, Alberta, Canada.

Hechtman, L. (1991). Resilience and vulnerability in long-term outcomes of attention deficit hyperactivity disorders. *Canadian Journal of Psychiatry* 36:415–21.

Hertzman, C. (1994). The life long impact of childhood experiences: A population health perspective. *Daedelus* 123:167–80.

Hetherington, E. M. (1989). Coping with family transitions: Winners, losers, and survivors. *Child Development* 60:1–14.

Kagan, J. (1994). *Galen's Prophecy: Temperament in Human Nature*. New York: Basic Books.

Kessler, R. C., and McLeod, J. D. (1984). Sex differences in vulnerability to undesirable life events. *American Sociological Review* 49:620–31.

Kitashima, M. (1997, summer). Lessons from my life. *Resiliency in Action*, 30–36.

Klohnen, E. C., Vanderwater, E. A., and Young, A. (1996). Negotiating the middle years: Ego-resiliency and successful midlife adjustment in women. *Psychology and Aging* 11:431–42.

Koppitz, E. (1964). *The Bender-Gestalt Test for Young Children*. New York: Grune and Stratton.

Kroger, J. (2000). *Identity Development: Adolescence through Adulthood*. Thousand Oaks, Calif.: Sage Publishing Co.

Lachman, M. E., and James, J. B. (eds.). (1998). *Multiple Paths of Midlife Development*. Chicago: University of Chicago Press.

Laub, J. H., and Sampson, R. J. (1993). Turning points in the life course: Why change matters to the study of crime. *Criminology* 31:301–25.

Laub, J. H., and Sampson, R. J. (1995). The long-term reach of adolescent competence: Socioeconomic achievement in the lives of disadvantaged men. In A. Colby, J. James, & D. Hart (eds.), *Competence and Character through Life*, 89–112. Chicago: University of Chicago Press.

Leadbeater, B. (2000, March). Strengths building research and policy. Paper presented at the 32d Banff International Conference on Behavioral Science, Banff, Alberta, Canada.

Levinson, D. J. (1978). *The Seasons of a Man's Life*. New York: Knopf.

Levinson, D. J. (in collaboration with J. D. Levinson). (1996). *The Seasons of a Woman's Life*. New York: Ballantine Books.

Livson, N., and Peskin, H. (1967). Prediction of adult psychological health in a longitudinal study. *Journal of Abnormal Psychology* 72:509–18.

Lohmöller, J. B. (1984). *LVPS Manual with Partial Least Square Estimates.* Cologne: Zentralarchiv für Empirische Sozialforschung.

Long, J. V., and Vaillant, G. E. (1984). Natural History of male psychological health, XI: Escape from the underclass. *American Journal of Psychiatry* 141:341–46.

Luthar, S., Cicchetti, D., and Becker, B. (2000). The construct of resilience: A critical evaluation and guidelines for future work. *Child Development* 71 (3):543–62.

MacArthur Foundation Research Network on Successful Midlife Development. (1998). *The National Survey of Midlife in U.S. (MIDUS): Age and Gender Tables.* Vero Beach, Fla.: MIDMAC.

Magnusson, D. (1988). *Individual Development from an Interactional Perspective: A Longitudinal Study.* Hillsdale, N.J.: Erlbaum.

Magnusson, D. (1998). The logic and implications of a person-oriented approach. In R. B. Cairns, L. R. Bergman, and J. Kagan (eds.), *Methods and Models for Studying the Individual,* 33–64. Thousand Oaks, Calif.: Sage Publishing Co.

Marks, N. F. (1996). Flying solo at midlife: Gender, marital status, and psychological well-being. *Journal of Marriage and the Family* 58:917–32.

Masten, A. S. (1994). Resilience in individual development: Successful adaptation despite risk and adversity. In M. C. Wang and E. W. Gordon (eds.), *Educational Resilience in Inner City America: Challenges and Prospects,* 1–25. Hillsdale, N.J.: Erlbaum.

Masten, A. S., and Coatsworth, J. D. (1998, February). The development of competence in favorable and unfavorable environments: Lessons from research on successful children. *American Psychologist,* 205–20.

Masten, A. S., and Garmezy, N. (1985). Risk, vulnerability and protective factors in developmental psychopathology. In D. B. Lahey and A. E. Kadzin (eds.), *Advances in Clinical Child Psychology* 8:1–51. New York: Plenum Press.

McClelland, D., and Franz, C. E. (1992). Motivational and other sources of work accomplishments in midlife: A longitudinal study. *Journal of Personality* 60:679–707.

McCord, J. (1983). A forty year perspective on the effects of child abuse and neglect. *Child Abuse and Neglect* 7:265–70.

Mednick, S. A., Cudeck, R., Griffith, J. J., Talovic, S. A., and Schulsinger, F. (1984). The Danish high risk project (1962–1982): Recent methods and findings. In N. S. Watt, E. J. Anthony, L. C. Wynne, and J. E. Rolf (eds.), *Children at*

Risk for Schizophrenia: A Longitudinal Perspective, 21–42. New York: Cambridge University Press.

Miller, M. (1996). Relevance of resilience to individuals with learning disabilities. *International Journal of Disability, Development and Education* 43:255–69.

Moffit, T. (1993). Adolescence-limited and life-course persistent anti-social behavior: A developmental taxonomy. *Psychological Review* 100:674–701.

Moskovitz, S. (1983). *Love despite Hate: Child Survivors of the Holocaust and Their Adult Lives*. New York: Schocken.

Norusis, J. J. (1985). *SPSS: Advanced Statistics Guide*. New York: McGraw Hill.

Novicki, S. (1971). Correlates of locus of control in secondary school populations. *Developmental Psychology* 4:477–78.

O'Connell Higgins, G. (1994). *Resilient Adults: Overcoming a Cruel Past*. San Francisco: Jossey-Bass.

Opp, G., Fingerle, M., and Freytag, A. (eds.). (1999). *Was Kinder Stärkt: Erziehung zwischen Risiko und Resilience*. Munich/Basel: Reinhardt.

Osofsky, J. (1990, winter). Risk and protective factors for teenage mothers and their infants. *Newsletter of the Society for Research in Child Development*, 1–2.

Parnas, J., Cannon, T. D., Jacobsen, B., Schulsinger, H., Schulsinger, F., and Mednick, S. A. (1993). Lifetime DSM-III-R diagnostic outcomes in the offspring of schizophrenic mothers: Results from the Copenhagen High Risk Study. *Archives of General Psychiatry* 56:707–14.

Rachman, S. (1979). The concept of required helpfulness. *Behavior Research and Therapy* 17:1–16.

Reiff, H. B., Gerber, P. J., and Ginsberg, R. (1997). *Exceeding Expectations: Successful Adults with Learning Disabilities*. Austin, Tex.: Pro-Ed.

Rende, R., and Plomin, R. (1993). Families at risk for psychopathology: Who becomes affected and why? *Development and Psychopathology* 5:529–40.

Ridley, M. (1999). *Genome: The Autobiography of a Species in Twenty-Three Chapters*. New York: HarperCollins.

Robins, L. N. (1966). *Deviant Children Grown Up*. Baltimore: Williams and Wilkins (1974 ed., New York: Krieger).

Robins, L. N. (1978). Study of childhood predictors of adult outcomes: Replication from longitudinal studies. *Psychological Medicine* 8:611–22.

Robins, L. N., and Rutter, M. (eds.). (1990). *Straight and Devious Pathways from Childhood to Adulthood*. New York: Cambridge University Press.

Rogan, L. L., and Hartman, D. (1990). Adult outcomes of learning disabled students ten years after initial follow-up. *Learning Disabilities Focus* 5:91–102.

Rotter, J. (1966). General expectations for internal or external control of reinforcement. *Psychological Monographs* 80 (1), Whole No. 609.

Rubin, L. B. (1996). *The Transcendent Child: Tales of Triumph over the Past*. New York: Basic Books.

Rutter, M. (1987). Psychosocial resilience and protective mechanisms. *American Journal of Orthopsychiatry* 57:316–31.

Rutter, M. (1989). Pathways from childhood to adult life. *Journal of Child Psychology and Psychiatry and Allied Disciplines* 30:23–51.

Rutter, M. (1996). Transitions and turning points in developmental psychopathology as applied to the age span between childhood and mid-adulthood. *International Journal of Behavioral Development* 19:603–26.

Rutter, M. (2000). Resilience reconsidered: Conceptual considerations, empirical findings and policy implications. In J. P. Shonkoff and S. J. Meisels (eds.), *Handbook of Early Childhood Intervention*, 2d ed., 651–82. New York: Cambridge University Press.

Rutter, M., Champion, L., Quinton, D., Maughan, P., and Pickles, A. (1995). Understanding individual differences in environmental risk exposure. In P. Moen, G. H. Elder Jr., and K. Lüscher (eds.), *Examining Lives in Context: Perspectives on the Ecology of Human Development*, 61–96. Washington, D.C.: American Psychological Association.

Rutter, M., and Quinton, D. (1984). Long-term follow-up of women institutionalized in childhood: Factors promoting good functioning in adult life. *British Journal of Developmental Psychology* 18:225–34.

Rutter, M., and Smith, D. J. (1995). Towards causal explanations of time trends in psychosocial disorders of young people. In M. Rutter and D. J. Smith (eds.), *Psychosocial Disorders in Young People: Time Trends and Their Causes*, 782–807. New York: Wiley.

Rydelius, P. A. (1981). Children of alcoholic fathers: Their social adjustment and their health status over 20 years. *Acta Paediatrica Scandinavica*, supplement no. 286.

Ryff, C. D. (1989). Happiness is everything or is it? Explorations on the meaning of psychological well-being. *Journal of Personality and Social Psychology* 57:1069–81.

Ryff, C. D., and Singer, B. (1996). Psychological well-being: Meaning, measurement, and implications for psychotherapy research. *Psychotherapy and Psychosomatics* 65:14–23.

Ryff, C. D., Singer, B., Love, G. D., and Essex, M. J. (1998). Resilience in adulthood and later life: Defining features and dynamic processes. In J. Lomranz (ed.), *Handbook of Aging and Mental Health: An Integrative Approach*, 69–96. New York: Plenum.

Scarr, S. (1992). Developmental theories for the 1990's: development and individual differences. *Child Development* 63:1–19.

SCAT (Cooperative School and College Ability Tests). (1966). Princeton, N.J.: Cooperative Tests and Services, Educational Testing Service.

Schorr, L. (1988). *Within Our Reach : Breaking the Cycle of Disadvantage*. New York: Anchor Press.

Shapiro, D. (1996, November 11). Invincible kids. *U.S. News and World Report*, 53–71.

Sheehy, G. (1995). *New Passages : Mapping Your Life across Time*. New York: Random House.

Snarey, J. R., and Vaillant, G. E. (1985). How lower and working-class youth become middle class adults: The association between ego-defense mechanisms and upward social mobility. *Child Development* 56:899–910.

Spekman, N. J., Goldberg, R. J., and Herman, K. L. (1992). Learning disabled children growing up: A search for factors related to success in the young adult years. *Learning Disability Research and Practice* 2:161–70.

Staudinger, U. M., Marsiske, M., and Bates, P. B. (1993). Resilience and levels of reserve capacity in later adulthood: Perspectives from life span theory. *Development and Psychopathology* 5:541–56.

STEP (Sequential Tests of Educational Progress). (1966). Princeton, N.J.: Cooperative Tests and Services, Educational Testing Service.

Terman, L. M., and Oden, M. H. (1959). *The Gifted Group at Midlife: Thirty-Five-Year Follow-up of the Gifted Child*. Stanford, Calif.: Stanford University Press.

Thurstone, L., and Thurstone, T. G. (1954). *SRA Primary Mental Abilities Examiners' Manual*. Chicago: Science Research Associates.

Tierney, J. P., and Grossman, J. B. (1996). *Making a Difference: An Impact Study of Big Brothers/Big Sisters*. Philadelphia: Public/Private Ventures.

U.S. Bureau of the Census. (1986). *Current Population Survey 1986*. Washington, D.C.: U.S. Government Printing Office.

U.S. Bureau of the Census. (1997). *Statistical Abstract of the United States: The National Data Book*. Washington, D.C.: U.S. Government Printing Office.

Vaillant, G. E. (1976). Natural history of male psychological health, V: The relation of choice of ego-mechanisms of defense to adult adjustment. *Archives of General Psychiatry* 33:535–45.

Vaillant, G. E. (1977). *Adaptation to Life*. Boston: Little Brown.

Vaillant, G. E. (1983). *The Natural History of Alcoholism*. Cambridge: Harvard University Press.

Vaillant, G. E. (1984). The study of adult development at Harvard Medical School. In S. A. Mednick, M. Harway, and K. M. Finello (eds.), *Handbook of Longitudinal Research*, vol. 2: *Teenage and Adult Cohorts*, 315–27. New York: Praeger.

Vaillant, G. E. (1993). *The Wisdom of the Ego*. Cambridge: Harvard University Press.

Vaillant, G. E., and Milofsky, E. S. (1980). Natural history of male psychological health, IX: Empirical evidence for Erikson's model of the life cycle. *American Journal of Psychiatry* 137:1348–59.

Vaillant, G. E., and Vaillant, C. O. (1981). Natural history of male psychological health, X: Work as a predictor of positive mental health. *American Journal of Psychiatry* 138:1433–40.

Vogel, S. A., Hruby, P. J., and Adelman, P. B. (1993). Educational and psychological factors in successful and unsuccessful college students with learning disabilities. *Learning Disabilities Research and Practice* 8:35–43.

Werner, E. E. (1989). Children of the Garden Island. *Scientific American* 260:106–11.

Werner, E. E. (1993a). Risk and resilience in individuals with learning disabilities. *Learning Disabilities Research and Practice* 8 (1):28–34.

Werner, E. E. (1993b). Risk, resilience, and recovery: Perspectives from the Kauai Longitudinal Study. *Development and Psychopathology* 5:503–15.

Werner, E. E. (1995). Resilience in development. *Current Directions in Psychological Science* 4:81–85.

Werner, E. E. (1997). Vulnerable but invincible: High risk children from birth to adulthood. *Acta Paediatrica* 86, supplement no. 422:103–5.

Werner, E. E. (1999). Risk and protective factors in the lives of children with high-incidence disabilities. In R. Gallimore, L. P. Bernheimer, D. L. MacMillan, D. L. Speece, and S. Vaughn (eds.), *Developmental Perspectives on Children with High-Incidence Disabilities*, 15–32. Mahwah, N.J.: Erlbaum.

Werner, E. E. (2000a). Protective factors and resilience. In J. P. Shonkoff and S. J. Meisels (eds.), *Handbook of Early Intervention*, 2d ed., 115–34. New York: Cambridge University Press.

Werner, E. E. (2000b). *Through the Eyes of Innocents: Children Witness World War II*. Boulder, Colo.: Westview Press.

Werner, E. E., Bierman, J. M., and French, F. E. (1971). *The Children of Kauai: A Longitudinal Study from the Prenatal Period to Age Ten*. Honolulu: University of Hawaii Press.

Werner, E. E., and Johnson, J. L. (1999). Can we apply resilience? In M. D. Glantz, J. L. Johnson, and L. Huffman (eds.), *Resilience and Development: Positive Life Adaptations*, 259–68. New York: Plenum Press.

Werner, E. E., Randolph, S. M., and Masten, A. S. (1996, March). Fostering resiliency in kids: Overcoming adversity. Proceedings of a Congressional Breakfast Seminar. Washington, D. C.: Consortium of Social Sciences Associates.

Werner, E. E., and Smith, R. S. (1977). *Kauai's Children Come of Age.* Honolulu: University of Hawaii Press.

Werner, E. E., and Smith, R. S. (1982). *Vulnerable but Invincible: A Longitudinal Study of Resilient Children and Youth.* New York: McGraw Hill (paperback eds. 1989, 1998, New York: Adams, Bannister, Cox).

Werner, E. E. and Smith, R. S. (1992). *Overcoming the Odds: High Risk Children from Birth to Adulthood.* Ithaca, N.Y.: Cornell University Press.

West, D. J. (1982). *Delinquency: Its Roots, Careers, and Prospects.* London: Heinemann.

Widom, C. S., and Ames, A. (1988). Biology and female crime. In T. Moffit and S. A. Mednick (eds.), *Biological Contributions to Crime Causation,* 308–31. Dordrecht: Martinus Nijhoff.

Wilson, J. O., and Hernstein, R. (1985). *Crime and Human Nature.* New York: Simon and Schuster.

Wolfgang, M. E., Thornberry, T. P., and Figlio, R. M. (1987). *From Boy to Man–From Delinquency to Crime.* Chicago: University of Chicago Press.

Woodsworth, M. (1979). *Roots of Delinquency.* London: Martin Robinson.

□

INDEX

Note: Page numbers with an *f* indicate figures; those with a *t* indicate tables.

Men
  coping skills of, 148–53
  discriminant function analyses of,
    158–59
  emotional support for, 70–71, 77
  job satisfaction of, 59–61, 153–56, 154f
  military service and, 5, 6
  mobility of, 33
  protective factors for, 107–8
  relationships of, 156–57
  self-esteem of, 157–58
  single, 73–74
  with troubled adolescence, 106–8
  unemployment rate among, 40
  See also Adults; Midlife cohort
Mental health services, 22
  adult admissions for, 105–6
  for adults with troubled childhood,
    110–12, 169
  class action suit for, 22–23
  for learning disabilities, 134
  long-term, 102
  resilience and, 71, 77
  seeking of, 50
Mental illness, 30
  delinquency and, 102, 104–5, 120
  incidence of, 37
  life-threatening experiences and, 115–
    16
  among midlife cohort, 49
  parental, 64–65, 95, 145–46
    coping with, 170–72
    sibling relationships and, 66–67
  perinatal stress and, 105–6, 108, 141,
    144
  psychotherapy for, 110–12, 169
  records of, 33
  religious groups and, 112–15
  risk factors for, 57
  troubled youth and, 102–3, 106
  See also specific types
Mental retardation, 141, 144–45
Midlife cohort, 38–55, 165–76
  children of, 44–46
  community service among, 48
  coping problems among, 54–55
  defining experiences of, 50–52
  divorce among, 43
  education of, 39–40
  health problems of, 171–72
  marital status of, 41–44
  participants in, 35–36

relationships of, 47–48
  parental, 46–47
  sibling, 47
  remarriage and, 41–44
  risk factors among, 56
  stressors of, 48–49
  substance abuse among, 49
  work experience in, 40–41
  See also Adults; Kauai Longitudinal
    Study
Midlife Development in the U.S.
  (MIDUS), 14, 38
  satisfaction with life and, 52, 166
  See also MacArthur Foundation
    Research Network on Successful
    Midlife Development
Migraines, 69
Military service
  delinquency and, 126–28
  education and, 39–40
  mobility and, 33–34
  poverty and, 5, 6
  as turning point, 13, 51
Miller, M., 139
Mormons, 114–15
Mortality rates, 35, 120, 144
Moskovitz, Sarah, 11
Mother-child relationships, 161
  as buffer, 5
  as defining experience, 52
  delinquency and, 7
  learning disabilities and, 133, 136
  social policy and, 176–77
Mothers
  absent, 11
  education of, 28, 107–8
  family coping and, 152–53
  older, 53
  See also Parents; Teenage mothers

National Collaborative Project (NCP), 105
National Longitudinal Alcohol
  Epidemiologic Survey, 145
National Survey of Midlife in the United
  States, 35
Norusis, J. J., 149
Novicki Locus of Control Scale, 30, 55
  for learning disabilities, 135–36
  for teenage mothers, 87

Oakland Adolescent Growth Study, 4
Obsessive-compulsive disorder, 102

Opp, G., 164
Osofsky, J., 82–84
Outreach programs, 82
Overcoming the Odds, 102, 150, 159, 171, 172

Packard Foundation, David & Lucille, 178
Parents
  adult relationships with, 36, 46–47, 64–66, 75
  care of, 8
  death of, 47–48, 50
  delinquency and, 119, 122, 126, 130–31
  emotional support from, 50, 51
  expectations of, 63–64
  family coping and, 152–53
  learning disabilities and, 133, 136
  of midlife cohort, 44–46
  psychopathology of, 64–65, 95, 145–46
    coping with, 170–72
    sibling relationships and, 66–67
  schizophrenia in, 10–11, 105–6, 145
  "substitute," 58, 139
  of teenage mothers, 88–89
  See also Childcare; Mothers
Parnas, J., 7
Peers, adult relationships with, 36
Perinatal complications, 26–27, 141–45
  mental illness and, 105–6, 108
  as risk factors, 142–44
  troubled youth and, 103
  See also Stressors
Permissiveness, 7, 45
Phenylketonuria, 181
Physical attractiveness, 5
Pineapple plantations, 19
"Planful competence," 4–5
Posttraumatic stress disorder, 11, 34
Poverty
  as childhood stressor, 103
  coping with, 170
  delinquency and, 121
  military service and, 5
  research on, 4–6
  teenage mothers and, 94–95
Pregnancy
  "hysterical," 71
  teenage, 30
    among African Americans, 8–9, 36
    perinatal stress and, 144
    risk factors for, 57

worries about, 69
  See also Teenage mothers
Prenatal stressors. *See under* Stressors
Primary Mental Abilities (PMA) test, 28, 151, 159
  for delinquents, 121
  job satisfaction and, 156
  perinatal stress and, 143–44
  self-esteem and, 157
  teenage mothers and, 89
Primary Mental Abilities (PMA) test mean scores, troubled youth and, 108
Prospective studies. *See under* Longitudinal studies
Protective factors, 13, 141–63, 172–74
  definition of, 3
  for delinquent youth, 125–31
  in families, 152–53
  for learning disabilities, 138–40
  research on
    European, 9–12
    U.S., 3–9
  for teenage mothers, 88–89
  for troubled youth, 107–9
  See also Resilience; Stressors
Psychological Well-Being. *See* Scales of Psychological Well-Being
Psychosocial Disorders in Young People, 180
Psychotherapy. *See* Mental health services
Public policy implications, 176–83
Public/Private Ventures (P/PV), 179

Queen Lili'uokalani Children's Center, 90

Rachman, S., 75
Reiff, H. B., 139
Religion
  community service and, 48
  delinquency and, 129–30
  emotional support and, 70, 77
  importance of, 52, 169
  mental problems and, 112–15
  parenting and, 45, 46
  teenage mothers and, 91, 101
Remarriage, 41–44
  delinquency and, 129
  resilience and, 73
  stepchildren and, 42
  among teenage mothers, 89
  See also Divorce; Spouse/mate
Rende, R., 182
"Reserve capacity," 4

❑

About the authors

Emmy E. Werner is a developmental psychologist and Research Professor in Human Development at the University of California at Davis, with previous appointments at the University of California at Berkeley, the National Institutes of Health in Bethesda, Maryland, and the Institute of Child Development at the University of Minnesota. She is the senior author of four earlier books on the Kauai Longitudinal Study, including *Vulnerable but Invincible* (1989) and *Overcoming the Odds* (1992). She has written several books about children who overcame great odds during the westward migration (*Pioneer Children on the Journey West*, 1995), during the American Civil War (*Reluctant Witnesses*, 1998), and during World War II (*Through the Eyes of Innocents*, 2000). She is a fellow of the American Psychological Society and recipient of the 1999 SRCD Award for Distinguished Scientific Contributions of Child Development and of the Dolley Madison Award for outstanding lifetime contributions to the development and well-being of young children and families.

Ruth S. Smith is a licensed clinical psychologist who lives on the island of Kauai and has been in private practice there for over 25 years. Her professional experience includes work at the University of Washington Child Guidance Clinic, the Merrill Palmer School in Detroit, and with the State of Hawaii Division of Mental Health and Head Start. She taught courses at the University of Hawaii and Kauai Community College. She is the co-author (with Emmy Werner) of three previous books on the Kauai Longitudinal Study: *Kauai's Children Come of Age, Vulnerable but Invincible,* and *Overcoming the Odds,* and of several publications related to the earlier phases of the study.

CPSIA information can be obtained
at www.ICGtesting.com
Printed in the USA
LVOW03s0400211117

557038LV00007B/668/P